Rethinking the South African Crisis

NATIONALISM, POPULISM, HEGEMONY

GILLIAN HART

THE UNIVERSITY OF GEORGIA PRESS

Athens & London

Published outside South Africa in 2014 by the University of Georgia Press

Athens, Georgia 30602

www.ugapress.org

by arrangement with University of KwaZulu-Natal Press

© 2013 by Gillian Hart

Set by Patricia Comrie

Manufactured by Thomson Shore

The paper in this book meets the guidelines for permanence and durability of the Committee on Production Guidelines for Book Longevity of the Council on Library Resources.

Most University of Georgia Press titles are available from popular e-book vendors.

Printed in the United States of America

18 17 16 15 14 P 5 4 3 2 1

Library of Congress Cataloging-in-Publication Data

Hart, Gillian Patricia, author.

    Rethinking the South African crisis : nationalism, populism, hegemony / Gillian Hart.

        pages cm. — (Geographies of justice and social transformation ; 20)

    "Published outside South Africa in 2014 by the University of Georgia Press [. . .] by arrangement with University of KwaZulu-Natal Press"—Title page verso.

ISBN 978-0-8203-4716-5 (hardcover : alk. paper) — ISBN 0-8203-4716-7 (hardcover : alk. paper) — ISBN 978-0-8203-4717-2 (pbk. : alk. paper) — ISBN 0-8203-4717-5 (pbk. : alk. paper)

    1. African National Congress—History—21st century. 2. Local government—South Africa.

3. Equality—South Africa. 4. Post-apartheid era—South Africa. 5. Social change—South Africa.

6. Protest movements—South Africa. 7. South Africa—Politics and government—1994–

I. Title. II. Series: Geographies of justice and social transformation ; 20.

    JS7533.A2H37 2014

    320.968—dc23

                                                                                2013045534

British Library Cataloging-in-Publication Data available

Dedicated to the memory of Hope Hale Davis,
Allan Pred and Sheila Weinberg.

Contents

Preface and Acknowledgements

Writing this book has been painful and difficult. Looking back to the euphoria of 1994, it is emphatically not the book I would have wanted to write as the twentieth anniversary of liberation approaches. The Marikana massacre exploded on 16 August 2012, just as I was trying to bring the book to closure. Marikana and its aftermath confirmed many of the arguments I was making. At the same time it forced me to rethink the larger framing of the book – and it was through that process that I came to focus on longstanding debates about the crisis in South Africa.

Like my 2002 publication *Disabling Globalization*, this book is grounded in Ladysmith and Newcastle – two former white towns and adjacent black townships in KwaZulu-Natal that constitute key vantage points from which I have tried to grasp post-apartheid transformations since 1994, and to which I have returned regularly – although since 2006 I have focused more on Ladysmith. Nonetheless, this book has a distinctively different personality, and has moved in different directions. Covering the first phase of the post-apartheid order (1994–2000), *Disabling Globalization* is a sustained ethnographic monograph – albeit one that refused to stay in place and took off for East Asia. The present book started life as a series of academic articles and journalistic pieces propelled by my efforts to comprehend the seismic political, economic and social upheavals that have rocked South Africa since the turn of the millennium. As I tried to piece these writings together, however, it became clear that this was not just a collection of essays, and that a larger argument was insistently trying to emerge.

* * *

Through this decade-long process I have been helped, sustained, encouraged and stimulated by an extraordinary array of friends and colleagues in South Africa who have contributed to the book in ways that extend beyond what they ever could have imagined. Many will not agree with my interpretations, and should in no way be held responsible for them. Those to whom I am deeply grateful include the late Neville Alexander, Peter Alexander, Shireen Ally, Mercia Andrews, Brian Ashley, Richard Ballard, Franco Barchiesi, Ahmed Bawa, Sthembiso Bhengu, Patrick Bond, Phil Bonner, Debby Bonnin, Keith Breckenridge, Shirley Brooks, Sakhela Buhlungu, Catherine Burns, Yunus Carrim, Sharad Chari, Ivor Chipkin, Jackie Cock, Ashwin Desai, Andries du Toit, Jackie Dugard, Alfred Duma, Alwin Fortuin, Celeste Fortuin, Bill Freund, Mary Galvin, Mark Gevisser, Stephen Greenberg, Jeff Guy, Lucas Holtzhausen, Mark Hunter, Vashna Jagarnath, Mazibuko Jara, Bridget Kenny, Francie Lund, Busi Madonsela, Brij Maharaj, Hein Marais, Gerry Maré, Monique Marks, Dudu Mazibuko, Cyril Mchunu, M. Mdakane, Bheki Mncube, Andile Mngxitama, David Moore, Sarah Mosoetsa, Julie Muir, Prishani Naidoo, Tubby Narendas, Andrew Nash, Michael Neocosmos, Trevor Ngwane, Noor Nieftagodien, Rienus Niemand, Lungisile Ntsebeza, David Ntseng, Sophie Oldfield, Vishnu Padayachee, Devan Pillay, Richard Pithouse, Melanie Samson, Vish Satgar, Maxwell Shabalala, Priska Shabalala, Ari Sitas, Jabulani Sithole, Ash Sompersad, Alison Todes, Henk van der Merwe, Ahmed Veriava, Astrid von Kotze, Thembisa Waetjen, Eddie Webster, Mark Weinberg, Michelle Williams, Nomkhosi Xulu, S'bu Zikode and Thamsanqa Zwane.

Many of the ideas in this book have been forged and sharpened in interaction with students in Berkeley and South Africa; while I cannot acknowledge them individually, I owe them an enormous debt of gratitude. My thanks as well to colleagues and friends in Berkeley and beyond, the Gruppo Gramsci, and to participants and respondents in seminars and lectures over the past decade who have profoundly shaped my thinking.

As she did with *Disabling Globalization*, Sally Hines at UKZN Press has played a central role in helping to usher this book into the world with her support, wisdom, intellectual acuity and nudging at various points along the way – an editor *extraordinaire*! Darin Jensen conceived the design of the cover, bringing to it a combination of aesthetic flair and sensitivity to the relationship between the cover and the text. I am also grateful to Blessing Ngobeni for allowing us to use his powerfully compelling painting. Luis Flores provided magnificent research assistance, and helped me to reframe key arguments. My thanks as well to Celia Braves for her superb indexing, completed in record time.

In the final phases of writing the book I benefited tremendously from careful and constructive readings by Richard Ballard, Sharad Chari, Mark Hunter, Stefan Kipfer, Hein Marais, Ari Sitas and Michael Watts. I have taken most (although not all) of their excellent advice, much of it delivered rapidly under tight time constraints. The remaining problems are mine alone!

Jean Lave has played a central role in this project from the very beginning, and it is impossible to acknowledge fully the depth and extent of her contributions. The book has evolved through the dialectical processes of intellectual engagement to which we are both so profoundly committed, combined with staunch friendship. As part of this process, she has also been my most rigorous critic, providing detailed comments on almost every page.

The usual disclaimers do not apply to David Szanton. He has been so deeply entangled in the formation of this book that it is as much his as mine.

Note to the U.S. Edition

South Africa after Mandela?

Alongside the remarkable transition, the Mandela Decade left behind a profound sense of failure felt by the very people who struggled to create a non-racial and diverse nation (Sitas 2010: 24).

[Mandela's] ideological legacy – in South Africa and globally – is startlingly complex. He has provided inspiration for the struggles of oppressed people throughout the world, and he has made himself a symbol of reconciliation in a world in which their oppression continues. To understand his historical role, and come to terms with his legacy, we need to see how his greatness and his limitations stem from the same source (Nash 1999b).[1]

Amid the planetary outpouring of grief following Nelson Mandela's death on 5 December 2013, fierce debates erupted over his role and legacy in post-apartheid South Africa. Anticipating these debates, the eminent novelist Zakes Mda – son of A. P. Mda, one of the cofounders of the African National Congress (ANC) Youth League in the 1940s who worked closely with Mandela – warned against polarized portrayals of Mandela. 'Mandela saved my country from a bloodbath but his focus on the symbols of reconciliation was at the expense of real economic reform in South Africa', Mda asserted in a 6 December article titled 'Nelson Mandela: Neither Sell-out nor Saint' (*Guardian*).

Mda's warnings against sanctifying Mandela received short shrift in the flood of obituaries in the mainstream media, many of which depicted the great man as a messiah who flew over from Robben Island to single-handedly save South Africans from themselves. A number of such encomiums came from those who had demonized Mandela as a terrorist prior to 1990. For the ever-provocative Slavoj Žižek, these crocodile tears were proof that 'if Nelson Mandela really had won, he wouldn't be seen as a universal hero' (*Guardian*, 9 December).

Also on 9 December, the conservative commentator Andrew Ross Sorkin posted 'How Mandela Shifted Views on Freedom of Markets' on the *New York Times DealBook* website, which was quickly reposted and widely cited. Immediately following his release in February 1990, Sorkin notes, Mandela declared inconceivable any change to the ANC's policy of nationalizing the mines, banks, and monopoly industries. Two years later, he returned from the World Economic Forum at Davos to inform his comrades, 'Chaps, we have to choose. We either keep nationalization and get no investment, or we modify our own attitude and get investment'. Sorkin concludes that Mandela's embrace of capitalism and free markets had undermined his dream of 'a democratic and free society in which all persons live together in harmony and with equal opportunities'. The *New York Times* of 15 December carried a far more sophisticated analysis by T. O. Molefe titled 'Mandela's Unfinished Revolution', insisting on the imperative for an economic revolution if South Africa is to continue on the path to reconciliation. While not referring specifically to either Sorkin or Molefe, Bill Keller – a *New York Times* op-ed columnist and former bureau chief in South Africa – sprang to Mandela's defense, albeit in terms that may not have pleased him: 'The examples of neighboring Zimbabwe and other liberated nations that redistributed themselves into economic collapse argue for Mandela's choice', Keller avers, going on to note that 'he found in the business moguls men a bit like himself: coolheaded, ambitious, practical leaders . . . his sympathies were with success' (*New York Times Magazine*, 29 December).

Recent books by Sampie Terreblanche and Ronnie Kasrils discussed in Chapter 4 of this book shed new light on the process through which what Kasrils calls the Faustian pact between the ANC and capital was forged. Even if one rejects the 'great man' theory of history that (with some exceptions) informs much of the recent debate around Mandela in the mainstream media, the question remains of his role in this process in relation to the transition more generally.

In the most elaborate left analysis published immediately following Mandela's death – a thirty-two-page essay titled 'Did He Jump or Was He Pushed?' (*Counterpunch*, 6 December) – Patrick Bond concludes 'perhaps he did both'. Many left analysts beyond South Africa portray Mandela as a pragmatist who had been dislodged from his socialist commitments by circumstances beyond his control. For instance, asking why Mandela didn't become the Chavez of Africa, Vijay Prashad opined it was because he came to power in the wrong decade.[2] Others go back to his earlier statements to claim that he was never a radical in the first place.

While sidestepping 'Mandela as sell-out' narratives, such interpretations are problematically one-sided. They rest on excessively narrow understandings of the transition in terms of 'elite pacting' and neoliberalism and fail to appreciate the complexity of Mandela's commitments and legacy. Addressing these issues is important. Mandela's passing has fundamentally changed the ethico-political terrain in South Africa, and the stakes in how we interpret his role and legacy going forward are considerable within as well as beyond South Africa.

The central argument of this book is the need to rethink the transition from apartheid in terms of what I am calling simultaneous and ongoing processes of de-nationalization and re-nationalization that are playing out in relation to one another in increasingly conflictual ways. Before suggesting how this reframing speaks to the question of South Africa after Mandela, let me turn to 'Mandela's Democracy' – a powerfully incisive analysis by Andrew Nash published in 1999 that is complementary in key ways with the argument of this book on the contested and historically constituted character of nationalism in relation to political economy.

With some exceptions, both mainstream and left commentaries on Mandela following his death have either neglected or brushed aside the powerful African dimensions of his praxis. At best they acknowledge that Mandela's confidence derived from his royal lineage. Yet what Nash calls Mandela's 'tribal model' of democracy is absolutely central to understanding how, as he puts it in the epigraph, Mandela's greatness and his limitations stem from the same source. The moral framework embodied in this model was crucial to the role Mandela played in helping to avert a bloodbath, while at the same time making room for his and the ANC's capitulation to capital.

In developing this argument, Nash notes that this model embodies a conception of the precolonial African past that emerged in the 1940s 'after the integrity of tribal society itself had been destroyed, making any real return to its conditions impossible' (1999b: 3).[3] It started as a protest against the exclusion of urban, educated Africans from what they saw as their rightful position in the class hierarchy of capitalist society and served also to mobilize a dispossessed proletariat around democratic demands. A key figure in its development was Anton Lembede, an Africanist philosopher and first-elected president of the ANC Youth League, who died in 1947. Lembede elaborated the idea of a radically democratic and egalitarian African past, and some of Mandela's later recollections of his childhood experience in the abaThembu Great Place follow verbatim Lembede's formulations, Nash points out. At the same time, Mandela adapted, elaborated, and extended the tribal model of democracy along liberal lines. He emphasized the moral integrity of the leader as opposed to the hereditary position of the chief; the leader's tolerance of criticism and commitment to open debate; the collective context in which decisions are made and the leader's role in listening to all sides and forging consensus; and the role of the democratic leader in helping all communities to reconcile their differences harmoniously.

This model has been simultaneously enabling and disabling. It created 'a moral framework for South African politics in which Africanist and Western liberal elements were integrated in so instinctive and original a way that Mandela himself could probably not have said where one ended and the other began' (Nash 1999b: 5). Yet it also required a fatal ambiguity on questions of capitalism and socialism, because 'to the extent that this question divides society, the leader who is to take on the consensus-interpreting role required by the tribal model of democracy can give his allegiance to neither, without endangering the tribal model itself' (ibid.). This argument allows us to see how, going back to the Freedom Charter of 1955, Mandela maintained an entirely consistent position:

> It appears both to those who praise Mandela as a realist, and those who denounce him as a traitor, that he had abandoned all he had stood for before. But there is no betrayal in his record. He has simply remained true to the underlying premise which had animated his economic thought all along: the need for the leader to make use of his prestige to put forward as the tribal consensus the position which was most capable of avoiding overt division. Once it became apparent that 'the hostility of business-men towards nationalization' was more than even the prestige of Mandela could alter, his prestige had to be used for the cause of privatization. The capitalist market had become the meeting place of the global tribe! (Nash 1999b: 6)

In the only recent commentary of which I am aware that draws on Nash's analysis, Jacob Dlamini observed that 'the trouble with Mandela is not that he thought like a chief [as Blade Nzimande claimed in 1997] but that he, as a symbol of the better angels of our nature, made things too easy for South Africans'; the challenge now is to fashion a new and different politics to confront the tough issues.[4] In his 1998 book *South Africa: Limits to Change*, Hein Marais made a related point: 'South Africa's providence was that Nelson Mandela created a temporary recess in which a sense of unity or nationhood could sink a few tenuous roots'; but, Marais went on to note, 'that interval of reconciliation and precarious stability has commonly been confused with a transition that still has to run its course' (265).

As I write in January 2014, a startlingly new politics is in fact taking shape in South Africa. In addition to the formation of the Economic Freedom Fighters in July 2013 (see the Coda to this book), a huge rift has torn apart the powerful Congress of South African Trade Unions (COSATU). On 20 December 2013 the large and influential National Union of Metalworkers of South Africa (NUMSA) declared that the

ANC had abandoned the Freedom Charter and that NUMSA would not support the ANC (or any other political party) in the 2014 elections. NUMSA also called on President Jacob Zuma to resign and announced that it would form a new united front to co-ordinate struggles in the workplace in a way similar to the United Democratic Front in the 1980s. Although NUMSA technically still remains in the Congress of South African Trade Unions (COSATU), this move represents a seismic shift in the South African political landscape that signals the erosion of the tripartite alliance of the ANC, COSATU, and the South African Communist Party (SACP) that has governed South Africa for the past twenty years. There is a palpable sense of excitement for many on the left in South Africa, for whom these developments seem to open up the possibility of confronting the rule of capital and realizing the promises of a more just society. Others view with dismay the possibility that NUMSA might ally with the Economic Freedom Fighters in an effort to reach beyond the shrinking industrial workplaces to connect with alienated youth, for whom the prospect of a stable job is no more than a chimera.

It is in the context of this shifting political landscape that the challenge of assessing both Mandela's legacy and the course of the transition over the past twenty years assumes added importance. In concluding, let me suggest in broad outline how the arguments of this book, especially when taken in conjunction with Nash's analysis of Mandela's democracy, speak to the question of South Africa after Mandela.

My argument about the need to rethink the transition in terms of de-nationalization and re-nationalization turns on the imperative to take seriously questions of nationalism in relation to political economy. At the moment when the ANC and other political parties were unbanned in 1990, the South African 'nation' did not exist: it had to be produced. Simultaneously, powerful South African conglomerates were straining to break away from the confines of the national economy and to reconnect with the increasingly financialized global economy from which they had been partially excluded during the 1980s by sanctions, exchange controls, and the heightening crisis of the apartheid state.

'De-nationalization' refers to alliances with the ANC through which corporate capital defined the terms of reconnection with the global economy, as well as to the forces unleashed in the process that have intensified inequality. It includes – but also precedes and extends beyond – the extremely conservative package of neoliberal macro-economic policies set in place in 1996.

At the same time I identify three key sets of re-nationalizing practices and processes: (1) inclusive discourses of the 'Rainbow Nation' associated with Mandela; (2) the ANC government's continuing use of harsh late apartheid-era anti-immigration legislation premised on control, exclusion, and expulsion that rebounded the nation to produce what some have called 'Fortress South Africa' within which xenophobia has exploded; and (3) specifically South African expressions of African nationalism embodied in the political keywords of the ANC alliance: the 'national question' and the National Democratic Revolution (NDR).

Rethinking the South Africa Crisis shows how these practices and processes of de-nationalization and re-nationalization, operating in relation to one another in the arenas of everyday life, are key to understanding how the ANC's hegemony has been unraveling over the past decade. They shed light as well on the forces generating populist politics – including the rise of the Economic Freedom Fighters. The book also shows how capital needs the ANC to keep the lid on things, which it tries to do with re-nationalization, even while the processes of de-nationalization are rendering this project increasingly impossible.

The book concludes with reflections on contemporary South Africa through lenses adapted from Antonio Gramsci as well as Frantz Fanon, who warned specifically against the elevation of the great leader: 'There is no demiurge, no illustrious man taking responsibility for everything, but . . . the demiurge is the people and the magic lies in their hands alone' (Fanon 2004: 138). In remarkably similar ways, Gramsci and Fanon insisted on the importance of democratic processes through which subaltern classes come to develop more critical and coherent understandings as a basis for collective action.

With this in mind, NUMSA's challenge to the ANC alliance following shortly after Mandela's passing is hugely significant. Most immediately, it acknowledges the respite that Mandela's democracy helped make possible, while also recognizing its limits. On the question of possibilities for a viable new politics to the left of the ANC and the SACP, all that can be said with certainty is that there will be unexpected twists and turns. Yet at the risk of allowing optimism of the will to overtake pessimism of the intellect, one can at least raise the possibility of NUMSA and others retrieving and renovating their histories of democratic organizing from the 1970s and 1980s.

Let me cite for example the town of Ladysmith and its surrounding townships, one of the municipalities in which I have been working since 1994. Through the 1990s and into the early part of the 2000s the Ladysmith townships were highly organized and mobilized, and local councilors were held tightly to account. Of great importance was the presence in Ladysmith in the mid-1950s of Govan Mbeki, who was tried and imprisoned on Robben Island with Mandela. In addition, from the late 1970s NUMSA and its predecessor played a crucial role in shaping local politics in Ladysmith by linking together struggles in multiple arenas (Hart 2002a). Although the remarkable levels of mobilization in Ladysmith have eroded, there is at least a possibility that histories and memories could be reignited in the present.

Both the present book and my earlier volume suggest that any possibility for an alternative politics must be grounded in local historical geographies and must also be capable of forging connections with dynamics beyond the local. NUMSA has confronted the ANC alliance with its greatest challenge to date at a moment when the destructive forces unleashed by the ANC's compromise with capital, along with the fragilities of those forces, have become clearly evident. Perhaps the time has come to temper pessimism of the intellect with some optimism of the will?

Berkeley, California
15 January 2014

Notes

1. Andrew Nash, 1999b, 'Mandela's Democracy', *Monthly Review* 50 (11), http://monthlyreview.org/1999/04/01/mandelas-democracy.
2. Vijay Prishad, 2013, 'Remembering Mandela', *Vikalp: People's Perspectives on Change*, December, http://www.vikalp.ind.in/2013/12/remembering-mandela-vijay-prashad.html.
3. Nash underscores, 'In calling this the tribal model of democracy, I am seeking mainly to describe a current in the ideological history of modern capitalism, and am not taking a position about the extent to which precolonial Africa conformed to this ideology or not' (1999b: 2).
4. Jacob Dlamini, 2013, 'Mandela Leaves Behind a Complex Legacy', *Financial Mail*, 12 December, http://www.financialmail.co.za/coverstory/2013/12/12/mandela-leaves-behind-a-complex-legacy.

Abbreviations

ANC	African National Congress
APF	Anti-Privatisation Forum
BEE	Black Economic Empowerment
COSATU	Congress of South African Trade Unions
CST	Colonialism of a Special Type
DA	Democratic Alliance
EXCO	executive committee
GDP	gross domestic product
GEAR	Growth, Employment and Redistribution strategy
HSRC	Human Sciences Research Council
IFP	Inkatha Freedom Party
JSE	Johannesburg Stock Exchange
LPM	Landless People's Movement
LRAD	Land Reform for Agricultural Development
MEC	minerals energy complex
MKMVA	Umkhonto we Sizwe Military Veterans Association
NDR	National Democratic Revolution
NEC	National Executive Committee
NGO	non-governmental organisation
NNP	New National Party
NSM	new social movements
NWCRA	Newcastle West Concerned Residents Association
RDP	Reconstruction and Development Programme
SACP	South African Communist Party
TRC	Truth and Reconciliation Commission
US	United States
WSSD	World Summit on Sustainable Development

1

Contours of Crisis in South Africa

A crisis occurs, sometimes lasting for decades. This exceptional duration means that incurable structural contradictions have revealed themselves . . . and that, despite this, the political forces which are struggling to conserve and defend the existing structure itself are making every effort to cure them, within certain limits, and to overcome them. These incessant and persistent efforts . . . form the terrain of the 'conjunctural', and it is upon this terrain that the forces of opposition organise (Gramsci 1971: 178; Q13 §17).

Confronting the Present

On Thursday, 16 August 2012, South African police and para-military units opened fire on striking mineworkers near the town of Marikana in the north-west platinum belt, killing 34 strikers and injuring another 78. Televised images ricocheted around the world, seeming to support the official story that mineworkers attacked police who then retaliated in self-defence. Yet mounting evidence shows that most of the killings subsequently took place in an area sheltered by rocks that served as an open-air latrine for workers and their families living in the nearby shack settlement of Nkaneng. Out of view of the media, it appears, police assassinated some of the strikers at close range.[1] In addition, eyewitnesses and researchers assert that the initial, widely publicised round of killings was in fact precipitated by police actions. Marikana, in other words, was far more a military operation than an exercise in community policing.

The Marikana massacre was the single most traumatic event of the post-apartheid era, evoking images and memories of police brutality at Sharpeville in 1960 and the Soweto uprising in 1976. Along with the corpses, hopeful visions of a new South Africa lay shattered on the killing fields of Marikana.

Over the weekend following the massacre, Julius Malema – the firebrand former leader of the African National Congress (ANC) Youth League – was cheered by a large crowd of angry mineworkers and their families in Marikana at a moment when ANC officials were terrified to set foot in the area. There and on subsequent occasions, Malema reiterated his claims that white settlers had stolen the rich natural resources of South Africa, and his calls for nationalisation of the mines. Marikana also launched a series of other strikes that swept through urban and rural South Africa. In a revealing commentary the following Monday, Peter Bruce, editor of the influential Johannesburg newspaper *Business Day*, confessed to his own traumatic response to this turn of events:

> What's scary about Marikana is that, for the first time, for me, the fact that the ANC and its government do not have the handle they once did on the African majority has come home. The party is already losing the middle classes. If they are now also losing the marginal and the dispossessed, what is left? . . . To misquote Winston Churchill: it's not just the beginning of the end. It's the end of the beginning of the end (*Business Day*, 20 August 2012).[2]

The beginning of the end, I suggest, was the Bredell land occupation in early July 2001, when thousands of hopeful settlers 'bought' tiny plots on a barren stretch of land between Johannesburg and Pretoria, and ANC officials moved swiftly and violently to evict them.[3] Bredell precipitated a profound moral crisis for the ANC government. It also fed into pressures that had been mounting since the mid-1990s, when the ANC's conservative policies and opening to the global economy dashed hopes of material improvement for many black South Africans. Some of these pressures then found vociferous expression in oppositional movements that burst onto the global stage at the World Conference Against Racism in Durban in August 2001, and the World Summit on Sustainable Development in Johannesburg in 2002. Following the bitter disappointments of the 1990s, the rise of what came to be called 'new social movements' – such as the Anti-Privatisation Forum and the Landless Peoples' Movement – renewed faith in South Africa as a site of hope for many on the left. Activists within and beyond the country heralded the movements as embodiments of counter-hegemonic globalisation and transnational civil society fighting against the ravages of neoliberal capitalism.

Yet this optimism was short-lived: by 2003/04 many of these movements were in a state of disarray. Since then we have witnessed the emergence and proliferation of expressions of popular anger and discontent extending far beyond the reach of the first round of new social movements. These seemingly disparate mobilisations can usefully be understood in the same frame in terms of 'movement beyond movements'. First, extremely violent outbursts of so-called service delivery protests erupted after the national elections in April 2004, and swept through the country.[4] Often accompanied by intense rage, these municipal rebellions have become an entrenched feature of everyday life in the heavily segregated black townships and shack settlements of post-apartheid South Africa. Yet these uprisings coexist with what on the surface appears as remarkable acquiescence to appalling material conditions, and with ongoing (albeit uneven) electoral support for the ANC.

Popular support for Jacob Zuma in the second half of the 2000s constitutes a second dimension of 'movement beyond movements'. Gathering force in 2005, this groundswell of support propelled him into the presidency of the ANC in December 2007, and of the country in May 2009 – despite his having been charged with rape (for which he was acquitted) and threatened with charges of corruption. A third manifestation burst violently on to the scene in May 2008, when 62 people defined as foreigners were brutally murdered, and hundreds of thousands more displaced. The rampage subsided, but everyday forms of xenophobia preceded the pogroms and remain a defining feature of life for many Africans from other parts of the continent – as well as some black South Africans defined as excessively 'foreign'.

In 2010 yet another expression of anger emerged in the form of demands by the ANC Youth League and its vociferous then-President Julius Malema for 'economic freedom in our lifetime' – and, more specifically, for nationalisation of the mines as well as expropriation without compensation of land stolen by whites. Much attention and public commentary has focused on the controversial and flamboyant figure of Malema, who was dismissed from the ANC in April 2012 and faces fraud, corruption and tax evasion charges. Yet there is uneasy recognition that the anger and alienation of large and growing numbers of young men and women rendered 'surplus' to the requirements of capital will continue to burgeon even if Malema disappears.

Proliferating expressions of popular discontent over the decade of the 2000s have gone hand in hand with increasing government interventionism. Since 2001 we have witnessed intensified official efforts to manage poverty; rising expenditure at all levels of government; and amplified official 'pro-poor' and 'developmental' rhetoric. Together with a number of other shifts in official discourses and practices, these moves represent significant departures from harsh home-grown structural adjustment in the first phase of the post-apartheid era (1994–2000).[5] While it may be tempting to dismiss such efforts as sheep's clothing draped over a neoliberal capitalist wolf, we do so at our peril because they represent part of an ongoing official battle to contain and control popular discontent. This battle intensified over the decade of the 2000s, accompanied by growing tensions within and between the ANC and its alliance partners, and by the ramping up of populist politics that some see tending towards fascism. As is often the case, the rise of populist politics in South Africa over the 2000s has also gone hand in hand with multiple, proliferating expressions of nationalism.

While this book primarily focuses on South Africa, the processes and challenges it grapples with are far more widespread. South Africa is an extreme but far from exceptional embodiment of forces at play in many regions of the world: (1) massive concentrations of wealth alongside the mushrooming of 'wageless life'[6] (or what an administrator of the Bundesbank calls 'populations with no productive function');[7] (2) oppositional politics that are assuming a multiplicity of forms: the Tea Party in the United States (US), explosive Hindu nationalism in India, widespread anti-Muslim and xenophobic sentiments in much of Euro-America, the re-emergence of fascism in Austria and other parts of Europe on the one hand – and, on the other, the uprisings in the Arab world, the Occupy movement and the anti-austerity movements in Greece, Italy and Spain; and (3) official efforts at containment ranging from liberal biopolitical interventions targeting specific populations (often in the name of security) to increasingly common police brutality and rampant militarism.

Defying the hopes and promises of liberation in the early 1990s, South Africa has come to exemplify all these dimensions in a form that is both extreme and deeply racialised – and the political stakes in how we interpret them are exceedingly high.

Rethinking the Transition from Apartheid

In *Disabling Globalization: Places of Power in Post-Apartheid South Africa* (2002a) I argued that local government was emerging as a key site of contractions in the first phase of post-apartheid restructuring (1994–2000). Over the decade of the 2000s, I maintain in this book, it has become *the* key site of contradictions. Broadly speaking, local government has become the impossible terrain of official efforts to manage poverty and deprivation in a racially inflected capitalist society marked by massive inequalities and increasingly precarious livelihoods for the large majority of the population. Ironically, attempts to render technical that which is inherently political are feeding into and amplifying the proliferation of populist politics.

While local government contradictions have their own specificities, they cannot be understood simply in local terms. 'Neoliberalism' – understood as a class project and manifestation of global economic forces, as well as a rationality of rule – has become the dominant frame for many critical understandings of post-apartheid South Africa, yet, while important, it is inadequate to the task.[8] In this book I suggest that the turbulent, shifting forces taking shape in the arenas of everyday life need to be situated in relation to simultaneous practices and processes of *de-nationalisation* and *re-nationalisation.* Deeply in tension with each other, de-nationalisation and re-nationalisation enable new angles of understanding the transition from apartheid.

At the moment when former president F.W. de Klerk unbanned the ANC and other liberation movements in 1990, the 'South African nation' was deeply in question. Quite literally, it had to be conjured into existence from the rubble of a deeply divided past. At precisely that moment, powerful South African conglomerates were straining at the leash to break away from confines of any sort of national economy and reconnect with the increasingly financialised global economy, from which they had been partially excluded during the 1980s by the heightening crisis of the apartheid state.[9]

De-nationalisation refers to alliances through which corporate capital defined the terms of reconnection with the global economy, as well as to the forces unleashed in the process. As such, it encompasses but extends beyond the extremely conservative package of neoliberal macro-economic policies set in place in 1996. The most compelling analysis of changing relations between corporate capital, the global economy and the South African state highlights what Ben Fine and others call the minerals energy complex that has shaped capitalist accumulation in South Africa since the minerals discoveries in the second half of the nineteenth century, and that remains in force today. This analysis, as we shall see, directs attention to the heavily concentrated character of South African corporate capital; the highly advantageous terms on which these conglomerates engineered their re-engagement with the global economy after the fall of apartheid through their relations with strategically placed forces in the ANC; how the conglomerates have restructured and de-nationalised their operations; massive and escalating capital flight; the formation of a small but powerful black capitalist class allied with white corporate capital; understandings of the 'economy' fostered through these alliances; their ongoing influence over ANC government policy; and multiple ways these forces continue to play into and intensify brutal inequalities and the degradation of livelihoods of a large proportion of the black South African population.

It is important to emphasise that de-nationalisation does *not* refer to political intervention in the 'economy' conceived as a separate sphere. It signals instead the simultaneously economic, political and cultural practices and processes that are generating ongoing inequality and 'surplus' populations, and the conflicts that surround them. De-nationalisation focuses attention on the historical and geographical specificities of southern African racial capitalism and settler colonialism, their interconnections with forces at play in other parts of the world, and their modes of reconnecting with the increasingly financialised global political economy in the post-apartheid period. The forces of de-nationalisation continue to shape the present – but they can only be understood in relation to, and deeply entangled with, practices and processes of re-nationalisation.

One can, I suggest, discern three key dimensions in which re-nationalising practices and processes have taken place. First are inclusive discourses of the 'rainbow nation' associated with Nelson Mandela that Ari Sitas (2010) calls 'indigenerality' – the liberal, ecclesiastical discourse of forgiveness that made possible the negotiations to end apartheid, and found further expression in the Truth and Reconciliation Commission. Discourses of inclusion were not just imposed from above – like the 'national question' discussed later they had (and to some degree still have) popular appeal. Yet, as Sitas argues, they abstracted from and papered over historical geographies of racial oppression, exploitation and racialised dispossession – and were falling apart by the end of the 'Mandela decade'.

A second key dimension of official post-apartheid re-nationalisation is found in the ANC government's immigration policies and practices. Indigenerality and rainbowism coincided with what Jonathan Crush (1999a) calls 'Fortress South Africa' – the ANC government's latching onto apartheid-era immigration legislation premised on control, exclusion and expulsion. The Aliens Control Act was repealed in 2002, but the bounding of the nation through immigration policy and practices – as well as popular vigilantism, abuses by police and brutal detention of 'aliens' – have ramped up and fed into xenophobia.

Third, the most important elements of post-apartheid nationalism are embodied in the keywords of the ANC Alliance: the 'national question' and the National Democratic Revolution (NDR).[10] The NDR refers to the first stage in a two-stage theory of revolution adopted by the South African Communist Party (SACP) in 1962 and subsequently by the ANC, in which the overthrow of the apartheid state would inaugurate a phase of bourgeois national democracy that would pave the way for the second-stage socialist revolution. This aspect of re-nationalisation highlights that it is not a separable 'political' process, but is crucially about making the case for accommodation of the inequalities of post-apartheid capitalism as a transitory phenomenon, to be superseded by the (ever-retreating) second phase. Forged in the context of fierce debates over race, class and nationalism since the first part of the twentieth century; elaborated during the anti-apartheid struggle; and reworked in the context of the transition, these terms carry deep popular resonance. Within the ANC Alliance, the NDR has become a site of increasingly vociferous contestation in which articulations of race, class, sexuality, gender, custom and tradition figure prominently.[11]

Practices and processes of de-nationalisation and re-nationalisation, understood in relation to one another, are crucial to comprehending the amplifying tensions and contradictions through which the ANC's hegemonic project has been unravelling over the past decade. ANC hegemony hinges crucially on official articulations of nationalism and claims to moral authority through leadership of the liberation movement – an authority that has severely eroded over the decade of the 2000s. At the same time, many popular struggles over the material conditions of life and livelihood that erupt in local arenas are simultaneously struggles over the meanings of the nation and liberation, now rooted in a profound sense of betrayal – struggles that can and do move in dramatically different directions.

Taken together, the dialectical relations of de-nationalisation and re-nationalisation define the contours of post-apartheid South Africa's passive revolution. This concept comes from Antonio Gramsci, the Italian scholar-revolutionary jailed by Mussolini in 1926 until shortly before his death in 1937. Gramsci initially used it to interpret how the Risorgimento (the national unification of Italy in the latter part of the nineteenth century) played into the rise of fascism. In the course of his *Prison Notebooks* he extended and elaborated the concept, and suggested its wider relevance.[12] Passive revolution refers not just to a top-down seizure of power by the bourgeoisie in the face of challenges from below. Rather, it involves the overthrow of some older social forms and the institution of new ones, combined with a deliberate and structural pacification of subaltern classes – it combines, in other words, both a 'progressive' or 'modernising' revolution of sorts, *and* its passive deformation (Thomas 2012: 35–6).

Part of what is illuminating about the concept of passive revolution is its deeply spatio-historical and comparative character that is helpful in thinking about forces at play in South Africa in relation to those in other regions of the world – in terms of their specificities *and* interconnections. For Gramsci, passive revolution was not an abstract model that can simply be applied or against which specific 'cases' can be measured. The challenge, both analytical and political, is to rework – or as Gramsci might have said 'translate'

– it in relation to the forces thrown up by a different set of circumstances. I will suggest that developing a concept of passive revolution that is adequate to contemporary challenges requires building on Gramsci's work, but also moving beyond it with the help of Frantz Fanon (1963, 2004), Henri Lefebvre ([1974] 1991), and strands of feminist theory, as well as in conversation with debates over post-colonial nationalisms.[13]

First, though, let me situate this book (and its title) in a longer lineage of debate and analysis of South African conditions that draws on Gramsci. In 1981 John Saul and Stephen Gelb published *The Crisis in South Africa* (updated by Saul in 1986), which represented the first Marxist analysis of the reformist thrust by the Botha regime in the late 1970s and early 1980s. Serious economic difficulties in the 1970s had, they argued, deepened into an organic crisis, forcing capital and the apartheid state into a desperate search for palliative measures. Drawing on Stuart Hall's (1981) reading of Gramsci, they anticipated that capital's 'formative action' would run aground because co-optation was far too limited and exclusionary to pre-empt the demands of the mass of the population. Reformism did, however, provide new space for political organisation and opposition, and new grievances around which to organise. The result would be growing coalescence of community and workplace struggles against a system with no claim to legitimacy. At the same time, the closeness of the exiled liberation movement to mass struggles in the townships meant that the ANC was unlikely to accept anything short of a fundamental redistribution of political and economic power.

What Saul and Gelb did not foresee, as Sitas (2010: 35) points out, was how the corporate bourgeoisie would fight for their own 'revolution within the revolution' – aided, of course, by the collapse of the Soviet Union and the global triumph of neoliberal forms of capitalism. Revisiting Saul and Gelb's arguments, Carolyn Bassett (2008) focuses on how South African corporate capital wrung concessions out of the ANC in the early 1990s, as well as shaping understandings of the economy, and defining the terms of their re-engagement with the global economy – an account that is broadly in accordance with that of a number of other analysts discussed more fully in Chapter 4. Corporate capital, she maintains, has been *too* successful, winning so many concessions and giving up so little in terms of supporting reforms to benefit the majority that the reform programme is inherently unstable. Bassett also invokes Gramsci's theory of passive revolution – which she defines as 'change imposed from above designed to maintain the economic and political system' with only passive consent from the masses – to argue that the ANC has been forced to rely on 'domination' rather than 'hegemony' to consolidate the new order (2008: 185-6).

In a broadly similar analysis published at the same time as Bassett's, Vishwas Satgar (2008) drew on passive revolution – which he defined as 'a non-hegemonic form of class rule' – to argue that what he calls an Afro-neoliberal class project within the ANC has used restructuring and globalisation of the South African economy to advance its interests, while at the same time demobilising popular forces and blocking fundamental transformation. Hein Marais sharply contests this analysis, arguing that the '"passive revolution" schema paints a tantalising but simplistic picture' (2011: 398). Maintaining that 'one of the great feats of the transition has been the marshalling of sufficient consent to avoid social instability' (2011: 399), he insists as well that seeing the South African transition as an example of reform from above 'plays down the extent to which popular energies and organisations eventually helped to shape the terms of the political settlement and bring about key new arrangements' (2011: 399).

This debate turns around an excessively narrow understanding of passive revolution in terms of domination as opposed to hegemony. In Chapter 6, I address these and other issues related to passive revolution, pointing to the uses as well as the limits of the concept, and suggesting how it needs to be translated in relation to post-apartheid South Africa.

Along with a number of other critics of the post-apartheid order, Bassett's and Satgar's focus is on what I am calling de-nationalisation. The dynamics of de-nationalisation are crucially important but insufficient for grasping the turbulent forces driving the ongoing crisis in contemporary South Africa. Of great importance as well are multi-dimensional practices and processes of *re-nationalisation* that, operating in relation to de-nationalisation, are linked to the erosion of ANC hegemony and the ramping up of populist politics.

Accordingly, let us turn to crucial questions about how best to understand complex, contradictory and changing issues of nationalism in relation to political economy.

Contending with Nationalism/s

> Although the ANC has been an explicitly nationalist movement, few studies have dealt with the specificity of its nationalism. Even fewer studies have taken the next step: to factor nationalism into their analysis of current events (Chipkin 2004: 335).

> [N]ationalism has proved an uncomfortable *anomaly* for Marxist theory and, precisely for that reason, has been largely elided rather than confronted (Anderson [1983] 1991: 3; emphasis in original).

For many critical observers and activists in South Africa today, dislike of nationalism is producing a dangerous disavowal and neglect. African and Afrikaner nationalisms have long been anathema for the liberal right. At the same time, many scholars and activists on the left dismiss as 'exhausted' official expressions of nationalism. There is also a widespread tendency to celebrate oppositional movements as embodying a post-nationalist (indeed cosmopolitan) cutting edge, while refusing to take seriously popular sentiments that fail to fit a post-nationalist mould.

While this combined neglect and disavowal of nationalism is by no means peculiar to South Africa, it resonates with some of the many ironies of South African liberation – its coincidence in the early 1990s with the global triumph of neoliberal forms of market capitalism and liberal democracy, together with the horrendous violence in Bosnia, Rwanda and elsewhere perpetrated in the name of ethnic nationalism. These forces fed into influential claims about the irrelevance of the nation in an increasingly borderless world, combined with the horrors and dangers of nationalism as an atavistic holdover: if nationalism is not already dead, in other words, then it should be.

There are, of course, exceptions to this general neglect of nationalism in South Africa.[14] Prominent among them is Ivor Chipkin's book entitled *Do South Africans Exist? Nationalism, Democracy and the Identity of 'the People'* (2007). Its core argument is that democracy (conceived as a form of society) and African nationalism are totally antithetical.[15] Maintaining that in the name of freedom nationalists 'substitute the goal of a democratic society for that of the nation' (2007: 119), Chipkin wants us to dispense with nationalism, and opt instead for a radical democratic citizenship. The irony here is that, as one of the very few who have called for careful, serious attention to post-apartheid nationalism, Chipkin ends up in effect wishing it away – in much the same way as those who refuse to take it on.

Forged in the crucible of struggles against colonialism and apartheid, post-liberation nationalisms cannot simply be shrugged off or wished away. The challenge instead is to grasp their popular appeal, and work towards critical understandings that can help to denaturalise increasingly dangerous articulations of nationalism. In other words, we have to think *with* nationalism *against* nationalism – and this entails beginning with taken-for-granted understandings in order to denaturalise the meanings of nation and liberation in relation to the rapidly changing world in which we find ourselves.

What are the conceptual tools that we might use for refashioning understandings of nationalism rather than just wishing it away? For this I argue that relational conceptions of the production of space in the work of Lefebvre ([1974] 1991) are extremely useful. In taking issue with what I called 'impact models' of globalisation in

Disabling Globalization (2002a), I made extensive use of Lefebvre's conception of space not as a passive backdrop or empty container, but rather as actively produced through power-laden practices that are simultaneously material and meaningful. Closely related are ideas of place (however large or small) not as a bounded unit, but as nodal points of interconnection in socially produced space, the boundaries of which always need to be critically interrogated (Massey 1994).

These concepts of the production of space are especially powerful tools for dismantling notions of the nation-state as a naturally bounded unit, as Manu Goswami (2002, 2004) has demonstrated in her reconstructions of key theories of nationalism, beginning with Benedict Anderson's *Imagined Communities* ([1983] 1991) – by far the most influential theory of nationalism in our time.[16]

Nationalism, nation-ness and nationality, Anderson argued, are cultural *artefacts* of a particular kind, capable of arousing deep emotional legitimacy and profound attachments. These artefacts were not simply invented, as several influential theories would have it.[17] Invention implies 'fabrication' and 'falsity', whereas nations understood as imagined communities 'are to be distinguished not by their falsity/genuineness, but by the style in which they are imagined' (1991: 6). The nation is imagined as a *community* 'because, regardless of the actual inequality and exploitation that may prevail in each, the nation is always conceived as a deep, horizontal comradeship' (1991: 7).

In Anderson's schema, 'the creation of these artefacts towards the end of the eighteenth century was the spontaneous distillation of a complex "crossing" of discrete historical forces; but that once created, they became "modular," capable of being transplanted, with varying degrees of self-consciousness, to a great variety of social terrains, to merge and be merged with a correspondingly wide variety of political and ideological constellations' (1991: 4). It was the 'convergence of capitalism and print technology on the fatal diversity of human language' (1991: 46) that made possible the proliferation of the modern nation as imagined community.

Anderson then identifies four categories of modular nationalism, beginning with an early form of modern nationalism pioneered in the Americas in the late eighteenth and early nineteenth centuries. The end of national liberation movements in the Americas coincided with the onset of the age of nationalism in Europe (1820 to 1920), which 'changed the face of the Old World' (Anderson 1991: 67). Within Europe he distinguishes between popular 'linguistic' nationalisms in the earlier part of the nineteenth century, and conservative 'official' nationalisms in the second half of the century that 'were *responses* by power-groups – primarily, but not exclusively dynastic and aristocratic – threatened with exclusion from, or marginalization in, popular imagined communities' (1991: 110; emphasis in original). Finally, what Anderson calls the 'last wave' of twentieth-century nationalisms in the colonial territories of Asia and Africa have their own character but are 'nonetheless incomprehensible except in terms of the succession of models we have been considering' (1991: 113).

Anderson's positing Asian and African anti- and post-colonial nationalisms as copies of their Euro-American predecessors provoked a storm of critique, as well as a tendency to set aside socio-historical analysis to focus on the symbolic and discursive aspects of nationalism.[18] In her critique of Anderson, Goswami (2002, 2004) charts what in my view is a far more productive way forward. The problem with Anderson's concept of modularity, she argues, is that it delinks the *circulation* of nationalist models from their ongoing contexts of *production* – a consequence of 'Anderson's almost exclusive focus on print-media rather than the new form of social relations established by capitalism' (Goswami 2002: 780). This understanding fails to address vital questions: the conditions that shape the openness of actors to particular nationalist models and visions of nationhood; the felt salience of particular national imaginings; and 'the clustering of nationalist movements at particular socio-historical conjunctures' (2002: 781).

While not dispensing with a concept of modularity, Goswami outlines a revised understanding that recognises both the durability and depth of the nation form and its reified status in relation to the changing global conditions of its production. Rather than the linear diffusion of abstract models from a Euro-American West to the rest, she argues, we need a spatio-historical understanding of how the practices, conceptual categories and institutions associated with the nation-state and nationalism have come to appear natural in distinct but interconnected contexts.[19] The fundamental lineaments of the nation form were set in the era of high imperialism (1870–1914) – the period of rapid capitalist and colonial expansion that coincided with high nationalism.[20] In addition to nationalist movements in Europe during this period, she points out:

> What bears emphasis is the temporal and institutional *synchronicity* of struggles to establish an internally homogeneous, sovereign space of nationness in a number of imperial-national (Germany, United States, Japan) and colonial/semi-colonial contexts (*swadeshi* in India, the boycott movement in China, state rationalization in Thailand). While these movements were fashioned by local social relations and power struggles, their temporal simultaneity, structural similarities, and competitive logic were conditioned by their location within a single, increasingly interdependent, and hierarchically organized global space-time (Goswami 2002: 788; emphasis added).

Goswami goes on to note that the centralisation and territorialisation of colonial state power in South Asia (India) and North Africa (Egypt and Algeria) 'unwittingly made possible and directed the dynamics and character of emergent anti-colonial movements' (2002: 790).

Although southern Africa does not feature in Goswami's account, this region that Cecil John Rhodes saw as his personal stomping ground played a central role in the formative period of high imperialism and high nationalism. The South African War (1899–1901) was the defining military conflict of the age of imperialism. It provided Britain with assured access to the world's largest supply of gold at the height of the gold standard; it inflamed the fierce Afrikaner nationalism that fortified the apartheid project later in the century; the post-war settlement between the British and the Boers from which the black population was excluded propelled the formation of the ANC; and Gandhi's formative experiences in South Africa forged an important connection between African and Indian nationalisms.

Let me turn now to some broader considerations of what it means to rethink nationalisms in terms of a relational conception of the production of space. Most immediately important is that an explicitly spatio-historical understanding of nationalisms moves us beyond an unproductive impasse between, on the one hand, an economistic and functionalist understanding of nationalism as reflective of – or determined by – the economic 'base' (to which Anderson was in part responding); and, on the other hand, analyses focused on the discursive effects and meanings of national territory (many of which emerged as a critique of Anderson).[21] Both rely, in effect, on taken-for-granted understandings of the nation as a territorially bounded unit. A spatio-historical analysis overcomes the either/or tensions between structural/historical and cultural/discursive understandings of nationalism. Instead, it brings them into an integrated frame of understanding by focusing on the processes, practices and meanings entailed in the production of specific – but always interconnected – national spaces in relation to wider global conjunctures.

The contradictory and dialectical processes of de-nationalisation and re-nationalisation that form the focus of this book are firmly located within this spatio-historical frame of understanding. What they also pose is the imperative of extending this frame to come to grips with articulations of nationalism with class and race, as well as gender, sexuality and ethnicity, both historically and in the present. In *Disabling Globalization*, I made extensive use of the idea of articulation understood in the dual sense of 'joining together' and 'giving expression to' – an analytical tool that was partly forged in the context of earlier South African debates over race, class and nationalism by Stuart Hall (1980).[22] Since then I have extended and elaborated the idea of articulation – first in relation to contemporary South African debates (Hart 2007), and then to take account of Gramsci's theory of language (Hart 2013). In Chapters 4 and 5, I will use articulation as a way of setting de-nationalisation and re-nationalisation in motion in relation to one another.

More generally, in developing what I mean by de-nationalisation and re-nationalisation, I will bring Goswami's skilful deployment of Lefebvre into a frame of analysis that also includes Gramsci, Fanon and strands of feminist theory.[23] Both Gramsci and Fanon were deeply engaged with the dilemmas of national unification at different moments in the twentieth century – Gramsci with how the national unification of Italy in the 1860s fed into the rise of fascism in the 1920s; and Fanon with the imperatives and pitfalls of anti- and post-colonial nationalisms in Algeria and other parts of Africa. In *The Wretched of the Earth* completed shortly before his death in December 1961, Fanon grasped the dangers of post-colonial bourgeois nationalism with remarkable prescience. Both Gramsci and Fanon have figured prominently at different moments in South African struggles – Fanon was an important inspiration for Steve Biko and the Black Consciousness movement in the 1970s, and Gramsci's ideas helped fuel fierce struggles against the apartheid regime and racial capitalism in the 1980s, as well as analyses such as *The Crisis in South Africa*. In addition, as we shall see, they share remarkable similarities and complementarities. Indeed, Ato Sekyi-Otu, whose book *Fanon's Dialectic of Experience* (1996) was inspired by South African liberation, has gone so far as to call Gramsci a precocious Fanonian!

In Chapter 6, I will focus on how Fanon's emphasis on the imperative for working through and beyond taken-for-granted understandings of nationalism resonates closely with what Gramsci meant by the philosophy of praxis – namely the practices and processes of rendering fragmentary 'common sense' (that which is taken for granted) more coherent, enabling new forms of critical practice and collective action. Both Gramsci and Fanon were attentive to questions of language and meaning in relation to practice, and both provide insights that mesh closely with the

possibilities for critically interrogating taken-for-granted understandings of nationalism opened up by Goswami's deployment of
Lefebvre.

The question, then, is what would it mean to put these ideas to
work concretely in post-apartheid South Africa – bearing in mind
that Gramsci, Fanon and Lefebvre did not present us with abstract
models that can simply be 'applied' in different times and places?
The challenge, rather, is to rework – or 'translate' – the analyses
they gave us in relation to a different set of circumstances and
forces in order to generate new understandings.

Unfolding the Arguments

> [H]ow *could* we come to understand . . . the genesis of the present,
> along with the preconditions and processes involved, other than
> by starting from that present, working our way back to the past,
> and then retracing our steps? (Lefebvre [1974] 1991: 66; emphasis
> in original)

In this book I am deploying what Lefebvre ([1974] 1991: 65-7)
called a 'regressive-progressive' method.[24] As suggested in the
epigraph, it entails starting with a description of the present and
its contradictions; then moving to an explanation of the historical
production of the present, and from there to a moment of opening
to the future – and to the possibilities present in current contradictions. This dialectical method is grounded in Lefebvre's
understanding of the production of space, which, 'having attained
the conceptual and linguistic level, acts retroactively upon the past,
disclosing aspects and moments of it hitherto uncomprehended'
(Lefebvre [1974] 1991: 65). The past appears in a different light, he
went on to say, 'and hence the process whereby that past becomes
the present also takes on another aspect'.

What is entailed, in other words, are understandings of the
past – or of multiple pasts – that are adequate to the present, and
to envisaging different futures. In this book, the idea of rethinking

the transition from apartheid spatially as well as historically in terms of de-nationalisation in relation to re-nationalisation has grown out of my efforts to grasp, of necessity in a very partial way, how key elements of the past have become the present in a rapidly changing global conjuncture.

Before unfolding the arguments, let me reflect briefly on the relationship of this book to *Disabling Globalization* (2002a). Beginning in May 1994, I started tracing the first phase of the post-apartheid transition from the vantage points of Ladysmith and Newcastle – two former white towns and adjacent black townships in KwaZulu-Natal that were sites of forced removals of black South Africans from rural areas and their relocation in the townships; apartheid-era strategies of industrial decentralisation; and Taiwanese (and subsequently Chinese) investment. Although research for the book ended with local government elections in December 2000, it was the Bredell land occupation in July 2001 and the ANC's crackdown on it that brought the book to closure. Although shocking at the time, this sort of display of state coercion has since become routine and banal.

Bredell exemplified that book's focus on the 'land question' – the central importance of histories, memories and meanings of racialised dispossession, and their ongoing reverberations in the present. It also helped to crystallise an argument about the need to delink land issues from agriculture and individual restitution claims, and re-articulate them in broader and more collective terms to demand redistributive social change and livelihood guarantees. At that moment, when a variety of new social movements focused on specific issues were emerging, I tried to suggest how re-articulating the land question could potentially link together diverse demands, and thus help unite a broader opposition to the brutal neoliberal economic policies that were ravaging livelihoods. I also suggested how framing demands in terms of a social wage might contribute to forging alliances between at least some elements of organised labour and the newly emerging movements.

The collapse of oppositional movements combined with the turbulent forces that followed in the wake of Bredell have forced me to go back and rethink the transition from apartheid in ways that go beyond narratives of 'elite pacting' and neoliberalism. In part I have been compelled to engage seriously with the intertwining of race and nationalism in relation to histories of dispossession and accumulation. It has also meant returning to follow carefully the contradictions of local government that became clear in the first phase of my research in Ladysmith and Newcastle. Focusing not just on protest but the everyday struggles over the issues and practices of local government, my purpose is to convey how practices, conflicts and struggles in the arenas of everyday life feed into and are shaped by ongoing, conflictual relations between de-nationalisation and re-nationalisation – and how they have all changed in relation to one another.

Starting with Bredell, Chapter 2 tries to convey as vividly as possible the roiling waves of political turbulence that swept through South Africa in the first decade of the new millennium. A key point here is that what I am calling 'movement beyond movements' are not just 'bottom-up' responses to 'top-down' neoliberalism. In an effort to portray the dialectical processes through which protest and containment have taken shape in relation to one another, I focus on a series of events in specific places over the decade starting with the Bredell land occupation and culminating in the Marikana massacre. My aim is to show how these 'defining moments' capture key forces – both material and meaningful – and enable us to catch glimpses of the processes through which they have been (and are being) reworked in practice. I also highlight how new social movements and proliferating forms of 'movement beyond movements' have an irreducibly local dimension, each with its own specificities as well as multiple connections to forces at play elsewhere.

In Chapter 3, I follow through the argument that local government has become *the* key site of contradictions over the decade of the 2000s. Drawing on my ongoing research in Ladysmith and Newcastle since 1994, along with evidence from other regions of the country, I show how intensifying national efforts to surveil and control local government are rendering it more fragile, and how some of the ostensibly 'pro-poor' measures set in place in the 2000s are inflaming the popular anger they were designed to contain.

Understanding the 'local' not as a set of bounded units but as nodal points of interconnection in socially produced space means that we cannot comprehend local government contradictions only in local terms – and why it is essential to situate them in relation to how de-nationalisation and re-nationalisation are playing out in practice. Chapter 4 turns the spotlight of attention on the simultaneous, interconnected and tension-ridden processes of de-nationalisation and re-nationalisation through which the 'new South Africa' was produced. My account points inter alia to the need to go beyond debates over neoliberalism to grasp the devastating dynamics of South Africa's racial capitalist order, and how it has changed as it has become more fully incorporated into global circuits of accumulation. At the same time, these practices and processes of reconnection were made possible by the multi-dimensional efforts to produce the 'nation' outlined earlier – the rainbow nation, Fortress South Africa and multiple articulations of African nationalism – all in tension with one another. Spiralling struggles cast in terms of re-articulations of nationalism are intimately linked with de-nationalising forces propelling intensified inequality and conditions of wageless life. Rife with tensions, these simultaneous processes of re- and de-nationalisation were present at the birth of the 'new' South Africa and, as I suggest in Chapter 4, shed new light on some of the key forces that took shape in the first phase of the post-apartheid order (1994–2000).

In Chapter 5, I come back to the amplifying tensions outlined in Chapters 2 and 3 that gathered force over the decade of the 2000s – but equipped this time with concepts of de-nationalisation and re-nationalisation, brought together with a careful re-reading of Gramsci's theory of hegemony informed by recent scholarship as well as reflections on how we think about populism. The focus here is on how the ANC is 'struggling to conserve and defend the existing structure' and making every effort to cure the 'incurable structural contradictions that have revealed themselves', to borrow from Gramsci's reflections on crisis in the epigraph at the start of this chapter.

Simultaneous processes of de-nationalisation and re-nationalisation are crucial to understanding the ANC's hegemonic project, and the contradictory ways it plays out in practice. Official articulations of the 'nation' and 'liberation' are not just cynical manipulations from above, or manifestations of 'exhausted nationalism'. They carry powerful moral weight and connect with specific histories, memories and experiences of racial oppression, racialised dispossession and struggles against apartheid. Precisely because official articulations of nationalism tap into popular understandings of freedom, justice and liberation from racial oppression, they bolster the ruling bloc's hegemonic project in crucial ways. At the same time, because nationalist calls are linked to histories, memories and meanings of freedom struggles, redress for the wrongs of the past and visions of a new nation, they are vulnerable to counter-claims of betrayal – a vulnerability that is intensified by the fallout from processes of de-nationalisation. Accordingly, the post-apartheid ruling bloc's capacity to tap into deep veins of popular understandings of the 'national question' has formed the linchpin of its hegemonic power, as well as a growing source of instability that has fed into the proliferation and amplification of populist politics. Far from resolving the crisis in South Africa, the conquest of Malema has prolonged and intensified it, paving the way either for his return, or for the rise of another demagogic figure.

Chapter 6 returns to debates over the South African crisis, and considers what it might mean to understand the crisis through the lens of passive revolution. Gramsci's concept provides potentially powerful insights, I argue, but is also necessarily partial and in need of translation. Any effort to translate passive revolution in South Africa today has to attend to anti- and post-apartheid nationalisms. It is here that Fanon's insights are so important, for he recognised with great clarity the imperative of working through and beyond articulations of nationalism.[25] Essentially Fanon saw anti- and post-colonial nationalisms as simultaneously crucially important *and* profoundly dangerous. Rather than just excoriating a comprador bourgeoisie, he pointed to the difficult work entailed in what one might call denaturalising nationalisms: 'If nationalism is not explained, enriched, and deepened,' he argued, 'if it does not very quickly turn into a social and political consciousness, into humanism, then it leads to a dead end' (Fanon 2004: 142–4). Distinctly different from liberal humanism, Fanon's 'new humanism' bears close resemblance to what Gramsci meant by philosophy of praxis. Drawing on Sekyi-Otu (1996) I highlight the close complementarities between Gramsci and Fanon, and also suggest how passive revolution usefully strengthens these complementarities. The concluding section, 'Translating Passive Revolution in South Africa Today', picks up on these themes to reflect on the political stakes of understanding the dialectics of de-nationalisation and re-nationalisation as the specific form of South Africa's passive revolution.

Notes

1. See for example Alexander et al. (2013); Greg Marinovich, 'The Murder Fields of Marikana', http://dailymaverick.co.za/article/2012-08-30-the-murder-fields-of-marikana-the-cold-murder-fields-of-marikana; and David Bruce, 'The Truth about Marikana', *Sunday Times*, 9 September 2012.
2. http://www.bdlive.co.za/opinion/columnists/2012/08/20/the-thick-end-of-the-wedge-the-editors-notebook.
3. As I discuss later, Bredell marked the ending point of *Disabling Globalization* (Hart 2002a: 305–8).
4. As discussed in Chapter 2, these protests date back to the late 1990s but seem to have changed tenor in 2004.
5. For a comprehensive and compelling account of key dimensions of change in post-apartheid South Africa, see Marais (2011).
6. Denning (2010).
7. Cited by Smith (2011).

8. Elsewhere (Hart 2008) I have argued that analyses of neoliberalism in terms of class project, economic policy and governmentality remain necessarily partial, since they take hold on terrains that always exceed them.

9. With the crisis of apartheid in the 1980s, the combination of sanctions and exchange controls 'gave rise both to conglomeration across the economy . . . and the expansion of a huge and sophisticated financial system as cause and consequence of the internationally confined, but domestically spread, reach of South African conglomerates with Anglo-American in the lead' (Fine 2008: 2). See Ashman, Fine and Newman (2011: 12) for a fuller discussion of this process. In 1990 when the ANC was unbanned, five colossal conglomerates – encompassing mining and related manufacturing, banking, retail and insurance operations – controlled 84 per cent of the capitalisation of the JSE (Chabane, Goldstein and Roberts 2006: 553).

10. See Chapter 4.

11. As discussed more fully later, I am using the term 'articulation' here in the dual sense of 'linking together' and 'giving expression to' in a way that is closely attentive to issues of language and translation (Hart 2007, 2013).

12. In recent years there has been a surge of renewed interest in passive revolution in different regions of the world, along with some intense debate over its contemporary relevance that I reference in Chapter 5.

13. This argument builds on and elaborates work with Stefan Kipfer (Kipfer and Hart 2013), as well as an earlier formulation (Hart 2008).

14. I will discuss these more fully in Chapter 4.

15. Chipkin's rationale is that '[t]he citizen is hailed through democratic institutions and acts according to democratic norms – what I will call "ethical values". The national subject is produced in and through the nationalist movement, supplemented by state bodies if it comes to power . . . [T]he measure of the nation is not the degree to which the state realises the nation, but the degree to which the nation controls the state' (2007: 15).

16. In the second (1991) edition, Anderson added two 'appendices' to address what he describes as serious theoretical flaws in the first (1983) edition. Henceforth I shall be quoting from the second edition.

17. For example, Gellner ([1983] 2009) and Hobsbawm (1990).

18. Partha Chatterjee, one of Anderson's most vociferous critics, put it this way: 'If nationalisms in the rest of the world have to choose their imagined community from certain "modular" forms already made available to them by Europe and the Americas, what do they have left to imagine? History, it would seem, has decreed that we in the postcolonial world shall only be

perpetual consumers of modernity. Europe and the Americas, the only true subjects of history, have thought out on our behalf not only the script of colonial enlightenment and exploitation, but also that of our anticolonial resistance and postcolonial misery. Even our imaginations must remain forever colonized' (1993: 5). A prime example of the discursive turn is the volume *Nation and Narration* (1990) edited by Homi K. Bhabha. As Goswami observes, 'Bhabha's influential essays on nationalism present, in a distilled form, this move from nationalism to nation, from a sociological to a discursive optic, and from the identity of the nation to its difference' (2002: 774).

19. In *Producing India: From Colonial Economy to National Space*, Goswami sheds new light on Indian nationalism *both* by placing it 'within and against the wider historical-geographical field of its emergence' (2004: 6), *and* by illuminating in vivid detail 'the multiple, overlapping, and densely intertwined' socio-economic and cultural processes and practices in the multiple arenas of everyday life through which the conception of India as a bounded space and economy was brought into being. These practices and processes made possible a language of national unity and development, she shows, while also engendering terrifying violence and conflict in the present (2004: 5). *Producing India* provides new insights into eruptions of violent forms of Hindu nationalism since the early 1990s, and underscores the political and theoretical importance of denaturalising nationalisms.

20. Of relevance here is Polanyi's ([1994] 2001) theory of imperialism that emphasises how Germany and other European powers used imperial ventures to protect themselves from the ravages of the gold standard during this period. See also the important caveats laid out by Silver and Arrighi (2003), who emphasise the importance of British dominance of the global economy, and Britain's access to the resources of India.

21. For an incisive critique of Chatterjee (1986, 1993), see Goswami (2004: 21–6).

22. Anne McClintock (1995) also makes use of the idea of articulation in her innovative analysis of how class, race, gender and sexuality work in and through one another in practice.

23. Relations between Gramsci, Fanon, Lefebvre and feminist theory are discussed more fully in Kipfer and Hart (2013).

24. I am indebted to Stefan Kipfer (personal communication) for pointing out that Lefebvre first used this method in an article on rural sociology published in 1953, which tries to marry different methods (notably field work and structural historiography); that it underpinned his effort in *The Production of Space* to historicise space in a non-evolutionary and dialectical fashion,

drawing on the concept of uneven development; and that Lefebvre wanted to demonstrate (in response to Sartre's appropriation of the term) that his method builds directly on Marx's Notes on Method in the 1857 Introduction to the *Grundrisse*.

25. In South Africa today Fanon is deployed in a variety of ways, often to denounce the comprador national bourgeoisie (e.g., Bond 2011). Nigel Gibson (2011a), Richard Pithouse and others have written extensively on Fanon in relation to Abahlali baseMjondolo (see http://www.abahlali.org); see also the articles in Gibson (2011b), as well as Mbembe (http://mg.co.za/article/2011-12-23-fanons-nightmare-our-reality) and Pithouse (2012a). Fanon also remains relevant to ongoing work on Steve Biko (e.g., Mngxitama, Alexander and Gibson 2008; Mangcu 2012). Relatively little attention, however, has been given to Fanon's insistence on the imperative to work through and beyond nationalisms.

2

From Bredell to Marikana

The Dialectics of Protest and Containment

STARTING WITH THE Bredell land occupation and ending with
the Marikana massacre, this chapter draws on ethnographic
engagements, media reports, cartoons and other sources to convey
as graphically as possible the turbulent forces that erupted over the
(long) decade of the 2000s: proliferating expressions of popular
discontent coexisting with often sullen acquiescence to ANC rule
by many who feel sidelined and betrayed by the post-apartheid order;
efforts by the successive ruling blocs in the ANC government to
contain and capture this mutinous energy, to borrow a phrase from
Sitas (2010: 190); and intensifying battles within and between the
ANC and its alliance partners, as well as the ANC Youth League.

Focusing on a sequence of 'defining moments' – a series of
events in specific places that have unfolded in relation to one
another – my purpose is to provide insights into how the processes
that form the focus of later chapters have been produced in practice
in the multiple, interconnected arenas of everyday life.

Defining Moments
Bredell, June–July 2001[1]
In late June 2001, a small group of people allegedly belonging to
the Pan Africanist Congress (a party with a minimal political base)
'sold' tiny plots carved from Bredell, a barren patch of land between
Johannesburg and Pretoria, for R25 (approximately $3) to thousands
of hopeful settlers who immediately started erecting ramshackle
shelters. The occupation provoked a national uproar in which
spectres of Zimbabwe were widely invoked, and the ANC govern-

ment moved swiftly to evict the settlers using the 1959 Trespass Act, an apartheid law kept on the statute books after 1994 (Marais 2011: 450). Television broadcasts carried images, eerily reminiscent of the apartheid era, showing heavily armed police – supported by the hated and feared East Rand (now Ekurhuleni) Dog Unit – pushing people into armoured vehicles, while many who had evaded arrest declared their defiance of the state. Other vivid images include the Minister of Housing Sankie Mthembi-Mahanyele beating a hasty retreat in her Mercedes-Benz as angry settlers shouted '*Hamba! Hamba!*' (Go away! Go away!); Minister of Land Affairs Thoko Didiza declaring on television that 'when foreign investors see a decisive government acting in the way we are acting, it sends the message that the government won't tolerate such acts from whomever'; and Didiza proclaiming that 'these people must go back to where they came from' as 'Red Ants' (workers in red overalls employed by a private company to which the removals were outsourced) ripped apart the rudimentary shelters. The last shack left standing was that of an 80-year-old woman, that had been consecrated as a church – and even the Red Ants hesitated before ripping it apart.

Although protests over the evictions were quickly contained, the moral fallout reverberated powerfully through South African society. Bredell represented a dramatic conjunctural moment, exposing the cracks and fissures that accompanied what Saul (2001) called the ANC's efforts to build its hegemonic project on the altar of the marketplace. Most immediately Bredell shone the spotlight of attention on the fierce extremes of wealth and poverty that intensified in the 1990s, despite a degree of deracialisation in the upper reaches of the income distribution.[2] By chance – but very significantly – the day before the Bredell occupation began, a coalition comprising the Congress of South African Trade Unions (COSATU), the Treatment Action Campaign and a number of churches issued a press release calling for a universal Basic Income Grant of R100 a month.[3]

In the *Mail & Guardian* of 13 July 2001, the inimitable cartoonist Zapiro offered scathing commentary on this hegemonic crisis of the post-apartheid state.

13 July 2001

While Bredell was about far more than access to land, it exposed the 'land question' as a particularly vulnerable flank in the ANC's armoury of state. Less than two weeks after the Bredell evictions, on 23–24 July 2001, the Landless People's Movement (LPM) was launched in Johannesburg to protest the snail's pace of land reform, and its framing in terms of a 'willing buyer, willing seller' model.[4] The LPM was established under the auspices of the National Land Committee – an umbrella organisation of non-governmental organisations (NGOs), with affiliates in each of the provinces, set up since the late 1970s to oppose forced removals. After 1994 a number of land activists moved from NGOs into government, at the same time that NGOs affiliated with the National Land Committee were conscripted into playing an increasingly state-like role in the countryside, implementing government policies (James 2002). Their growing frustration with what were widely seen as deeply flawed policies of land reform was one of the factors feeding into the formation of the LPM.[5] Another factor was the anger of black tenants over ongoing abuses on white-owned farms despite the Extension of Security of Tenure Act, which, some critics alleged, simply instructed white farmers on how to go about evicting tenants. Events in Zimbabwe also helped to propel the formation of the LPM, as did connections with the Brazilian Landless Workers' Movement and Via Campesina.[6]

Bredell also turned the spotlight of attention on urban-based movements opposing the rising costs of basic services – mainly water and electricity – along with widespread cutoffs of these services by municipal officials, as well as evictions from township housing for rent arrears. What sparked these struggles were neoliberal principles of cost recovery through which many township residents confronted sharply higher prices for water and electricity, as well as cutoffs for those who failed to pay.[7] Based primarily in the main metropolitan centres, these movements – loosely grouped into the Anti-Privatisation Forum (APF) – included the Soweto Electricity Crisis Committee, the Concerned Citizens Forum in certain townships in the Durban metropolitan region and the Anti-Eviction Campaign in Cape Town.[8] Directed most immediately against the institutions of local government these urban movements are (or were), as Leonard Gentle (2002:18) observed, 'defensive struggles against the immediate oppressor – the local government functionary cutting off their water, evicting workers from their houses or suspending electricity connections'. In the first phase of local government restructuring (1994–2001), as we shall see in Chapter 3, black townships had been starved of resources for urban services – a consequence of the negotiated political settlement as well as fiscal austerity.

Johannesburg, August 2002
If Bredell exposed major fissures in the ANC's hegemonic project, the UN-sponsored World Conference Against Racism less than two months later provided the stage on which the newly formed movements burst into global prominence – in fact, a rehearsal for a much larger and more dramatic display a year later in 2002.

For many within and beyond government, the status of the World Summit on Sustainable Development (WSSD) as the largest conference in the world marked South Africa's emergence as a global player. At the same time, the burgeoning new social movements were a major source of official anxiety, as was the prospect of transnational anti-globalisation activists arriving in South Africa.

The week before the launch of the WSSD, a group of LPM protestors marched to the office of the premier of Gauteng protesting recent forced removals and evictions in the province. Police attacked the protestors with tear gas and batons, and arrested 77 of the estimated 1 000 protestors.[9] They were released from what had been John Vorster Square, the notorious apartheid police headquarters, after spending two nights in prison. Together with the APF the LPM held a protest on 24 August, the day before the launch of the WSSD, on the campus of the University of the Witwatersrand to coincide with the international conference on globalisation. At around 6 p.m., the protestors asked the audience to accompany them on a march to the nearby John Vorster Square. Here are some of my notes from this event:

> *Rows of police vehicles are parked just outside the entrance to Wits. Yet on the surface, at least, the mood appears remarkably relaxed as a fairly large crowd – including a number of children – assembles outside the Great Hall and receives candles. Within a few minutes, there is a series of what sound like gunshots, and the air is filled with stinking smoke. Immediately, large numbers of people are running towards me, some of them screaming in fear. It turns out that as the marchers in front moved into Jorissen Street, a row of police in riot gear fired stun grenades – with no warning at all. Several people have been injured by the stun grenades, and one arrested.*

A week later, on 31 August, what came to be called the Social Movements Indaba staged a spectacular march from the shacks and open sewers of Alexandra township in north-east Johannesburg to the glitzy fortress of Sandton in the north-west, where the official meetings were being held. Of great significance was the sharp contrast between the huge, rollicking March of Movements bedecked in red T-shirts, and the embarrassingly meagre turnout for an ANC-sponsored rally in Alexandra addressed by Thabo Mbeki.

Much of the left commentary following the WSSD march was strongly celebratory. Indymedia South Africa, for example, proclaimed that 'August 31 2002 will go down in history as the beginning of a new movement in South Africa and the world – a movement that asserts the power of people over delegated leaders and representatives in government, NGOs, political parties and the bureaucratised trade union movement; the power of people over profits and the interests of the rich; the power of collective, democratic action in the creation of another world outside of capitalism'. Yet in retrospect it has become clear that the movements were deeply fractured even then – and quite far from constituting a counter-hegemonic pole, as some had claimed at the time of the marches. There was, as Stephen Greenberg (2002) pointed out shortly after the WSSD, a paradox of growing grassroots opposition and militant action, along with a sharpening of divisions within and among movements, and growing tensions in relations with NGOs.[10]

Some of these tensions were, in fact, quite evident at the time of the WSSD, when the LPM bused in some 5 000 people from all corners of the country to participate in a 'Week of the Landless' at Shareworld, a derelict theme park on the outskirts of Soweto. What Shareworld made clear was the extraordinary array of interests and agendas yoked together under the LPM's banner of 'Land, Food, Jobs!' Participants defining themselves as the 'landless' included not only farm labourers and tenants, but also chiefs, school teachers and other professionals, disgruntled restitution claimants and a number of residents of informal settlements in the Gauteng area – some of whom came into fairly explosive conflict with one another, and with NGO representatives, over the course of the week. Tensions between the LPM and the APF also sprang into public view during the Social Movements Indaba march when sharp debate erupted over the LPM's support for Mugabe.[11] Further divisions

within and between NGOs and oppositional movements subsequently emerged.[12]

The chasm between these 'new' social movements and the 'old'
left of the ANC Alliance – COSATU and the SACP – was even
wider. In his commentary on the absence of any participation of
traditional formations of the working class in rural and urban
movements, Gentle (2002: 19) pointed to the trade union movement's failure to come to grips with the recomposition of the
working class towards sharply higher unemployment, increased
informalisation, changing male-female ratios and the emergence of
what he called a new urban-rural commuter status. He went on to
suggest that struggles around landlessness, evictions and electricity
and water cutoffs offered opportunities for the labour movement
'to experiment with new forms of organisation that are more
conducive to organising the unemployed and retrenched workers
or casual workers and workers in the informal sector. Their "site of
struggle" is not so much the regular workplace, but somewhere
between the workplace and the township' (2002: 19). In the same
issue of the *South African Labour Bulletin* (December 2002), I pressed
into service some of the key arguments of *Disabling Globalization* to
suggest how land, labour and livelihood struggles are deeply
interconnected, and how re-articulating the 'land question' in terms
of a social wage might enable 'new' social movements and organised
labour to forge alliances with one another, as well as across the
rural-urban divide (see Chapter 1).

At the time both COSATU and the SACP were in a heavily
embattled position within the ANC Alliance, stemming in large
part from their fierce opposition to the ANC's conservative turn as
well as internal divisions.[13] Emblematic of this conflict at the time
was a series of interviews that Jeremy Cronin, Deputy Secretary
General of the SACP, conducted with Helena Sheehan between
2001 and 2002, in which he reflected critically inter alia on the
ANC's position in relation to neoliberal capitalism, popular
demobilisation and the bureaucratisation of the ANC that he termed
'Zanufication' (Cronin 2001, 2002a), conjuring up the rapidly de-

teriorating situation in Zimbabwe. On the same day that the WSSD was launched (25 August 2002) there were reports that the ANC National Executive Committee (NEC) had sharply rebuked Cronin, forcing him to recant.[14] According to Jimmy Seepe, 'Mbeki berated critics of the ANC who have interpreted the public apology by Cronin as a sign of "intolerance, authoritarianism and dictatorship". Their positions, he said, showed they had an objective interest in disunity within the ANC and the alliance.'

COSATU's run-ins with the ANC were more overt and spectacular. In August 2001, shortly before the start of the World Conference Against Racism, COSATU called on its 1.8 million members to go on a two-day national strike against the privatisation of national assets. According to a press report on the strike on 29 August:

> Public Enterprises Minister Jeff Radebe, who heads the privatisation effort, said there could be no turning back from the commitment to restructure state-owned corporations. 'We have made it very clear that the essence of our economic policy is not going to change . . . Right now, the issue of restructuring is African National Congress (ANC) policy and we have to implement it to its natural conclusion,' he said.[15]

In fact, as we shall see, in the mid-term review of October 2003, the Mbeki administration started to signal its retreat from pushing privatisation to its 'natural conclusion', and a turn to trying to make parastatals serve 'developmental' purposes.

COSATU maintained a low profile during the WSSD, carefully distancing itself from the new social movements. Yet deep tensions between the unions and the Mbeki ruling bloc became powerfully evident in early October 2002, when COSATU organised another two-day national strike to protest the government's privatisation programme – a move that coincided with the Mbeki forces lashing out fiercely against their critics from the left in the run-up to the ANC conference in December 2002.

Stellenbosch, 16–20 December 2002

17 December 2002

The ANC's 51st policy conference held at Stellenbosch in December 2002 was widely seen as a moment of triumph for Mbeki, when he definitively vanquished critics of neoliberalism and privatisation from within and beyond the ANC Alliance.[16] Yet, as one observer presciently noted at the time, 'while the ANC has proven to be a political bulldog in dealing with political foes, it has weakened internally'.[17]

In September 2002 immediately following the WSSD, strategically placed ANC figures sprang into action, excoriating the 'ultra-left anti-neoliberal coalition' and effectively lumping together the new social movements and the left within the ANC Alliance, despite their deep estrangement from one another. A series of documents issued by the ANC in the latter part of 2002 is very revealing.[18] Although varied in official authorship, the language and logic of these diatribes are remarkably consistent. In addition to accusing the 'anti-neoliberal coalition' of telling blatant lies and waging a war against 'our government and the progressive forces of our country', the documents raise ominous questions about whose interests this coalition is serving. All three accuse the 'coalition' of acting in alliance with 'real neoliberals' (i.e., the predominantly white Democratic Alliance or DA) and with foreign elements hostile to the ANC, seeking to carry out 'a counter-revolutionary offensive against the national democratic revolution'.

Mbeki reiterated this theme almost word-for-word in his address to an ANC policy conference in late September 2002, asserting that 'we have radically reduced the capacity of the opponents of the national democratic revolution to conduct a campaign of terror against the revolution', while at the same time accusing 'left sectarian factions' of occupying 'the same trench with the anti-socialist forces' in their joint efforts to impede the national liberation movement.[19] The 'Strategy and Tactics' document prepared for the December 2002 conference is replete with references to the NDR, describing the ANC as the 'leader of the national democratic struggle, a disciplined force of the Left, organised to conduct consistent struggle in the interests of the poor'. As I argue more fully in Chapter 4, these deployments of the language of the NDR as part of an arsenal to discipline the 'ultra-left' represent a significant shift in official articulations of nationalism.

In addition to re-electing Mbeki as president with no opposition, the conference elected Minister of Finance Trevor Manuel to the top position in the NEC – a result widely seen as a strong endorsement for the government's conservative macro-economic policies and a further sign of the defeat of the left within the alliance.

The conference also highlighted a key point of tension between COSATU and the Mbeki wing within the ANC – namely proposals for a universal Basic Income Grant. In October 2002 the NEC rejected the Basic Income Grant, opting instead for an increase in coverage of the Child Support Grant. The conference effectively sidelined COSATU's support for the Basic Income Grant, and in his State of the Nation speech in February 2003 Mbeki made no mention of it – although he did assert that a key purpose of the Growth, Employment and Redistribution (GEAR) strategy had been 'to generate the resources for us to address the social needs of our people', and that, as a result of its successes, 'this year will see a further expansion of services to the people'.[20] He added, however, that 'government must act to ensure that we reduce the number of people dependent on social welfare, increasing the numbers that rely for their livelihood on normal participation in the economy'. By July 2003, he had invented (some would say dredged up) a language for talking about the nature of poverty and its treatment that was both new and remarkably retro.

Tshwane (Pretoria), 29 July 2003

Following a Cabinet Lekgotla[21] on 29 July 2003, Mbeki appeared at a media briefing and made the following announcement:

> Now, this is, as it were, the modern part of South Africa, with your aeroplanes and your computers and the people sitting around this room, who read and write and so on. We, all of us, we are this modern sector . . . So, you then have this large part of South Africa, which is relatively uneducated. It is unskilled. *It is not required in terms of modern society.* I am saying 'required' in the sense of employability. So, we have recognised this from the beginning, that large numbers of our people are poor and are in this condition. You can make the interventions we make about modernisation of the economy and so on, but it wouldn't necessarily have an impact on them, because of that degree of marginalisation. Therefore, you needed to make different sorts of intervention (emphasis added).[22]

This was an enormously important moment, marking a key turning point in what one might call the government of poverty.

Official discourses of a First and Second Economy figured prominently in the ANC's 'Ten Year Review' later in 2003, its manifesto for the 2004 election, Mbeki's State of the Nation address in February 2004, his opening address to parliament in May 2004 and a slew of statements by lesser luminaries.[23] One of the clearest and strongest articulations can be found in 'Transform the Second Economy' on the ANC *Today* website, that links language of a Second Economy to that of a developmental state – a term that the

ANC government in the 1990s had been careful to limit to local government:

> Contrary to arguments about minimal state intervention in the economy, we must proceed on the basis of the critical need for the state to be involved in the transformation of the Second Economy. This state intervention must entail detailed planning and implementation of comprehensive development programmes, fully accepting the concept of a developmental state.[24]

At the same time, leading ANC figures were quick to make clear that planned intervention in the Second Economy did not in any way reduce official commitment to rapid capital accumulation driven by market forces.

A first step towards a more ostensibly 'pro-poor' stance can be traced to 2001 when Minister of Water Affairs and Forestry Ronnie Kasrils inaugurated a policy to provide free basic water that became linked with Municipal Indigent Policy – the vagaries of which form the focus of Chapter 3. Also in 2001, Vishnu Padayachee and Imraan Valodia (2001) discerned signs of 'changing GEAR' – including an economic growth strategy that suggested a retreat from the Washington Consensus, and a somewhat more interventionist stance in infrastructural development, industrial policy and labour market interventions. Even so, the launch of the Second Economy in 2003 heralded a qualitatively new phase in the post-apartheid order. It marked the moment when the Mbeki administration moved decisively in overtly interventionist directions, flexing its muscles as a self-defined 'developmental state' – at the same time as it reverted to a much older lexicon of a dual economy.

There is now an extensive body of writing on First/Second Economy, much of it critical of the dualistic framing and pointing to the deep interconnections between racially inflected structures of wealth and poverty in South Africa.[25] My own contribution to the debates was to suggest that the discourse of the Second Economy can be seen as part of an effort to contain the challenges exemplified by oppositional movements that reached their zenith at the time of the WSSD, and render them subject to government intervention.[26] What is significant about this discourse is the way it defines a segment of society that is superfluous to the 'modern' economy, and in need of paternal guidance – those falling within this category are citizens, but second class. As such they are deserving of a modicum of social security, but on tightly disciplined and conditional terms.

Strategies to identify and treat a 'backward' segment of society also goes a long way towards explaining the vehemence with which powerful figures in the ANC have dismissed proposals for a modest universal income grant. Mbeki's response to a question about the Basic Income Grant at the July 2003 press conference on the Cabinet Lekgotla is quite revealing: 'To introduce a system of social support, which indiscriminately gives to a millionaire R100 and to this poor old lady on a pension R100, it really doesn't make sense' – a totally specious argument that neglects the proposed claw-back from higher income taxpayers. The reason why the ANC government has consistently rejected the Basic Income Grant, I suggest, is precisely *because* it is a universal grant – and therefore lacks points of leverage for instilling in its recipients the 'correct' attitudes and aspirations. This consideration sheds light on former Minister of Trade and Industry Alec Erwin's remark that 'the problem with the Basic Income Grant is not the money but the idea'.[27]

There is another dimension of this moment in July 2003 of great significance, made clear by Mark Gevisser in his magisterial biography of Mbeki, subtitled *The Dream Deferred* (2007). Confirming the importance for Mbeki of his invention of the two economies, Gevisser cites an interview with Joel Netshitenzhe, a close confidante of Mbeki at the time, who explained that when Mbeki tried to sell GEAR to the left in 1996, 'his starting point was *Das Kapital*. He used Marx to defend GEAR. Now, as he is developing his "two economies" ideas, he goes to EU policies and practices, and what the EU does with its underdeveloped regions. And he draws his conclusions from there . . .' (Gevisser 2007: 780). Gevisser goes on to recount his own meeting with Mbeki in July 2004, in the afterglow of national elections that April in which the ANC increased its majority to 69.7 per cent, up from 66.4 per cent in 1999:[28]

> Mbeki himself told me that it was precisely his burgeoning sense of empowerment that enabled him to act decisively on poverty, for the first time since he introduced GEAR eight years previously. It was all about being able to leverage resources effectively because he was finally in full control of the economy. Even without private sector investment, the state itself actually had 'volumes of capital' which it could inject into the economy; volumes the ANC did not know how to access – or even know how to find – in its first fragile years in power (2007: 780).

Yet, as Gevisser himself points out in discussing what he aptly calls 'the poisoned well of post-apartheid South African politics' (2007: 675), the Cabinet subcommittee on arms procurement that Mbeki chaired from 1996–99 approved R30 billion in spending on military hardware, a figure that ultimately doubled due to the unstable rand: 'nothing in the South African transition illustrates . . . "the dream deferred" more trenchantly than the spectacle of an ANC government committed to redistribution and a "better life for all" dropping nearly R60 billion on submarines, frigates, and fighter jets at a time when it was trying to cap spending on everything else' (2007: 676). In Chapter 3, I shall come back to explore the ramping-up in (non-military) government spending since 2003/04, especially in relation to local government.

During the same interview in July 2004, Mbeki cast aside any possibility of what he termed 'some big eruption', speaking of 'a much greater sense of joy in South Africa today' (Gevisser 2007: 781).[29] In retrospect these statements appear as the epitome of hubris, in its original Greek sense of calling forth the wrath of the gods. There were in fact signs that anticipated huge eruptions later in the decade – but to find them we have to go back to two moments in seemingly nondescript and distinctly unglamorous places.

Bergville, 6 December 2003

In December 2003 I received a phone call in Durban from Alfred
Duma, a veteran who served time on Robben Island, inviting me
to an *imbizo* in Bergville, a rural area, about 45 kilometres from
Ladysmith/Ezakheni where he lives. From the isiZulu word meaning
a gathering called by a king or traditional leader, *imbizo* has now
become a formal part of the South African government's lexicon:

> Government launched the *Imbizo* programme in 2001 as a period
> of intensified activity where all spheres of government – national,
> provincial and local – interact with the people across the country.
> The *Imbizo* initiative plays an important role as an interactive style of
> governance, which creates more space for public participation and
> involvement around interactive implementation of government's
> Programme of Action.[30]

This was going to be a very large and important event, Mr Duma
explained, at which Jacob Zuma (then Mbeki's deputy president)
would be present. I accepted with alacrity. To the best of my
knowledge, this event represented the first time that the ANC had
made a substantial foray into deep rural regions of KwaZulu-Natal,
then the exclusive territorial stronghold of the Zulu nationalist
Inkatha Freedom Party (IFP). Three years earlier, just before the
local government elections on 5 December 2000, I had accompanied
friends in Ladysmith on an ANC campaign trip to other rural areas
of the newly demarcated uThukela district municipality. On that
occasion there had been great trepidation about possible attacks by
the IFP, and several of the cars in the convoy were carrying weapons.
Clearly, the event to which I had been invited was in preparation
for the national and provincial elections scheduled for April 2004.

Another reason why I was intrigued was that in August 2003
the director of the National Prosecuting Authority, Bulelani Ngcuka,
announced that Zuma's involvement in the arms deal had produced
prima facie evidence of corruption. The allegations turned around
a R500 000 annual bribe paid by the French arms manufacturer

Thales, facilitated by Zuma's financial adviser Schabir Shaik. Ngcuka explained at a media briefing that the National Prosecuting Authority had decided not to charge Zuma because they considered the case to be 'unwinnable' in court. Herein lay the first rumblings of the massive eruption that transformed the landscape of South African politics in the second half of the decade.

The Bergville *imbizo* was, indeed, a major event. It was held in a tent with seating for 5 000 people, pitched on a flat-topped hillock at the end of a bumpy, muddy dirt road (this being the middle of the rainy season). There was a massive military and police presence, and one could only gain access to the tent by going through a metal detector and tight security check. Mr Duma and I were ushered into front-row seats, in recognition of his having worked with Zuma. All the top ANC figures in the province were assembled – but it was only when the meeting had been called to order that Zuma was helicoptered in, entering the tent amidst enthusiastic cheers and ululations. Sitting in the front made it difficult to observe the audience. I had the distinct impression, though, that much of the noise was coming from younger people, while many of the older people I was able to observe were more reserved – hardly surprising in this IFP stronghold.

Strikingly clear, though, was Zuma's capacity to connect with the audience in language that resonated powerfully, and called forth animated responses. The most insistent issue that came up during the *imbizo* was that of water. A number of speakers from the floor pointed out that this region was rich in water, but that most of it was being piped to Gauteng province. ANC officials promised to change this – as well as to provide more houses, schools, clinics and jobs. They also exhorted the audience to vote for the ANC, explaining that they could do so secretly without incurring the wrath of traditional leaders. Zuma's skilful wooing tied in seamlessly with animated expressions of Christianity, communism and Zulu masculinity – including song and dance performances by inspirational gospel singers, vigorous renditions of '*Ama komanisi*' (We are communists) and warrior dances.

It was only in 2005 that Zuma first performed his own legendary song 'Awaleth' Umshini Wami' (Bring me my machine gun) at the trial of Schabir Shaik who was convicted of fraud in June that year, feeding into the forces that propelled Zuma into the presidency of the ANC in 2007, and the country in 2009. Before tracing this process, we need to attend to another event that triggered huge upheavals in the second half of the 2000s.

Harrismith, 30 August 2004

Travelling north-east from Bergville, one links up with the N3, the major highway between Durban and Johannesburg from which one catches a glimpse of Harrismith, a former white town in the Free State province, and its neighbouring black township Intabazwe. Let us go now to Harrismith/Intabazwe, to a moment in time captured by three press reports:[31]

20 children shot in Harrismith protest

Monday, 30 August 2004

Twenty children were shot when police tried to disperse a group of protesters on the N3 highway outside Harrismith today, Free State police said.

Paul Kubheka, a police spokesperson, said about 4 500 youths, some called out of schools in the Intabazwe township of Harrismith, descended on the N3 highway this morning to highlight concerns about service delivery in the area.

'Steps were taken to calm them down but they forced their way onto the N3,' said Kubheka. 'This had serious implications because it is a national road.' Kubheka said police opened fire and two youths were hit with pellets, one in the leg and another in the hand. 'They were already on the road and there was no other way of controlling them,' Kubheka said.

Upon visiting a local hospital it was found that 18 other children were admitted after they were also shot with pellets. Kubheka said four other children were admitted with cuts and bruises after they had been pushed against a wire fence during the protest. None of the children were seriously injured. Kubheka said the highway was clear by 1pm but the children had moved into the township where they were setting tyres alight.

The area was being monitored by a large police contingent drawn from all the police units in the surrounding areas. 'Police are monitoring the situation. We are trying to avoid a confrontation.' Kubheka said the youths called themselves 'The Concerned Group' and appeared to be made up of many community organisations. – Sapa [South African Press Association]

Harrismith in mourning[32]
Thursday, 2 September 2004
Sibonelo Msomi
Ntabazwe Township in Harrismith was still in flames on Wednesday.

Burning tyres, scrap cars, stones and poles blocked roads as residents who feel neglected by the local Maluting-a-Phofung Municipality demonstrated their anger.

Late on Wednesday residents decided to embark on mass action to bring the township to a standstill – preventing any movement of people in or out.

This is to show that the township is mourning the death of Tebogo Moloi [Mkhonza], 17, who died on Monday after being shot by police during a protest march during which a crowd blockaded the N3 demanding government housing subsidies, improved water and electricity services, employment opportunities and development in the impoverished Free State town.

Premier Beatrice Marshoff was warned of possible riots here two weeks ago but the town exploded on Monday before she intervened. Marshoff confirmed this in Bloemfontein yesterday at a provincial meeting with mayors and speakers.

She said her office had been in contact with the Greater Harrismith Concerned Residents (GHCR) group, which complained about poor service from the local council.

'I was still waiting for more information about the issue when the situation got out of hand,' said the premier.

On Wednesday, children were sent home early from local schools and joined youths who were positioned on all street corners ready to act on orders to embark on further action.

GHCR chairman Neo Motaung said the situation is potentially explosive until Marshoff or President Thabo Mbeki intervene.

'We do not trust the mayor, Balekile Mzwango, and his councillors because they have failed us for years. They have failed to install water meters, provide us with free electricity, build low-cost government subsidy houses and create employment opportunities. All they did was to move businesses from Harrismith and develop Qwa Qwa at our expense.[33] There is no development here and we feel the pinch of unemployment,' said Motaung.

Motaung said the provincial ANC leadership has conducted a smear campaign against members of the GHCR. As a result, he said, Motaung has been kicked out of the local ANC branch, allegedly because of his role in complaining about poor services in Ntabazwe.

He said the group will aggressively embark on a campaign to force government to listen and respond to their demands.

'We will burn municipal vehicles in the township and destroy their properties if that is what we have to do to get their attention. We have lost patience now and already we have shown that we can mobilise people to bring the area into a standstill. *If further action is what will bring our demands to Mbeki's attention, we have the will to do that,*' he said [emphasis added].

GHCR Organiser Msizi Mavuso said anger is still burning in the township as police continue to assault and insult people in the streets of the township.

Harrismith: Shock video[34]
Sunday, 5 September 2004
Exclusive but shocking video footage in *City Press*'s possession shows how Harrismith police opened fire indiscriminately on demonstrators as they slowly crossed the N3 highway last week and then continued firing at them as they fled for cover.

This move led to the tragic death of 17-year-old Tebogo Mkhonza.

The video shows how the toyi-toying group slowly started crossing the highway. The demonstrators were not throwing stones, as some reports claimed, and their numbers were nowhere near the reported 4 500 claimed by police earlier this week.

Before the demonstrators were halfway across the road, police opened fire without any warning. The demonstrators turned and ran for cover.

Police, however, continued to fire at their backs. They also continued shooting as people fell to the ground. The video clearly identifies three police officers firing at the fleeing demonstrators, although more were involved in the shooting. The footage then shows at least four police officers grappling with a demonstrator and forcibly pushing him into the back of a police van.

In extremely disturbing footage, one then sees a badly injured and bleeding Mkhonza lying on the floor of a police van. Fellow demonstrators locked in the van are visibly upset by police inaction to call an ambulance. Mkhonza wailed in pain and battled to breathe with what looked like a chest wound.

The Harrismith protest was by no means the first municipal revolt of the post-apartheid era – such protests can be traced back to the late 1990s (Bond 2012). In early July 2004, for example, residents of Diepsloot, a shack settlement north of Johannesburg, staged a huge, angry march to protest housing conditions. Yet perhaps because of the killing of Tebogo Mkhonza, Harrismith has become iconic of thousands of so-called service delivery protests that have rocked the country – a deeply problematic term, as I discuss more fully in Chapter 3 where I locate municipal uprisings in relation to the broader contradictions of local government in the post-apartheid era.

Harrismith can also be seen as an instance of protracted, enraged protests following police brutality in other parts of the world: Paris in October 2005, when two teenage boys were electrocuted fleeing from police; Athens in December 2008, when a protesting teenager was killed by police; Tunisia in December 2010 when Mohamed Bouazizi set himself on fire after suffering humiliation by a police woman, sparking uprisings all over North Africa and the Middle East; and London in August 2011 when Mike Duggan had his face shot off by police, who then refused to answer to community members.

From Harrismith angry protests quickly spread to the towns of Vrede, Warden and Memel in the adjacent Phumelela municipality, and from there to the entire country. In October 2005, the Minister of Safety and Security announced that his department had recorded 881 illegal protests during the 2004/05 financial year – during which period there were 5 085 legal protests.[35] Peter Alexander (2010: 26) cites data provided by the Incident Registration Information System of the South African Police Service on 'public gatherings', the large majority of which appear to be protest related. According to these data, there were 34 610 'gatherings' between 2004/05 and 2007/08 of which 2 861 were defined as 'unrest-related', and 31 749 as 'peaceful'. In Chapter 3, I shall discuss two such 'gatherings' in late 2004 in Ladysmith and Newcastle.

The other institution that counts protests is Municipal IQ, a private firm that describes itself as 'a web-based data and intelligence service specialising in the monitoring and assessment of all of South Africa's 283 municipalities'. Their 'Hotspots Monitor', which issues press releases containing data on 'major protests' covered by the media, is suggestive of how much activity is *not* covered by the media (although the morning traffic report on the radio, SAfm 'Morning Live', regularly provides helpful information to motorists on which roads to avoid where protestors have erected barricades and are burning tires).

The most widely publicised of these protests took place in the town of Ficksburg in the Free State province on 13 April 2011. In the course of a large protest in the run-up to local government elections, police kicked and beat Andries Tatane with batons, and then shot him twice in the chest. Tatane, a 33-year-old mathematics teacher and community organiser, was unarmed. The murder was recorded on camera, and broadcast on the evening news by the South African Broadcasting Corporation, eliciting widespread shock. Yet David Bruce (2012) has shown that the Tatane killing

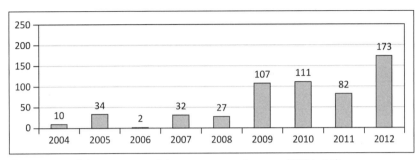

Figure 2.1 Major service delivery protests by year (2004–12).
Source: Municipal IQ, 'Hotspots Monitor', June 2013.

was not an aberration, as officials proclaimed.[36] Starting with the death of Tebogo Mkhonza in Harrismith, the policing of protests has become increasingly violent. In October 2012, a Multi-Level Government Initiative released a report claiming that protest activity rose dramatically in the first eight months of 2012, and that some 80 per cent of these protests were violent.

For purposes of the present discussion, three aspects of the upsurge in municipal rebellions are important to bear in mind. First, they coincided with significant weakening of the first round of oppositional new social movements.[37] The emergence of the Durban shack dwellers' movement (Abahlali baseMjondolo) in March 2005 represented a different dynamic of organisation and growth, despite official repression.[38] The key point, however, is that the municipal uprisings are taking place far beyond the reach of either generation of social movements – they exemplify precisely what I am calling 'movement beyond movements'.

Second, the amplifying waves of municipal protest have coincided with substantial increases in government spending along with far more actively interventionist moves by the ANC government, as we shall see in Chapter 3 – a dynamic that compels us to push well beyond conventional explanations cast in terms of poor service delivery, corrupt and inept municipal officials and councillors, or 'bottom-up' responses to 'top-down' neoliberalism.

A third consideration, to which we now turn, concerns the confluence of municipal uprisings with a second key dimension of movement beyond movements – the upsurge in popular support for Zuma following his dismissal as deputy president in mid-2005 just before the ANC's National General Council in June/July 2005.

Tshwane (Pretoria), 29 June – 3 July 2005

Mid-way between the ANC's 52nd national conference in Stellenbosch in December 2002 and the 53rd conference in Polokwane in December 2007, the ANC held its National General Council from 29 June – 3 July 2005 at the University of Pretoria 'to discuss and debate the strategic organisational and political issues facing the movement', the ANC website explains.[39] What the neatly organised set of documents accessible through the website does not tell us is the vehemently explosive character of the debate, in sharp contrast with the 2002 Stellenbosch conference. This was precisely the eruption that Mbeki had confidently dismissed a year earlier, and it foreshadowed his defeat at Polokwane in December 2007.

Several dramatic events earlier in June fed into the contentious terrain of the National General Council. On 2 June Judge Hillary Squires convicted Schabir Shaik of fraud, and found 'overwhelming' evidence of a 'corrupt relationship' with Zuma. On 14 June Mbeki appeared before a special session of both houses of parliament and declared that '. . . as President of the Republic I have come to the conclusion that the circumstances dictate that in the interests of the Honourable Deputy President, the government, our young democratic system, and our country, it would be best to release the Honourable Jacob Zuma from his responsibilities as Deputy President of the Republic and member of the Cabinet'.

On the opening day of the National General Council, 29 June, Zuma appeared in the Durban magistrates' court to face corruption charges. He received a standing ovation from the public gallery as he walked into court, and a dramatic show of support from a large crowd outside – many of them also shouting anti-Mbeki slogans, waving placards against Mbeki, and some burning images and cursing him using apartheid-era expletives. Feeding into this anger was Mbeki's appointment of Phumzile Mlambo-Ngcuka, wife of Zuma's accuser Bulelani Ngcuka, as deputy president in Zuma's place.

Appearing before the National General Council on 30 June, Zuma announced that he would not be participating in party structures during the course of his prosecution. Following a heated debate, the National General Council voted to reinstate Zuma to his position in the party. In effect, a widely representative body drawn from ANC branches overturned a decision by the National Working Committee, a small group close to Mbeki at the pinnacle of the ANC power structure.

On Sunday, 3 July, *City Press* newspaper carried a report on the National General Council by Seepe entitled 'Mbeki fights for ANC control':

> The battle lines were clearly drawn on Saturday evening between ANC president Thabo Mbeki and his deputy [in the ANC] Jacob Zuma over who will finally control the organisation . . . Since Thursday the plenary has been displaying a great deal of disdain for Mbeki and huge support for Zuma, who got himself 'reinstated' into the full glory of his position as number two man in the party, as well as an endorsement for the presidency in 2007 . . . The resolution to reinstate Zuma came amid songs praising him while denigrating Mbeki. Zuma's supporters were vocal in their excitement and saw their victory as putting Mbeki in his place . . . The show of support for Zuma at the NGC [National General Council] raises the question of whether Mbeki is now a lame-duck president who rules the country without overt support from his organisation.

On the same day, the *Sunday Independent* reported:

> The ANC's rank and file staged an uprecedented coup this week, using a closed session of the party's national general council to overrule its top leaders and throw Jacob Zuma another political lifeline . . .

Mbeki has never before been confronted by such open rebellion and his leadership so undermined.

These reports called forth an infuriated response from Smuts Ngonyama, Mbeki's spokesperson, strongly objecting to the language of 'battle line' and 'coups', and accusing the media of 'peddling its own truth about the National General Council'.

What is beyond dispute is that, in addition to reinstating Zuma to his position in the party, key proposals set forth by the Mbeki ruling bloc were overturned by the National General Council. In preparation for the National General Council, the ANC released a series of discussion documents: 'Development and Under-development', 'The National Question' and 'Unity in Diversity' as well as 'The Organisational Design of the ANC' and 'Guidelines on Discussion of Strategy and Tactics'.[40]

Most controversial was the 'Development and Underdevelop-ment' paper prepared by Jabu Moloketi, a conservative figure close to Mbeki, and which focused on 'bridging the divide between the First and Second Economy'. Its central thrust was that 'an increase in investment is only likely to result in an increase in employment if the cost of labour is reduced relative to capital'. The paper then proposes a dual labour market strategy, in which minimum wage and other collective bargaining agreements are waived in the lower segment of the labour market. The document unleashed fierce condemnation by the SACP and COSATU, who saw the Moloketi proposals as undermining the concessions to organised labour in the neoliberal turn of the 1990s. It also provoked a barrage of angry critique of the elitism of the ANC's Black Economic Empowerment (BEE) measures, making clear how BEE sits uneasily astride the discursive divide between the First and Second Economies.

Mbeki's moves to centralise power in the President's Office also came under heavy fire. Declaring that 'the ANC needs to reform its election and selection processes in order to restore sanity within the ranks and to reduce the contemporary commotion and factionalism', the 'Organisational Design' discussion paper proposed the formation of a permanent Electoral Commission that would 'take charge of the election process in the run up to and including election processes'. In effect, this was part of an effort to bring unruly branches and provincial structures under control by replacing branch-level lobbying with centralised, top-down selection – and it was vigorously rejected by the National General Council.

Another revealing statement in the 'Organisational Design' discussion paper reads as follows:

> We need to confront the reality that our branches as presently established are not adequate to reach and mobilise all the motive forces of the NDR behind the ANC. We must review the structural reach of the ANC such that the broad forces the ANC organised under the UDF [United Democratic Front] to topple apartheid rule, remain mobilised under the ANC's political and ideological hegemony.

The 'Consolidated Report on Sectoral Strategies' published in the wake of the National General Council is even more explicit about the limits of ANC structures at local level:

> The new situation has also seen the emergence of issue-based social movements, which mobilise around legitimate grievances, but do so in a manner that may conflict with programmes and values of the ANC. The principal cause of such developments, particularly the recent upheavals in a number of localities is the weakness of ANC structures and thus their inability to give leadership to communities.

The report goes on to recommend that '[w]e must reaffirm the ideological orientation of the ANC as that of "revolutionary African nationalism", and a "disciplined force of the left"', noting as well that '[w]e must actively strive to build ideological coherence and unity of action within the Alliance, in pursuit of the NDR and minimise contradictions and conflicts at practical level'.

In the last paper published before his death, Harold Wolpe (1995) presciently noted that conceptions of 'fundamental transformation' central to the NDR were likely to become a major source of contestation in the future – a point to which I return in far greater detail in Chapter 4. Most important for purposes of the present discussion is how the National General Council became, in effect, the crucible in which Wolpe's prophecy was fully realised. The explosive anger that erupted at the National General Council also underscores the double-edged character of articulations of nationalism as liberation – how they are key elements of the post-colonial hegemonic project, while at the same time deeply vulnerable to charges of betrayal.

These considerations are crucial to grasping the 'Zunami' – a term coined in the context of the ANC's 53rd national conference in Polokwane in December 2007, when the extent and intensity of popular support for Jacob Zuma was powerfully on display, catching many of the pundits who pronounce on South African politics by surprise. Common explanations for the Zunami cast in terms of a 'coalition of the disgruntled' are radically inadequate, as I argue more fully in Chapter 4. Instead, popular support for Zuma needs to be grasped as a key dimension of 'movement beyond movements' – the lineaments of which started to emerge with great clarity in the second half of 2005.

Ladysmith, September 2005 – March 2006

In the second half of 2005 I took a sabbatical from the University of California, Berkeley, in anticipation of local government elections that were due to take place towards the end of the year. Confronting a veritable conflagration of municipal protests, the ANC government decided to postpone the elections that eventually took place on 1 March 2006. I did, however, have the opportunity to observe how the battle for control of the ANC was playing out in everyday practice, and to participate in some extraordinary moments in this seemingly very ordinary place. Three events exemplify the amplifying tensions within the ANC Alliance at local, regional and provincial levels in KwaZulu-Natal.

28 July 2005: David Szanton and I arrived in Ladysmith in the late afternoon, and went directly to the ANC office. We were hoping to meet with a friend who had just been appointed a ward councillor in Ezakheni – the previous councillor had been recently dismissed on charges of corruption. 'I'm working very hard,' she exclaimed, going on to say, 'We're afraid of people toyi-toying in the streets.' A Local Election Team (LET) meeting was just getting underway, and we were invited to sit in. LET meetings are routine events in the run-up to elections, assembling representatives from ANC branches to chart strategy. In this ANC stronghold during the period prior to the 2000 local government elections, the campaign meetings, preparations and organisation I was able to observe ran like well-oiled machinery. This meeting was a rebellion by branch members against the ANC leadership. It was chaired by a regional ANC official who began by exhorting branch representatives to expand ANC membership in preparation for the election, make sure that ANC packs got out, and that they collected the R12 annual fee. As he was talking there was a palpable tension in the room, with people muttering to one another and shaking their heads. Shortly after he started talking he was interrupted by questions that focused around two key issues: the visit of the deputy president to Bergville the previous Sunday, and the appointment of a new municipal manager. Participants in the meeting became very vocal and vociferous, demanding to know why they had not been kept informed about these key issues. One after another women and men stood up and complained bitterly about how the leadership was simply ordering them around and telling them what to do, treating them like cattle while excluding them from vitally important events and decisions. At one point an infuriated man jumped up and shouted that 'the leadership must not privatise knowledge'!

27 November 2005: On this hot, steamy Sunday we met the provincial head of the Umkhonto we Sizwe Military Veterans Association (MKMVA), Mr Sibusiso Qwabe, in Durban and drove him to Ladysmith for the launch of the local branch of the MKMVA.[41] We had been asked to do so by Mr Duma, who explained that Mr Qwabe had been denied transport by the

> Mbeki-aligned leadership of the ANC in the province. Intense divisions within
> the provincial level ANC formed the central focus of our conversations on the
> trip to Ladysmith.[42] About 35 veterans were awaiting us in the ANC office,
> more or less evenly divided between women and men.[43]
>
> At the start of the meeting Mr Qwabe launched into a vigorous rendition
> of Jacob Zuma's theme song, 'Awuleth' Umshini Wami' (Bring me my
> machine gun), in which everyone participated.[44] 'What do we mean when
> we sing this song?' he asked as soon as the last strains had died away. 'We
> mean three things,' he continued, 'first we are angry; second we are disciplined;
> and third we are organised to change the situation.'

Liz Gunner has written brilliantly about the historical provenance
of the song in the struggle era and its powerful contemporary
resonances 'with its weighty solemnity carrying the gravitas of a
Zulu war song, the weight of heavy masculinity, echoes of the just
struggle for a free country, shards of anger of those who feel the
new dispensation has brought them nothing' (2008: 48). On the
occasion of the launch of the Ladysmith MKMVA, Mr Qwabe used
his interpretation of the meaning of the song to organise his speech.
He expounded in detail on how shabbily the veterans had been
treated by a highly educated technocratic elite in the ANC who
had not been on the front line of the struggle, but had seized power
and privilege for themselves and drove around in fancy cars while
most people were suffering. Picking up on the second theme, he
reminded the veterans of the discipline and determination that
their active participation in the struggle had instilled in them. From
there, he exhorted the veterans to throw their support behind Zuma,
and not believe lies that were being told about him – especially
those relating to his alleged rape of a 31-year-old woman several
weeks earlier, which, Mr Qwabe insisted, was a set-up by Zuma's
enemies. In Chapter 5, I discuss more fully Zuma's rape trial the
following April and its larger significance, as well as the role of the
MKMVA in consolidating support for Zuma prior to Polokwane.[45]

In relation to themes that surfaced during the MKMVA launch,
let me touch briefly on different reports of an event on 2 December

2006, at the reburial in Pietermaritzburg of Moses Mabhida, a senior figure in the SACP who died in exile in Mozambique in 1986 and with whom many veterans identified closely. Mbeki's biographer Gevisser reports on this event as follows:

> Here, during his [Mbeki's] speech, he was booed and jeered at by a crowd of Zuma supporters: wearing ANC tee shirts, they broke into Zuma's trademark song of rebellion, the struggle standard *Umshini Wami* ('Bring me my machine gun'), and prevented Mbeki from continuing. It was a repetition of the thuggish disrespect Zuma supporters had shown towards Mbeki throughout their hero's court appearances, singing aggressively rude songs about him and his family and burning tee shirts and posters bearing his image. At the Mabhida funeral, Zuma made a show of bringing his supporters to order, but the event degenerated into chaos (2007: 790).

A report of the same event in the *Mail & Guardian* the following Friday (8 December 2006) cited Zuma supporters' anger over what they saw as attempts by those in the Mbeki camp to 'hijack Zuma's long-standing ambition to return Mabhida's body and claim his legacy'. Zuma is seen as Mabhida's protégé, the report goes on to note, and therefore feels he has the right to claim his legacy: 'It is significant for the Zuma camp that Mabhida died literally in Zuma's hands [arms?] in a foreign country and in a "house of exile".' The report also cites a senior ANC provincial leader known to be close to Zuma asserting that 'it was not fitting that the Mbeki camp, "characterised by highly educated ANC members, who were not in the trenches during the revolutionary struggle", were going to "rob Zuma of his moment in the sun"'.

This was not the first time that President Mbeki was booed off the stage. An earlier event took place in Ezakheni township outside Ladysmith, on another hot and steamy Sunday three months after the MKMVA launch and just before local government elections held on Wednesday, 1 March.

28 February 2006: On this peak day of campaigning for the local government elections, Mbeki was scheduled to address residents of D Section in Ezakheni who were threatening to boycott elections in their ward and disrupt voting in other wards. They were infuriated because their candidate for ward councillor had been rejected by regional and provincial ANC officials, who had insisted that a woman candidate run instead. Mbeki was scheduled to land at the small Ladysmith airport at around 9 a.m., and go directly from there to D Section. It was raining that morning, and a crowd of us waiting at Ladysmith airport were told that the plan had changed. Mbeki would be landing in the larger and safer Pietermaritzburg airport, and going first to Wembezi township outside Estcourt where IFP members were threatening to turn the township into a no-go zone for the election. In fact, it was only around 4 p.m. that Mbeki's entourage arrived in Ezakheni. By that point, many in the large crowd were drunk and probably all of them angry. Officials were trying to mollify the crowd with loud music and dancing on the makeshift stage – but there were also a large contingent of police, and sharpshooters positioned on surrounding rooftops. Accompanied by the proposed replacement candidate and provincial ANC officials, Mbeki came on stage and began to introduce her. At that moment the crowd surged towards the stage shouting 'Phansi, phansi!' (Down, down!) and gesturing downward with their thumbs. A row of police at the front of the stage moved to push the crowd back, and sharpshooters stood and took aim. In this incredibly tense moment Mbeki ripped off his ANC T-shirt and tossed it into the crowd, exposing his naked torso. This swift, unexpected move disarmed the crowd. There were momentary expressions of disbelief – and then people started laughing and shouting for everyone on stage to hand over their T-shirts. They obliged, with women scurrying to find something with which to cover their breasts. An aide handed Mbeki a jacket and the shirtless dignitaries were hustled from the stage into their limousines, which shot out of the township as fast as the pot-holed roads would allow. In the somewhat shell-shocked aftermath of this extraordinary event, I asked several people for their impression of what had just happened. The dominant response was that it was 'undignified' – a response, I must admit, that struck me as deeply unfair, given the likely mayhem that Mbeki had adroitly averted. What this event reflected, though, was popular anger and resentment towards Mbeki and his regime that far exceeded any 'coalition of the disgruntled'.

Contrary to widespread expectations of massive boycotts of local government elections the following Wednesday, in the country as a whole the ANC Alliance actually increased its share of the vote from 60 per cent in the 2000 local elections to 66 per cent, with a very similar turnout rate. These aggregates unquestionably mask local contingencies and shifts in different directions.[46] Yet, as Susan Booysen (2007) has observed in an insightful paper entitled 'With the Ballot and the Brick', it is also the case that many of the poorest South Africans have come to regard protest as a legitimate and necessary form of political action – at the same time that they continue to support the ANC vis-à-vis other political parties. In Ladysmith – and many other parts of the country, I suspect – people were very clear that they were voting for Zuma.

Polokwane, 16–20 December 2007

Polokwane (formerly Pietersburg) in the northernmost province of Limpopo is a small, nondescript previously white town rather like Harrismith and Ladysmith, adjacent to a large black township, Seshego, that was part of the Lebowa Bantustan. This product of apartheid geography has come to signify the fiercest battle ever fought in the nearly 100-year history of the ANC that erupted at its 53rd national conference. The internecine bloodbath was precipitated by Mbeki's decision to run for a third term as president of the ANC, even though the South African constitution prevented him from standing for a third term as president of the country. His plan, as Marais (2011: 364) puts it, 'was to usher Phumzile Mlambo-Ngcuka in as South Africa's first female president [in the 2009 national elections], while he would continue to wield decisive influence from behind the screen'. It was, as Marais notes, 'a pompous, foolhardy manoeuvre', and it led to Mbeki's humiliating defeat at the hands of delegates elected by ANC branches.

Popular anger towards the ruling bloc was powerfully evident at the conference, especially on the first day when thousands of delegates hissed at Mbeki, and broke into singing '*Umshini Wami*' immediately following his two-and-a-half-hour speech. They also made soccer hand gestures indicating that a player should be taken off the field. Delegates then shouted down conference chair Mosiuoa Lekota – a strong Mbeki supporter, openly critical of Zuma – who was forced to cede the platform to Zuma's chosen deputy, Kgalema Motlanthe.

For two and a half years, the prospect of Zuma's ascension to the ANC throne had terrified a significant chunk of South Africa's bourgeoisie, both black and white – with much of this terror finding expression in terms of 'populism'. 'Waiting for the Barbarians', an article by Vukani Mde and Karima Brown in *Business Day* on 31 October 2005, is the most incisive piece of mainstream press commentary of which I am aware during this period between the National General Council and Polokwane:

> In the conventional analysis of the ANC crisis, Zuma is the choice of the 'disaffected' in the ANC, who see in him a chance to return to the centre of decision-making. The marginalisation of the 'disaffected' forces – the Congress of South African Trade Unions (COSATU) and South African Communist Party (SACP), the ANC Youth League, sections of business and the left of the ANC – is the result of Mbeki's autocratic and exclusive leadership style.
>
> If Zuma represents the 'disaffected', this analysis tells us that Mbeki represents a necessary modernising project that cannot but leave behind some of the ANC's historical baggage. It follows from this that Mbeki is driving the shedding of the party's historical character as a broad movement, and turning it into a modern political party in the pursuit of power.
>
> This extends to our stance on the continent. Mbeki leads a movement to shake off Africa's old kleptocracy, despite his lapses in Zimbabwe. Zuma is the stereotype of the Big Man in Africa, embracing the continent's proclivity for excess.
>
> If one buys into this broad analysis of the Zuma/Mbeki divide, a number of seemingly neutral and 'obvious' value judgements can be made. Zuma represents the past, which may or may not have been glorious while it lasted. Mbeki represents a necessary future,

unpalatable and hard-nosed though it may be. That Zuma is the accused in a corruption trial of course adds weight to these value judgements.

To choose between Mbeki and Zuma is to choose between two competing futures. One is characterised by rationality and the rule of law, a strong state that punches above its weight internationally and is economically 'well managed'.

The other future – the Zuma-SACP-Cosatu scenario – is a slide into South American-style lethargy. We will have a parasitic state that fleeces the middle classes while the rulers loot the fiscus. We will lose our place in the international arena and our economic policies will be 'populist'. Our legal institutions will be weakened to the point of being irrelevant.

But, the article goes on to point out, the 'corrupt Zuma, anti-corruption Mbeki' portrayal conveniently ignores the 'clear symptoms of crony capitalism' under Mbeki's stewardship, including the official quashing of investigation into the arms deal:

It is a mark of Mbeki's successful image management that he now finds himself cloaked in the robes of an anticorruption crusader, instead of being held responsible for the slide that has occurred under his rule.

The decline, which is inextricably linked to Mbeki's stated project to nurture a black elite, is there for all to see, and is lamented by the same crowd who predict damnation should Mbeki be succeeded by a populist. So why do they paint post-1994 SA as a development model that is at peril from populists should the forces of rationality fail to protect it? Answer this question, and the class bias of much commentary on Zuma and Mbeki becomes obvious.

Now it is true that the SA built over the last 11 years has been a roaring success for some. There has been a phenomenal growth in the ranks of the black middle class. It is equally true that the beneficiaries of the past decade stand to lose should the seeming tide of a populist revival under Zuma fail to be arrested. That is why support for Mbeki is a class preference. It is not a preference for modernity over backwardness, or democracy over anarchy. Nor is it a preference for the rule of law over corruption.

This is not to dismiss those who paint doomsday scenarios of life under the Zuma crowd. Their panic is real, but it is not premised on what they would have us believe it is. It is less about the good of the country and the defence of democratic institutions than it is about a sense of foreboding about lost privilege. With Zuma – or anyone like him – in the Union Buildings, the barbarians will have truly breached the gate, pissed on the lawn and generally spoiled the party.

But to get the full picture of what is happening in SA, it is also necessary to ask who precisely Zuma's supporters are. This will show us the class fissures that underlie the contest for the ANC. The Zuma base – sometimes derided as the 'masses', or the 'crowd' – generally are not privy to the apocalyptic predictions peddled in 'quality' newspapers. Even if they could somehow be reached and be told directly how miserable things would get with Zuma in charge, they would be inclined not to be moved, since things are miserable for them now.

What the Zuma fallout exposes is the extent to which Mbeki's metaphor of two SAs is in fact a reality. But these two SAs are divided by their class experiences more than their race heritage.

That Zuma has been courted and funded by business interests is an indication of the fluidity of the succession tussle. Many in business recognise the Zuma phenomenon for what it is: the first real chance that the accommodation that the ANC crafted with capital may be endangered. *These interests, which are no different from those promoted by and supportive of Mbeki, have opted for a different management strategy. They are hard at work to co-opt Zuma so that he too may serve their interests* [emphasis added].

SA need not fear the implications of the Zuma/Mbeki fallout. It does not portend the end of our democracy as we know it. It may well invigorate democracy. It represents a full frontal assault on the class consensus that has until now been our developmental paradigm.

Shortly before the Polokwane conference, Zuma travelled to India, the United Kingdom and the US to calm the jitters of nervous capitalists, and impress upon them his good intentions. I was able to observe one version of this performance at first hand on 5 December 2007, when Zuma addressed a small group of academics and business people at a lunch sponsored by the Institute for International Studies at the University of California, Berkeley.[47] In his speech, delivered with considerable elan, Zuma started out emphasising the need for political stability and economic growth. He went on to outline the role of the ANC in bringing about the transition from apartheid, along with the inclusive, democratic process through which the constitution emerged: 'This is not a country that depends on a leader,' he insisted, going on to note that 'we play in a framework determined by the constitution; no individual or party can take us in a different direction'. Zuma then turned to the question of the economy – carefully separated in good liberal fashion from that of politics. Here are some of his comments, taken from my notes:

> We have established a political system that no one can complain about. Our economic policies have been balanced up to now. They have withstood turbulences in different parts of the world. However, we are still faced with a first economy and a second economy. The question is how to put them together. This goes with [the question of] the plight of the poor. Some say that the gap between the rich and the poor has increased. There has been a big increase in the number of people in the cities living in informal settlements. We need thinking people to say how to address the poverty issue. This is the issue we are debating within the alliance and the progressive forces. What policies do we need? We are having this debate with the participation of the trade unions and the SACP. Where do we go? The challenge is to bridge the gap between the First and Second Economies to address the plight of the people. How to address this problem? We want scholars to help: how do we grow the economy and address the plight of the people? Education is critical. A high percentage of the

21 December 2007

unemployed people are unskilled. A big chunk of them are
unemployable because they have no skills. The country cannot develop
when people are not educated. Human capital is essential. We have
not done enough to address this issue. Rural development is also
very important – how do you do that? People are flocking into the
cities because there is no economy in the rural areas. We do have
policies in general terms. But how do we implement them? I come
from a university situated in a rural area. I am the chancellor [an
honorary position in South Africa]. I am running a pilot project of
toilets in rural areas. You can't solve problems of sewage in rural
areas in the same way as in the cities. I spoke to Billiton – they
understand. They put in septic tanks in rural areas. [More generally]
sewage, water and electricity must be put in rural areas. We want to
establish a relationship with this university. Professor Vilakazi in South
Africa says that development must go from rural to urban. This is an
issue we are debating all the time . . . We have a surplus while people
are starving. The system has tried to do something – but we need to
do more.

Zuma's appropriation of Mbeki's discourse of a First and Second Economy in this context is especially interesting and significant.

In his acceptance speech at the close of the Polokwane conference on 20 December, Zuma assiduously reassured domestic and international capital that nothing would change in terms of macro-economic policy – at the same time that he spoke of the importance of the SACP and COSATU in the ANC Alliance, and the imperatives for redistributive policies.

As is often the case, the most astute political commentary on Polokwane came from Zapiro.[48]

Ramaphosa, 18 May 2008

On the night of 11 May 2008 a group of men and women in a section of Alexandra township outside Johannesburg known as Beirut went on a pre-planned rampage. Wielding guns and other weapons and shouting '*Mayiphume inunu*' (Get rid of the insects), they attacked and killed foreign nationals, raped women, and looted and destroyed shacks and shops.[49] Xenophobic attacks spread like wildfire to other townships and informal settlements throughout the country. It was only after the army had been deployed that the violence subsided. On Monday, 26 May, Minister of Safety and Security Charles Ngakula announced that 'xenophobic violence against foreign nationals had been brought under control'.[50] Two weeks of horrifying violence left 62 people dead (a third of them South Africans from minority ethnic groups judged to be excessively foreign), dozens raped, some 700 wounded and over a hundred thousand displaced.

The shocking photograph that has become emblematic of what Sitas calls the xenocide – a man on his hands and knees engulfed in flames – was taken in Ramaphosa shack settlement on the East Rand at the height of the violence on Sunday, 18 May. The story of how reporter Beauregard Tromp worked to discover the identity of the man, Ernesto Alfabeto Nhamuave, accompany his remains to his home in Mozambique and attend his funeral bears retelling.[51]

Photo: Halden Krog

Anatomy of hatred[52]

23 May 2008

Beauregard Tromp

The man with the brush-cut wouldn't leave without his compatriot.

'Go, they are killing your people,' warned residents with whom the Mozambican shared a township plot.

The Ramaphosa township was alight. At least four people had already been killed by mobs sweeping through the neighbourhood, bent on driving out the Shangaans.

The bags of clothing the two men had meticulously hoarded for their journey home were on the carpet floor of the sparse shack.

When the two arrived almost a month ago, all they owned clothed their bodies. A generous neighbour had donated a foam mattress for the two to sleep on.

'Heita Mugza,' a neighbour would greet the two.

Living less than a metre apart on the small plot of land covered almost entirely by the four shacks on it, names were not important.

'Mugza' would suffice.

The two Mozambicans returned every evening in workmen's overalls splattered with drops of paint, occasionally returning home with empty paint tins.

When the first mutterings of the xenophobic violence that had engulfed Alexandra were spilling over into Ramaphosa, the two were warned that they should consider leaving.

By Saturday, neighbours were emphatic that they should go.

A man and woman, both Shangaans, would visit that afternoon and engage in serious discussion with the two 'Mugzas'.

By Sunday, the situation had reached crisis point. Two more foreigners had been killed. The township was alight in parts and smouldering in others.

Police dispersed the baying and crudely armed mobs, only to have them re-form minutes later.

The tall 'Mugza' finally arrived. The stove, the book *Karoo Blossom* and some old shoes would have to be left behind.

'Go through the back. We've already arranged with the neighbour,' said a sympathetic local resident, who we have, for her safety, identified as Laura.

For some reason, the two decided instead to walk down the road towards the circle where police had earlier dispersed hundreds of armed residents.

Short 'Mugza', dressed in a maroon jacket and green cargo pants, walked in front with a duffel bag over his shoulder.

Tall 'Mugza', dressed in a blue buttoned-down shirt and matching trousers, followed shortly behind, weighed down with bags of clothing and bedding.

As the two neared the circle, a shout went up. 'Run!' short 'Mugza' turned to shout at his compatriot in Shangaan.

The mob rushed, machetes and knives at the ready.

Short 'Mugza' made a dash over the empty taxi stand for the main road. A sea of bodies appeared around him.

Trapped, short 'Mugza' was pressed up against a wall, beaten and stabbed before a cement block was thrown on his head.

Tall 'Mugza' wouldn't get much further.

'First they pushed him against the fence and started beating him. Then they stabbed him. Then they threw the block of cement on top of him,' said Laura, who watched helplessly.

Four calls were made to Reiger Park police station, but nobody would answer the phone.

The nearby wooden stalls had already been stripped bare for the bonfire burning at the traffic circle.

Some of the mob took flaming pieces of wood and put it underneath a battered and bloody tall 'Mugza', who was already down on his hands and knees.

His screams did not reach the ears of the heavily armed police contingent some 100 metres away.

Dissatisfied with their first attempt, the mob wrapped tall 'Mugza' in his duvet cover and piled wood on top of him.

The fire got going. A mattress was thrown on top of the flaming man. The fire engulfed tall 'Mugza'.

A teenage girl was dispatched to run up the street to call the police. Others followed, each carrying the same message: 'They're killing the Shangaans.'

By the time police and journalists arrived on the scene, the crowd had dispersed and tall 'Mugza' was silent.

The only signs of life from the flaming man perched on his hands and knees were his weakly flailing hands.

By the time paramedics delivered the flaming man to Tambo Memorial Hospital, less than five minutes away, he would have succumbed to polytrauma – multiple injuries.

The flaming man would die with every breath he took as the fire scorched his lungs.

His compatriot would later also succumb to his wounds.

Four days later, his burnt clothes and duvet lie in the ashes where he fell.

The two arrived nameless in a country where better opportunities beckoned.

In the Germiston state mortuary, the two for now remain nameless among the other foreigners killed, destined for the anonymity of a pauper's burial.

They called him Mugza – more about Ernesto Alfabeto Nhamuave[53]
27 May 2008, *The Star*
Beauregard Tromp

The *Sunday Times'* Victor Khupiso gave us his name and spoke to a brother-in-law who said he would bury the body.

At the Germiston City Hall, two nondescript Mozambican men bedded down among their compatriots. Unlike the hundreds of weary bodies forced from their homes in Ramaphosa and Meyerton, the two brothers were there on Monday night to be close to their brother.

Fifty metres down the road, in a cold, steel, refrigerated hole, lay Ernesto Alfabeto Nhamuave.

For almost a week, the public knew him only as the flaming man. In Ramaphosa township, he was known simply as Mugza.

For Jose and Severiano he was a brother, a husband and a father who sought a better life in South Africa less than three months ago. Jose, a miner at South Deep Mine for 11 years, returned home regularly with money and gifts for the family. Severiano joined him four months ago.

Ernesto was struggling to make ends meet. As a security guard in Maputo, the money just wasn't enough to provide for his family of five.

A running joke in Maputo is that people would rather employ a security guard than install an alarm system because it's cheaper.

On Thursday, Jose and Severiano got a call from their brother-in-law, Francisco Kanze. Stabbed, beaten and with a cement block thrown on his head, Kanze would survive the attack on him and Ernesto in Ramaphosa on May 18.

The image of Ernesto burning to death would bring the reality of the xenophobic horror home to people around the world.

Although Jose and Severiano are strictly speaking cousins of Ernesto, the three grew up metres from each other near Inhambane, the tourism area 550km north of Maputo where hundreds of South Africans flock annually on holiday. Early on Monday morning, the pair were at Germiston mortuary to identify Ernesto's body.

Jose held no hope that it was all a mistake. All he wanted now was to take his brother home. The body was sent to Germiston mortuary, hospital officials assured. Body number 1247 was pulled out. This time the entire body was burnt. The face was unrecognisable. Only part of a leg and a foot had escaped relatively unharmed.

'I knew it was Ernesto because of his toes. He has a birth defect on his middle toe,' said Jose.

At the Germiston Community Hall, Mozambican official Edmundo Matenja has a ledger that is nearly full. Most of the names recorded in them are people looking for family members lost when they fled. At the back of the ledger is a list of six names, their fate known.

Ernesto Alfabeto Nhamuave would be number seven.

Family insist on seeing picture[54]
Seeds, song and tears for Ernesto
3 June 2008
Beauregard Tromp
They wanted to see it. They wanted to know how Ernesto had died. In the rural village of Vuca, 500km north of Maputo, the uncles who helped bring up Ernesto Nhamuave wanted to see how a mob of South Africans in an unknown township had set their son alight and watched him die. Early yesterday morning, the Nhamuave clan sank to their knees as one as their elders, Nowa, held a bowl filled with nuts and seeds for the kuphahla ceremony. 'This is your son, who went to South Africa to work. But he was killed there. He rests with you now,' said Nowa, choking back tears as he scattered the seed over the grave prepared for Ernesto.

At 5am Ernesto returned home. On May 18 Ernesto and his brother-in-law, Francisco Kanze, were hunted down by an angry mob in Ramaphosa township on the East Rand. Stabbed, beaten and bloodied, Francisco was left for dead before the mob turned their attention to tall and handsome Ernesto. By the time journalists and police arrived on the scene, a flaming Ernesto, perched on hands and knees, had stopped screaming.

More than 50 family members gathered in small groups early yesterday. As the lights approached in the distance, a wail rose as women greeted the body. The journey had taken 24 hours, as other victims of the xenophobic violence in South Africa were dropped off on the way.

The truck broke down, and the body was loaded on to a bakkie for the final leg. By 7am, the number of mourners had grown to more than 200. Some of the journalists who had witnessed the grisly scenes were there to take the story of the flaming man, Mugza, Ernesto, to its conclusion.

'They want to see,' Jose Nhamuave told photographer Simphiwe Nkwali. No. He could not. Since taking the pictures of Ernesto's death and tracking down Francisco to a hospital in Germiston, Nkwali had been drawn into the story. It was he, following the body from the mortuary in Johannesburg, who had ended up taking the body home on the back of his rented bakkie.

A priest lit a candle as family members crammed into Ernesto's tiny reed-and-thatch home.

'God, protect this body. Ancestors, we know this body should rest for a day inside his house, but we know Ernesto's spirit is already with us,' the priest continued. For a moment Ernesto's wife, Hortencia, raised her head from where she lay under the tarpaulin shade before she disappeared under a blanket. At his home, hands more adept at farming falteringly sewed a black cross on the white sheet over Ernesto's coffin.

Supported by elderly women, Hortencia shuffled slowly towards the home she shared with her husband. Traditionally the wife would be allowed one last look at her husband before he was committed to the earth. Less than halfway there strong arms grabbed hers, preventing her from falling in the fine grey sand. Singing hymns, the crowd moved towards the grave, a paraffin lamp lighting the way in the early morning. A weeping Alfabeto, held up by aunts, watched as his father's body was lowered into the grave.

With prayers and bible readings conducted in Citswa, a derivative of isiZulu, the crowd were occasionally prompted into song. Jesus walks with me, they sang. Click. Click. Click. A camera lens dropped. Photographer Shayne Robinson, perched on the edge of the grave with colleagues, wept. Nkwali's eyes welled. Handing over their cameras briefly, the photographers who witnessed the nightmare picked up shovels and became mourners.

On the coffin, first a straw mat was placed and then Ernesto's clothes were laid out – trousers and shoes at his feet, shirts and jackets at his torso. As family members shovelled sand into the grave, photographers who had witnessed the horror of May 18 joined in and helped them. As the crowd departed, the four white candles placed at the corners of the grave quickly succumbed to the gentle breeze.

Afterwards, mourners gathered in the compound. A member of the ANC's regional branch denounced the xenophobic violence sweeping South Africa, blaming gangs. The local Frelimo party secretary called on Mozambicans not to seek revenge. 'We are brothers,' both said.

Still, they wanted to see. Finally, the picture that had gone around the world and left South Africans shamed was shown. 'Ah, ah, ah.' Heads shook. 'Siyabonga,' [Thank you] they said.

The May 2008 pogroms were far from an isolated set of incidents. They were preceded by multiple warnings and incidents of xenophobic violence, and followed by further killings and threats as well as ongoing, everyday forms of xenophobia.

For purposes of the present discussion, I want to emphasise the significance of the timing of the pogroms – falling as they did in the interregnum between Polokwane and the May 2009 national and provincial elections. On 25 May, fully two weeks after the killings began in Alexandra, senior ANC officials finally fanned out across townships and informal settlements calling for peace and tolerance. There they encountered a furious response. Press reports tell of how visiting dignitaries were bombarded with complaints about lack of delivery of basic services, as well as the government's unwillingness to deal with the influx of immigrants.

The following account of Zuma's encounter with residents of shack settlements on the East Rand that day is especially telling:[55]

The African National Congress leader faced a barrage of angry questions as he faced a crowd of around 4,000 residents of shanty towns around Springs, 60 kilometres (37 miles) east of Johannesburg.

'Fighting won't solve your problems but will instead exacerbate them, and they will therefore remain unsolved,' he said. 'Peace should prevail and we must engage each other on whatever issues there might be,' said Zuma.

While the leader was loudly welcomed by the crowd – packed into a small community centre – he received an unusually tough response as members demanded the government deal with the influx of foreigners.

A young man shouting from the back of the hall urged Zuma to ensure government kept out foreigners from neighbouring countries.

'You talk to (Zimbabwe President Robert) Mugabe, you talk to (Mozambique President Armando) Guebuza. Tell them to tell their people they must not harass us in our country. This is our country.'

He said foreigners in the country were 'riding on the gravy train'.

'*We are looking to make you our president (in 2009 elections) so beware. If you are a stumbling block, we are going to kick you away*,' the man warned, as the crowd erupted with deafening support for the sentiments [emphasis added].

An old man near the front of the room complained that foreigners took away employment opportunities and undercut salaries for locals.

'If you don't do these things right, the fight will go forward,' he said.

Zuma attempted to appease the fractious crowd who wanted him to stay and listen to their grievances about public service delivery, lack of proper housing and sanitation.

'You cannot build South Africa without the help of your neighbours. Learn to lend a helping hand to them. Without these people our struggle would have been in vain,' Zuma said.

He promised to return to listen to the community's problems, insisting that peace first needed to prevail, as 'we can't listen to one another in an atmosphere of violence'.

Local resident Cannel Nxadi, 25, said the problems would stop 'when they take away all the foreigners, the robbers,' while 32-year-old Levy Mayisela warned that 'if they come back there is going to be another fight.'

Pietermaritzburg, 12 September 2008

On Sunday, 14 September, Lehman Brothers declared bankruptcy, plunging financial markets into turmoil and precipitating the massive meltdown of the global economy. In the weeks that followed, along with many other South Africans, I was glued to a television screen watching a local political drama unfold on local stations – and only occasionally switching to CNN and BBC to keep track of imploding markets.

The previous Friday in the Pietermaritzburg High Court, Justice Chris Nicholson effectively threw out corruption charges against Zuma and cleared the way to his becoming the next president of the country in the April 2009 elections. The immediate issue before the judge was whether the National Prosecuting Authority had failed in its obligation to allow Zuma to make legal representations against its decision to prosecute him. Based on an overview of huge volumes of documentary evidence, Nicholson's ruling went far beyond this issue. Referring to the 'titanic battle between Zuma and Mbeki', Nicholson ruled that there had been improper political interference in the prosecution of Zuma.[56] Outside court, Zuma's meeting with his supporters was remarkably sober. Assuming the stance of a wounded warrior, he broke into an isiZulu war song: 'I have wounds all over my body because of the warriors from my neighbourhood, they are all stamping, all over me,' Zuma sang.[57]

Following a marathon meeting, the ANC's NEC called for the resignation of Mbeki in the early hours of 20 September. On Sunday, 21 September, in a televised address to the nation, Mbeki resigned from the presidency – saying, among other things, that 'despite the economic advances we have made, I would be first to say that . . . the fruits of these positive results are still not fully and equally shared among our people, hence abject poverty coexisting side by side with extraordinary opulence'. The following day Deputy President Phumzile Mlambo-Ngcuka resigned, along with ten cabinet ministers and three deputy ministers.

Notably missing from the list was Manto Tshabalala-Msimang, Mbeki's criminally obdurate Minister of Health who had collaborated with him to deprive millions of South Africans suffering from HIV/AIDS of anti-retroviral treatment. On 25 September Kgalema Motlanthe was sworn into office as interim president of the country. He immediately removed Tshabalala-Msimang from her post, and replaced her with Barbara Hogan who moved swiftly to expand access to anti-retrovirals.

The next act in this political drama commenced on 8 October, when Mosiuoa Lekota (who had recently stepped down as Minister of Defence) called a news conference to exhort 'all who share our concerns to join a collective effort to defend our movement and our democracy' from ANC leaders who were deviating from the party's principles. Asked whether he was seeking marriage counselling or divorce from the ANC, he responded, 'it seems to me we have been serving today divorce papers'.[58] Watching this performance, I was reminded of an event in January 1991 – a gathering of civic associations at the Settler Monument in Grahamstown at which Lekota (known then by his soccer nickname 'Terror') announced that the United Democratic Front had accomplished its task, and must now hand the reins to the leadership of the ANC. Yet, he warned the crowd, they must remain vigilant, using the following parable to make his point:

> *There was once a woman who used to tell her husband when he made mistakes – but every time she did so, he beat her unmercifully. Eventually she gave up, and decided to keep quiet. One day, at an important function, he blew his nose and – without his knowing it – a big lump of snot landed on his forehead. His wife saw this, but kept quiet – and all through the day people laughed at him.*

'We don't want the ANC to be like the husband,' Terror declared. 'We must have the courage to tell the leadership when they are doing the wrong thing.' It was deeply ironic that less than eighteen years later he had taken on the role of the abused wife, leaving home and slamming the door.

Less than a month later Lekota moved into a new political home with Mbhazima Shilowa, another disgruntled Mbeki supporter. They announced the formation of a new party at a convention on 1 November, and launched the Congress of the People in Bloemfontein (where the ANC had been launched in 1912) on 16 December (a deeply significant public holiday in South Africa). The ANC went to court to prevent their appropriation of the name of the congress at which the Freedom Charter had been adopted in 1955 – a move that the Pretoria High Court dismissed on 12 December. By the following year yet another divorce took place when the alliance dubbed 'Shikota' was torn apart by internecine fighting.

In the national elections held on 22 April 2009 the ANC won 65.9 per cent of the vote, the DA 16.66 per cent and the Congress of the People 7.42 per cent. The Zuma administration had barely taken office when they were confronted by strikes and municipal uprisings on a scale that was unprecedented, and had at least something to do with the collapse of Lehman Brothers. The meltdown of the global economy that followed the Lehman collapse resulted in what has been called a 'jobs bloodbath' in South Africa, in which close to a million people are estimated to have been thrown out of work.

Soccer City, 2 July 2010

Writing in the *New York Times* shortly before the opening game of the FIFA World Cup on 11 June 2010, Gevisser offered a vivid reminder that the upcoming spectacle represented, among other things, an investment in post-apartheid nationalism:[59]

In Johannesburg, I am struck by the contrast between the two structures that will be used for the World Cup: the brutalist concrete apartheid-era Ellis Park stadium looming over inner-city decay on the one hand; the spherical and sculptural 'African Calabash' of Soccer City on the other.

Johannesburg brands itself as a 'World Class African City,' and the calabash was built to beam this impression to the world. But it serves another function too: at a time when it seems increasingly difficult to hold the Rainbow Nation together, it provides South Africans with the fantasy of containment within a single shared national identity.

At Ellis Park, you cannot but notice the grubby city all around you; at Soccer City, you enter an African dreamscape. And so the distance between them is not just the 20 kilometers on the impressive new Bus Rapid Transit system: it is the distance between a real, messy South Africa and the 'Mandela Miracle' fantasy that at times enables, and at time oppresses, the country.

Perhaps it's a journey we South Africans have to travel – at a time when our society is becoming more unequal, such performances of national pride may indeed be priceless.

On one level, the investment paid off handsomely (in addition to lining the pockets of FIFA officials to the tune of some $3.2 billion).[60] The World Cup spectacle conjured up a euphoric sense of national pride and unity that some likened to the first democratic elections in April 1994 when, as Bishop Desmond Tutu put it with his characteristic exuberance in *The Rainbow People of God* ([1996] 2006: 257), 'it was like falling in love . . . the sun is shining brighter, the flowers seem more beautiful, the birds sing more sweetly, and the people . . . have suddenly discovered that they are all South Africans'.

More than that, once that national team had been definitively defeated and Ghana made it to the quarter-finals, South Africans suddenly discovered that they were all Africans. The game against Uruguay on 2 July at Soccer City called forth an extraordinary surge of pan-African solidarity – intensified by a powerful sense of

15 July 2010

injustice when Uruguayan striker Luis Suárez's handball on the
goal line denied Ghana a victory. In response to Suárez's claim that
'the Hand of God now belongs to me', the *Sunday Times* of 4 July
captured pervasive sentiment with a front-page image of Suárez
with large red horns emblazoned with 'The Hand of the Devil'.[61]
The collective commiseration and heartbreak for a few days following
the game forged even stronger bonds of pan-African camaraderie
across all the usual chasms of South African society.

The irony was that these expressions of African solidarity
coexisted with widespread threats of xenophobic attacks as soon as
the World Cup was over – reminding us, as does Zapiro, of the
multiple, conflicting articulations of nationalism that can – and
do – pull in different directions.

Johannesburg–Pretoria, 27–28 October 2011

The day 27 October marks the anniversary of the birth of Oliver
Tambo, one of the great icons of the liberation struggle and former
president of the ANC. On that day in 2011, the ANC Youth League
organised a 'March for Economic Freedom in Our Lifetime'.
Estimated at between 5 000 and 8 000, the crowd of exuberant

marchers congregated in the centre of Johannesburg. Yellow-clad marshalls moved through the assembling crowd, giving instructions and preventing marchers from talking to reporters. The discipline caught on television contrasted sharply with a riotous scene almost two months earlier on 30 August 2011, when ANC Youth League supporters threw rocks and bottles at ANC headquarters in Johannesburg, and tried to storm the building. That was the first day of disciplinary hearings in which ANC officials charged Julius Malema and several of his lieutenants with bringing the organisation into disrepute – charges that culminated in their expulsion from the ANC in April 2012.

Embodying ANC Youth League demands for nationalisation of the mines and expropriation without compensation of white-owned land, the Economic Freedom march targeted three strategic institutions: the Chamber of Mines, the Johannesburg Stock Exchange (JSE) in Sandton 18 kilometres north of Johannesburg, and the Union Buildings in Pretoria a further 68 kilometres to the north. At around 5 p.m. weary marchers reached the JSE, where ANC Youth League officials presented a memorandum of grievances:[62]

'The people who are stealing our wealth must come on stage,' Malema said from the back of a truck converted into a stage outside the JSE. 'Down with white capital monopoly,' he chanted.

The league is demanding the nationalisation of mines and the introduction of probation programmes within companies to give youth skills in mining. The memorandum calls for better wages for mine-workers and the active involvement of mining companies in the development of the industry.

An official from the JSE received the league's memorandum. 'Thank you for the opportunity. We will take your demands to the executive,' he said.

This upset members of the crowd who started singing the controversial song Dubul'ibhunu (Shoot the Boer), which has been declared hate speech in court.

A hard core of marchers trudged on to Pretoria, where they camped overnight in a sports stadium. When Malema addressed the crowd at around 5 a.m., he directed much of his speech to instructing marchers how to answer questions. Here are some of my notes from his televised speech on the independent eTV channel:

> If they ask you why we are marching, you tell them we are marching because we want to live like whites. Everything whites have we want as well. We are demanding our land back which was stolen from us. When they came from wherever, they came from their small countries they didn't come with land – they found land. When they came from their small countries, they didn't come with minerals – they found gold and diamonds and platinum. That land, those minerals belong to us!

His speech at the Union Buildings later that morning, directed at the state and the ANC, was rather more reconciliatory:

> The fearlesss economic freedom fighters have walked the long walk to freedom. We are not fighting the government. We acknowledge the good work the government is doing. But we want more. This is our government. We elected this government – it was elected by yourselves. We will always come here if there are problems with this government. We love the ANC and are prepared to work with the ANC.

From the Union Buildings, a police escort whisked Malema to Oliver Tambo International Airport, where he boarded a charter flight to Mauritius to attend the wedding, reputed to have cost R15 million ($2 million), of property magnate David Mabilu whom the *Mail & Guardian* accused of having made his millions from buying land from one arm of government and reselling it to another.[63] The mainstream Sunday newspapers on 30 October made much of Malema's hypocrisy, highlighting his costume switch from Che Guevara beret and Mandela T-shirt to a luminous purple wedding outfit, and calling attention as well to his own allegedly ill-gotten gains. What they failed to point out was that the plentiful photo opportunities on a palm-fringed Mauritian beachfront with a luxury hotel in the background enabled Malema to demonstrate to his followers his capacity to live like the wealthiest whites.

Journalist Fiona Forde's biography of Julius Malema, felicitously entitled *An Inconvenient Youth*, appeared at the height of the ANC Youth League rebellion in the second half of 2011. Based on two years of engagement with Malema, Forde's biography contains several important pointers to an analysis that extends beyond the flamboyant figure of Malema. We shall return to engage the question of what such an analysis might entail in Chapter 5. Here I would like to call attention to several other defining moments that are directly salient to this analysis.

In April 2010, Forde accompanied Malema and seven other Youth League members on a visit to Zimbabwe. Her account provides a vivid illumination of the ANC Youth League's close relations with their counterparts in ZANU-PF, and their appropriations of Mugabean nationalism. It also sheds light on the ANC Youth League's vision of a southern African superpower, turbocharged by nationalising mineral wealth – most importantly platinum.[64] During his trip, Malema 'lauded President Robert Mugabe for his leadership, hailed Governor Gideon Gono as a financial genius for his creativity at the Reserve Bank, and pledged to breathe political life back into ZANU-PF at the expense of their unity government partners, the Movement for Democratic Change (MDC)' (Forde 2011: 187). His hosts declared him a brave young bull, and the new commander of southern Africa – and presented him with a herd of six cattle, including a prize-winning bull.

While the Youth League leadership was in Zimbabwe, Eugene Terre'Blanche, the extreme right-wing nationalist leader of the Afrikaner Weerstandsbeweging, was bludgeoned to death on his farm. Earlier that year Malema had resurrected the old struggle song, '*Dubul' iBhunu*' or 'Shoot the Boer' referred to above. Following Terre'Blanche's murder, the Afrikaner organisation Afriforum brought a hate-speech case against Malema for singing the song. Although the judgment went against Malema, in fact it played powerfully in his favour. As Forde puts it: 'In defending himself in that very high-profile trial, Malema not only became the custodian of ANC struggle songs, but a hero in the eyes of millions' (2011: 20).

Forde also issues a reminder that the constituency to which Malema directs his appeal extends beyond the very large numbers of disaffected young people to the millions more who subsist on social grants and handouts. In a *Sunday Times* article in September 2011 entitled 'Malema's Theory of White Power Caches Resounds', Jonny Steinberg reported on conversations with villagers in Lusikisiki in the former Transkei:

> In the spaza shops and shebeens and in family homesteads, nobody talks about any public figure as much as they do about Malema . . . Why does Malema occupy so privileged a place? After all, many villagers dislike him and would not miss him if his public life ended tomorrow. People nonetheless talk about him because the story he tells about our country has been received here as a revelation. He says that the moment black people won South Africa at the ballot box, whites began to hide power in invisible places: In multinational corporations and in the media, in laboratories and the judiciary, in closed systems of esoteric knowledge. He says his mission is to go and find power where it hides, and retrieve it. The moment Malema tells this story, people instantly recognise it as true. Even those who despise him do not doubt that he is correct . . . 'I had not thought of South Africa's transition to democracy the way Malema described it,' a villager told me. 'But once he said it, it seemed to be something I had always known.'[65]

Malema's claim that he can find hidden caches of white power sheds important light on how his conspicuous display of wealth demonstrates his capacity to find hidden money. It also serves as a reminder of how much is missed by those who emphasise his hypocrisy in championing the cause of the impoverished majority. The ANC's political suppression of Malema will come at a price, Steinberg notes, since he will be seen in many places as a person who spoke the truth. Also, he argues, Malema is foreshadowing what the ANC will in future years become: 'As it strains to maintain its support in places like Lusikisiki, it will increasingly represent itself as the vanguard of an insurgency against the powerful on behalf of the poor, complaining that the legislature and executive it controls are hollowed out and powerless.' As we shall see in Chapter 5, there are those – including the SACP – who go beyond Steinberg's prediction of escalating populist politics to perceive in Malema and his backers a sort of proto-fascism.

In April 2012 Malema and two other ANC Youth League officials were expelled from the ANC for bringing the organisation into disrepute, following a series of disciplinary hearings and appeals. At the time, four investigations of Malema's finances were underway: by the Hawks (the Directorate for Priority Crime Investigation), the Master of the High Court, the Public Protector and the South African Revenue Service. By September 2012 he was confronting charges of tax evasion, fraud, corruption and money laundering.

Marikana, 16 August 2012

> In the blazing North West summer sun Marikana workers sing about the abuse they suffer, about their dissatisfaction and their demands; they sing of their terrible experience and the massacre that changed everything.
>
> The lyrics of their songs are a venting of anger; anger at Lonmin, Jacob Zuma, the general secretary of the National Union of Mineworkers (NUM), Frans Baleni, and the union's president, Senzeni Zokwana. The words of praise to [be] found in the songs are for Julius Malema, for understanding and standing with them. The hope of those who sing them, is that their heartfelt words will go from their mouths to God's ear. Or at least drop into an ear of someone who dares to listen, and care.

Safasaphela isizwe esimnyama ngexa ya mapholisa . . .
Juju Malema uyasizela ngexayokubulawa
(The black nation is being extinguished because of the police . . .
Juju Malema is defending us because of police killing us).[66]

The strike is over. The dead, most of them, have been buried . . .
Even as the headlines mull the cost to the economy, sifting rumour
from fact and shifting focus to the next big strike and quantifying the
potential for greater unrest, Marikana will not recede from the public
consciousness very easily. Even as a sense of calm and normalcy returns
to the town, where goats steal spinach from street vendors, poetry
and music, cultural expressions of Marikana, not as a place, but as a
pivotal movement [moment?] in South African history have begun to
emerge.[67]

The strike is over
The dead must return
to work.[68]

The Marikana massacre was not just *a* pivotal moment; it was *the*
most momentous of the post-apartheid era, made all the more so
by its passage into popular culture. Militant labour strikes are a
common occurrence in present-day South Africa, much as they were
during the apartheid regime. What has made Marikana distinctive
is both the militaristic violence with which the coercive arm of the
state smashed down on striking workers, and the shocking clarity
with which Marikana and its aftermath laid bare the contours of
the South African crisis.

In *Marikana: A View from the Mountain and a Case to Answer*
(2013), Alexander and his colleagues speak of a 'triangle of torment'
linking the mining company Lonmin (headquartered in London
and listed on the London Stock Exchange), the police and the
National Union of Mineworkers, that can be situated within a larger
corporatist triangle that includes big business (especially mining
capital), the government/ANC, and COSATU (2012: 182). Located

at the centre of this triangle and embodying all three sides is Cyril Ramaphosa.

A key figure in the formation of the National Union of Mineworkers in the 1980s, Ramaphosa was its general secretary until 1991 and a major force behind a massive miners' strike in 1987. He was also the head of the ANC team that negotiated the end of apartheid, and Mandela's choice to take over as president of the ANC and the country in 1999. When Mbeki triumphed over him, Ramaphosa became a corporate giant (thanks to BEE deals), and one of the wealthiest men in Africa with a portfolio that included a 9 per cent share in Lonmin at the time of the massacre. In December 2012, he was elected deputy president of the ANC, and is widely expected to ascend to the position that Mandela envisioned for him. For many he is the closest figure South Africa has to a saviour, and a great deal of work is going into burnishing this image.[69]

Removing the tarnish of Ramaphosa's role in the Marikana massacre requires hard work. On 24 October 2012, *The Times* ran an article entitled 'Ramaphosa Exposed':

> Released by advocate Dali Mpofu – who is representing injured miners and more than 200 workers who were arrested – the e-mail correspondence with Lonmin executives portrays Ramaphosa as callous.
>
> In an e-mail to Albert Jamieson, Lonmin's chief commercial officer, a day before the August 16 shooting, Ramaphosa wrote: 'The terrible events that have unfolded cannot be described as a labour dispute. They are plainly dastardly criminal and must be characterised as such. There needs to be concomitant action to address this situation.'
>
> This is in stark contrast to the compassionate image Ramaphosa projected in the aftermath of the Marikana massacre, in which 34 miners were shot dead . . .
>
> Yesterday, Mpofu told the commission that the e-mails showed a direct 'toxic collusion' between Lonmin, Mineral Resources Minister Susan Shabangu's department, the police ministry, state security agencies and Ramaphosa.

'It is clear Ramaphosa was directly involved by advising what was to be done to address these "dastardly criminal actions", which he says must be characterised as such and dealt with effectively,' Mpofu said.[70]

Ironically, on 14 August 2012 – just as tensions in Marikana were escalating – the Bench Marks Foundation (a faith-based organisation focused on corporate responsibility) published a report calling attention to shocking conditions in the platinum mining belt entitled 'Living in the Platinum Mines Fields'.[71] On 17 August the Foundation issued a press statement, citing Bishop Jo Seoka (President of the South African Council of Churches and Chairperson of the Bench Marks Foundation) who was in Marikana at the time of the massacre. Here is an excerpt:

> The platinum mining companies appear on the surface to be socially responsible, respectful of communities and workers and contributing to host community development. 'Nothing can be further from the truth', says Bishop Seoka.
>
> The Bench Marks Foundation study pointed out that the platinum mines rely on labour brokers and subcontractors that employ workers at very low wages. The use of migrant and subcontracted labour, the living-out allowance and the overcrowding of townships and squatter camps housing mine workers is a recipe for disaster. If the truth be told it is shareholders in London and elsewhere that are to blame. Profits are being made at the expense of workers and communities and with the help of political patronage. Mine companies put politically connected people on their board, such as director generals and former ministers, which leads to a breakdown of democracy, of government oversight, and of regulatory authorities' power . . .
>
> 'Why is the South African government, represented by the South African police force choosing to open fire on its own people, in order to protect a corporation?' asks Seoka. The lives of black mine workers are clearly not worth much in the eyes of Lonmin or the government. Unfortunately, recent events at the Lonmin mine are only the tip of

the iceberg of the continuous exploitation by platinum mining houses of both mine workers and the surrounding mining communities.

What is happening at Lonmin is a horrific example that is symptomatic of a wider structural problem of exploitation by the mines. The benefits of mining are not reaching the workers or the surrounding communities. Lack of employment opportunities for local youth, squalid living conditions, unemployment and growing inequalities contribute to this mess.[72]

Concluding Observations: Local Crucibles of Contention

Marikana exemplifies how, when considered specifically and concretely, the proliferating expressions of popular discontent that I am calling 'movement beyond movements' embody points of coming together of multiply scaled forces and relations. In Marikana they include a mining house headquartered in London that has drawn its wealth from the rich mineral resources of southern Africa for over a century; the weakening grip of a once-powerful union whose senior officials are now caught up in close relations with the mining companies, including the formation of a jointly owned bank that extends credit to impoverished workers while the mining companies garnish wages; the perpetuation of migrant labour, only housed now in shacks rather than hostels; the eroding hegemony of the ANC government that forms the focus of Chapter 5; the licence to kill accorded to an increasingly militarised police force; and the political ambitions of Julius Malema and his wealthy backers. In Marikana these forces assumed a form that is extreme but not exceptional – in each of the instances of popular discontent described in this chapter it is possible to trace out vitally important trans-local relations and connections.

At the same time, all have an irreducibly 'local' dimension – each with its own specificities – through which subaltern populations situated in asymmetrical relations of power rework these forces in the multiple arenas of everyday life. These complicated reworkings that consistently escape the power of those who would contain and control them are not necessarily 'progressive' – but in their interconnections with forces at play elsewhere, they are major drivers of social change, including as we shall see the erosion of ANC hegemony.

In Chapter 3 we will start once again with local protest and conflict, but now to examine more deeply what 'local' we are talking about, and why it matters for a broader analysis of the South African crisis.

Notes

1. The description of Bredell is adapted from Hart (2002a, 2006a) and the discussion of the WSSD below from Hart (2006a).
2. For a summary of evidence on increasing poverty and inequality in this period, see Nattrass and Seekings (2002). In November 2002, Statistics SA released figures suggesting a decline in income of the poorest 50 per cent of the population between 1995 and 2000 (Terreblanche 2002: 474). Other Stats SA research suggests that the havoc wrought by unemployment and its associated drop in incomes was somewhat assuaged by R53 billion pumped into poor communities in the form of housing, electricity and water. In other words, asset poverty declined while income poverty increased. Yet, as critics point out, principles of cost recovery discussed below undermine these claims (see note 6 below).
3. The Basic Income Grant coalition grounded its demand in the report of the Commission of Inquiry into a Comprehensive Social Security System chaired by Vivian Taylor, which estimated that nearly 14 million people in the 40 per cent of poorest households (approximately 20 million people) do not qualify for any social security transfers. The coalition estimated that the Basic Income Grant would close the poverty gap by more than 80 per cent, and that the net cost would be R20–25 billion annually, with the majority of the cost recovered through progressive taxation.
4. For more on the LPM, see Greenberg (2002, 2004) and Mngxitama (2002).
5. At the time of Bredell, land redistribution had effectively come to a halt. Soon after assuming office in 1999, Didiza placed a moratorium on the main land redistribution initiative of the previous administration – the Settlement and Land Acquisition Grant, through which households earning less than R1 500 a month were eligible for a grant of R15 000 (later increased to R16 000) that they could use to purchase land on a 'willing buyer, willing seller' basis. In 2000, the Department of Land Affairs proposed a new programme entitled Land Reform for Agricultural Development (LRAD)

– the clear intent of which is to promote the development of a class of full-time black commercial farmers. LRAD only came online at the end of 2001, fully two years after the Settlement and Land Acquisition Grant had been put on hold, and in the context of a rising clamour for land. Essentially, LRAD tied land redistribution to the agenda of the national Department of Agriculture at a time when South African agriculture had one of the lowest levels of state protection in the world. For a detailed analysis of South African land reform and agricultural policy, see http://www.plaas.org.za.

6. For more on these movements and the relationships among them, see the Land Action Research Network (http://www.landaction.org).

7. See McDonald and Pape (2002), Ngwane (2003) and Bond (2004).

8. Dissatisfaction around these issues had been simmering since at least 1997, erupting in sporadic protests in different regions. According to McDonald and Pape (2002: 7), 'The Anti-Privatisation Forum (APF) began in Johannesburg as a response to the iGoli plan. Originally it included COSATU, several of its affiliates, a number of community-based structures and a range of left-wing political organisations. In Johannesburg, COSATU eventually pulled out of the APF because of conflict with other organisations. In 2000 and 2001, APFs were formed in other municipalities. In late 2001 a national meeting of the APFs was held to develop a national programme of action. While COSATU is not active in most of the APFs, SAMWU [South African Municipal Workers' Union], a leading COSATU affiliate, has taken a resolution to form APFs and has participated extensively in their development in most areas.'

9. The press statement issued by the LPM and the National Land Committee is available at http://www.focusweb.org/publications/press-statements/wssd-2002/arrest-2.html.

10. See, for example, how Ashwin Desai's celebratory account of oppositional movements in *We are the Poors* (2002) gave way to the far more circumspect observation that these movements confront the danger of 'remaining localized, particularistic, and single-issue focused' (2003).

11. In a sympathetic but critical overview of the state of the LPM in the second half of 2002, Stephen Greenberg noted in the context of the LPM's support for Mugabe that '[t]he failure of the LPM to distinguish between a mass-based land occupation movement and the desperate measures of a repressive nationalist government in crisis has created an obstacle to more thorough-going unity between the landless and the urban grassroots movements. In appearance, even if not in reality, the landless movement is perceived as unconcerned about democratic and worker rights. Uncritical support for

Zanu-PF and the Zimbabwean state suggests ideological contradiction and haziness in the landless movement' (2002: 8).

12. Conflicts among different NGO activists in the National Land Committee and its affiliates over the form and direction of the LPM intensified in the period following the WSSD, and in July 2003 some affiliates succeeded in ousting the director of the National Land Committee. Deborah James has pointed to the tension-ridden conditions in which land NGOs find themselves: 'On the one hand, the land NGOs see their role as one of challenging the state, moving it beyond what has come to be seen as its narrow, even Thatcherite, focus on the entrenching and restoring of property rights. On the other, however, much as these activists may want to commit themselves primarily to championing the informal rights of the poor, they are compelled by the insistent demands of their many constituents, and by financial considerations, to play a supportive role to the Department of Land Affairs in its implementing of the land reform programme' (2002: 15).

13. See Buhlungu (2002) for a useful analysis of the position of organised labour at the time, and Marais (2011) for an overview of shifting relations within the alliance.

14. Jimmy Seepe, 'Mbeki Roasts Cronin', 25 August 2002, http://www.news24. com/SouthAfrica/Politics/Mbeki-roasts-Cronin-20020825.

15. Brendan Boyle, 'National Strike Begins', 29 August 2001, http://www.fin24. com/Economy/National-strike-begins-20010829.

16. For an insightful discussion of how critiques from the left were sidelined at the national conference, see William Mervin Gumede, 'Who would dare lean to the left here?' *Sowetan*, 23 December 2002: 13; and for a clear statement of the disciplining of the left, see Dumisani Makhaye, 'Left, right in combat', *Sowetan*, 19 December 2002: 19.

17. Dumisani Hlope, '2002 belongs to Mbeki and the ANC', *City Press*, 29 December 2002: 9. See also Gevisser (2007: 774–5).

18. In September 2002, the Political Education Unit of the ANC issued a document entitled 'Contribution to the NEC/NWC Response to the "Cronin Interviews" on the Issue of Neoliberalism'. See also Dumisani Makhaye, 'Left Factionalism and the NDR', http://www.anc.org.za/docs/ anctoday/2002/at48.htm#art1. The quotations in this paragraph are from the first document, although they recur in the second. For critical responses from the SACP and COSATU respectively, see David Masondo, 'Right-wing Opportunism Masquerading as Revolutionary Democracy and Revolutionary Socialism: A Response to Moleketi and Jele', 2002, http:// www.sacp.org.za/main.php?ID=3054, and COSATU Central Executive Committee, 'Final Political Report', 5–7 November 2002.

19. 'Ultra-left transposes DA agenda on the ANC', *City Press*, 29 September 2002: 8. This accusation against the 'ultra-left' of being in cahoots with the right is discussed more fully in Chapter 5.
20. http://www.info.gov.za/speeches/2003/03021412521001.htm.
21. From the Setswana word meaning a community council, Cabinet Lekgotlas are strategic policy meetings held twice a year.
22. http://www.info.gov.za/speeches/2003/03080511461001.htm.
23. For documentation, see South African Regional Poverty Network, http://www.sarpn.org.za/documents/d0000830/index.php.
24. http://www.anc.org.za/ancdocs/anctoday/2004/text/at47.txt.
25. For a summary of this literature, see Marais (2011: 193–8), and a 2007 special issue of *Africanus* 37 (2).
26. My initial efforts to grapple with these shifts were in a 2004 paper entitled 'Beyond Neoliberalism? South African Developments in Historical and Comparative Perspective' in which I sought to situate these shifts taking place in South Africa in relation to broader moves in many other regions of the world in the 1990s towards what some have called revisionist neoliberal forms of capitalist development, and others define as neoliberal governmentality. The paper was originally prepared for the conference on 'Reviewing the First Decade of Development and Democracy in South Africa', Durban, 21–22 October 2004, organised by the School of Development Studies at the University of KwaZulu-Natal and subsequently published as Hart (2006b).
27. Mentioned by Francie Lund in a debate on the Basic Income Grant at the University of Natal, Durban, 31 October 2002.
28. It is also the case, though, that the percentage of voting-age South Africans who cast votes fell sharply from 86 per cent in 1994, to 72 per cent in 1999, and 58 per cent in 2004.
29. We should recall here that in May 2004 South Africa won the competition to host the 2010 Soccer World Cup.
30. http://www.info.gov.za/issues/imbizo/index.html.
31. Available at http://www.teleologie.org/TO/troubles/dossiers/afrique/afr_du_sud/04_afs_2/04_AFS_2.htm.
32. http://www.news24.com/SouthAfrica/News/Harrismith-in-mourning-20040901.
33. Qwa Qwa was part of an apartheid-era Bantustan, set up to attract industries to densely settled areas in the countryside so as to prevent black residents from migrating to metropolitan areas. Many of these labour-intensive industries collapsed following the opening of the South African economy to cheap imports in the mid-1990s.

34. http://www.news24.com/SouthAfrica/News/Harrismith-Shock-video-20040905.
35. These figures are contained in an article entitled '66 cops injured in illegal service delivery protests', *Cape Argus*, 13 October 2005. I am indebted to Patrick Bond for this reference.
36. http://www.sacsis.org.za/site/article/1455.
37. For analyses of these movements, see McKinley and Naidoo (2004) and Ballard et al. (2006).
38. See http://www.abahlali.org/.
39. http://www.anc.org.za/events.php?t=National%20General%20Council %20-%202005.
40. Copies of the documents and consolidated reports on the National General Council are available at http://www.anc.org.za/events.php?t=National%20 General%20Council%20-%202005. For a set of analyses of the first three documents, see Edighji (2005).
41. Umkhonto we Sizwe (Spear of the Nation) or MK was the name given to the armed wing of the ANC, formed in 1961 in response to the Sharpeville massacre the previous year.
42. For an illuminating report on these tensions, see http://mg.co.za/article/ 2007-04-26-kwazulu-natal-rebels-kowtow-to-mbeki.
43. The women and some of the men had been involved in Self-Defence Units – community policing units established in the early 1990s in the context of intense violence between the ANC and IFP. For a discussion of the violence in Ezakheni in this period, see Hart (2002a).
44. For Jacob Zuma's rendition of the song at his moment of triumph in Polokwane in 2007, see http://www.youtube.com/watch?v=lof6XJ8b1SU &feature=related.
45. For a discussion of the role of the MKMVA prior to Polokwane, see http: //mg.co.za/printformat/single/2007-09-13-mk-vets-mobilise-for-zuma/.
46. In D Section of Ezakheni, residents did in fact vote in the ANC's candidate – but she died in office six months later, and was replaced by their preferred candidate.
47. I was told that Zuma was interested in meeting academics, and a student in the Political Science department at the University of California, Berkeley had connections with him. South African press reports subsequently explained that Zuma had been invited by Stratfor (Strategic Forecasting Incorporated), described by *Fortune* magazine as 'one of the elite but low-profile private intelligence agencies that are increasingly relied on by multinational corporations, private investors, hedge funds and even the [US] government's own spy agencies, for the analysis of geopolitical risks'

(reported in an article entitled 'US intelligence firm sponsors Zuma trip', 6 December 2007, http://www.thetimes.co.za. George Friedman, the CEO of Stratfor, was favourably impressed by Zuma, according to this and other reports.

48. The shower attached to Zuma's head is now a permanent fixture of Zapiro cartoons – a reference to Zuma's claim during the rape trial that he showered to reduce his risk of infection following sex with an HIV-positive woman. In 2008 Zuma brought a R15-million (over $2 million) lawsuit against Zapiro for cartoons depicting Zuma about to rape Lady Justice – but he dropped the charges in 2012.

49. For a detailed account, see Misago et al. (2010).

50. http://mg.co.za/article/2008-05-26-minister-xenophobic-violence-under-control.

51. See also the website of Filmmakers Against Racism who produced an extraordinary set of documentaries in response to the violence: http://filmmakers-against-racism.blogspot.com/.

52. http://www.iol.co.za/news/south-africa/anatomy-of-hatred-1.401640.

53. http://www.highbeam.com/doc/1G1-179309856.html.

54. http://www.iol.co.za/news/south-africa/ernesto-s-spirit-is-already-with-us-1.402949.

55. http://www.africasia.com/services/news/newsitem.php?area=africa&item=080525182105.5wzwl2f7.php.

56. This ruling was overturned by the Supreme Court of Appeal on 12 January 2009.

57. http://mg.co.za/article/2008-09-12-zuma-i-am-a-wounded-warrior.

58. http://www.iol.co.za/news/politics/lekota-serves-divorce-papers-on-anc-1.419380.

59. http://www.nytimes.com/2010/06/08/opinion/08iht-edgevisser.html?scp=5&sq=mark+gevisser&st=nyt.

60. For an incisive set of critical reflections on the World Cup, see Cottle (2011).

61. http://www.flickr.com/photos/warrenski/4760660512/.

62. http://www.businessday.co.za/articles/Content.aspx?id=157251.

63. http://mg.co.za/article/2011-11-04-how-jujus-wedding-host-made-his-millions/.

64. South Africa currently supplies over 80 per cent of platinum on global markets. Zimbabwe's production is much smaller, but deposits are closer to the surface, making extraction easier and more profitable than in South Africa.

65. http://www.timeslive.co.za/opinion/columnists/2011/09/11/malema-s-theory-of-white-power-caches-resounds.

66. http://www.dailymaverick.co.za/article/2013-01-28-heartfelt-hard-painful-songs-of-marikana. This quotation has been lightly edited.
67. http://www.dailymaverick.co.za/article/2012-09-24-marikana-putting-words-to-tragedy.
68. Concluding stanza of Ari Sitas' poem, 'The Unending Hurt of Marikana', September 2012.
69. See, for example, Bill Keller's contribution to this project in the *New York Times Sunday Magazine*, 26 January 2013, http://www.nytimes.com/2013/01/27/magazine/could-cyril-ramaphosa-be-the-best-leader-south-africa-has-not-yet-had.html?ref=billkeller&_r=0.
70. http://www.timeslive.co.za/thetimes/2012/10/24/ramaphosa-exposed.
71. 'A Review of Platinum Mining in the Bojanela District of the North West Province', http://www.bench-marks.org.za/.
72. Press Statement, Bench Marks Foundation, http://www.bench-marks.org.za/.

3

The Unruly Terrains of Local Government

[R]eality produces a wealth of the most bizarre combinations. It is up to the theoretician to unravel these in order to discover fresh proof of his [sic] theory, to 'translate' into theoretical language the elements of historical life. It is not reality which should be expected to conform to the abstract schema. This will never happen (Gramsci 1971: 200; Q3 §48).

ON SATURDAY, 30 October 2004, residents of Ladysmith/Emnambithi marched through the town to protest the handing over of water control from the local municipality to the Uthukela Water Company – a public corporation launched in late June 2004 in north-western KwaZulu-Natal and encompassing three district municipalities. Despite its nominally public status, the company operated according to principles of cost recovery and immediately instituted a sharp increase in water tariffs. Protestors were infuriated by these increases, as well as by the rapid deterioration in water and sanitation services following the takeover – broken pipes, gushing hydrants, evil odours and raw sewage running in the streets and emptying into rivers. 'The whole town could unite behind us,' declared Cyril Mchunu, a trade unionist and one of the organisers of the march.

Under the headline 'Protesting Against High Water Tariffs', the *Ladysmith Gazette* on 5 November 2004 carried a report of how 'the community of Ladysmith took to the streets' and presented a memorandum of demands to the mayor of the district municipality, one of the shareholders in the Uthukela Water Company. In addition to the ANC, SACP and COSATU, the signatories included

95

the New National Party (NNP), the right-wing Freedom Front, the African Christian Democratic Party and the Ladysmith Chamber of Commerce. Only the DA and the IFP were missing. One of the photographs accompanying the report shows an elderly white municipal official marching alongside a row of toyi-toying young black men in ANC T-shirts.

The organisers of the Ladysmith march had tried, unsuccessfully, to co-ordinate with the ANC in Newcastle, about 100 kilometres to the north. Newcastle and its surrounding townships had also been incorporated in the Uthukela Water Company, and residents experienced similar increases in water tariffs and a major deteri-oration of water and sanitation services. Although the Newcastle ANC backed away from public protest, an organisation calling itself the Newcastle Concerned Residents Association staged some spectacular protests in the second half of 2004 – including an incident when several hundred township residents (including a number of older women) barged into a town council meeting and barricaded the doors. Terrified councillors called the police who threatened to bring in the dog squad to disperse the crowd – but, as one of the organisers later told me, 'we know they aren't allowed to use dogs – and in any case, how would the dogs know the dif-ference between the councillors and the Concerneds?' 'Eventually,' reported the *Newcastle Advertiser* on 1 October 2004, 'some calm was restored as the councillors held hostage agreed to listen to the ratepayers' demands'.

These two expressions of popular anger and local democracy certainly did not make it into the national press, and it is uncertain whether or not they are included in national statistics cited in Chapter 2 of the thousands of municipal uprisings during this period. In the larger scheme of things, and for all that they have a certain entertainment value, these events in Ladysmith and Newcastle appear pretty mundane and easily explained either by 'poor service delivery' or 'bottom-up resistance to top-down neoliberalism'.

In fact, both explanations are totally inadequate. My purpose in this chapter is to dig beneath the surface of these and other slightly out of the ordinary happenings in very 'ordinary' and unglamorous places, and suggest their larger significance.

In *Disabling Globalization* (2002a), I drew on historical and ethnographic research in Ladysmith and Newcastle between 1994 and 2000 to develop a broader argument about how local government had come to embody some of the key contradictions of the neoliberal post-apartheid era – namely the tensions between fierce fiscal austerity combined with massive new responsibilities for local government and pressures to commodify basic services on the one hand, and invocations of local participation, social justice and democracy on the other – with all of this playing out on viciously uneven terrains carved by the racial geographies of apartheid, and opening to the global economy.

My ethnographic research in Ladysmith and Newcastle for *Disabling Globalization* concluded with local government elections in December 2000. In retrospect, this was a major turning point in post-apartheid local government. Over the decade of the 2000s, this first phase of fiscal austerity and unfunded mandates has given way to an anxious interventionism – one that combines substantially larger transfers of resources from national to local government with escalating efforts to bring unruly local governments under control, and with programmes of municipal indigence designed to manage poverty.

During this period, I will argue, local government has crystallised as *the* key site of contradictions, confrontations and the making of political struggles in South Africa. Focusing again on Ladysmith and Newcastle but moving out from there, I am going to suggest how intensifying national efforts to surveil and control local government are rendering it more fragile. At the same time, I will show how some ostensibly 'pro-poor' measures are feeding into and inflaming the popular anger they were designed to contain.

The Shifting Contours of Local Government

A brief historical reconnaissance is in order, since urban and peri-urban black townships in South Africa have long been what Michael Watts (2003) calls 'ungovernable spaces'. Going back to the early 1980s, efforts to devolve fiscal and administrative responsibilities to so-called Black Local Authorities rapidly became the Achilles heel of the apartheid state in its reformist guise. Indeed, it was the linking together of township and workplace struggles that contributed to the demise of apartheid. What came in the 1990s to be dubbed a 'culture of non-payment' (for municipal services) was the continuation of an oppositional stance in black townships, where it soon became evident that the material benefits of political liberation for the large majority of the population would remain sharply circumscribed in the face of continued white privilege.

In retrospect we can see how, through local government restructuring in the 1990s, black townships and the former Bantustans bore the brunt of both post-apartheid negotiations and the harsh fiscal austerity of that decade. Apropos the former, William Mervin Gumede has reminded us how

> Mbeki played a key role in the agreement on local government that would see municipal elections and integration deferred until 2000. Until then, white municipalities continued to receive the lion's share of resources, while black local authorities had to make do on smaller budgets and fewer resources for larger populations. National Party negotiator Tertius Delport credited Mbeki with accommodating the NP's demands for checks and balances in respect of negotiated agreements on local government (2005: 78).

In 1995 (1996 in KwaZulu-Natal), there were in fact local government elections on the basis of around 830 'transitional council' demarcations in urban areas that cut across the racialised spaces defined by the Group Areas Act – but excluded rural regions and densely settled areas in the former Bantustans governed by traditional authorities. As Gumede points out, however, both budgets and voting arrangements in the transitional councils were designed to protect the privileged status of formerly 'white' suburbs. It was only in 2000 that a new system of municipal demarcations came into effect that fundamentally redrew the map of local government. The Municipal Demarcation Board slashed the number of local authorities to 284, incorporating rural and urban areas into single entities, and eliminating the disproportionate representation of former white areas. Outside the six major metropolitan areas, as we shall see, the new demarcations have generated powerful pressures for urban-rural redistribution from a limited base, along with fierce battles for access to and control over key resources – most importantly water.

Local governments in the first phase of restructuring (1994–2000) were not only rigged in favour of former white areas; they were also starved of resources while at the same time loaded with massive new responsibilities – in effect, unfunded mandates. Local governments in South Africa have historically been heavily dependent on revenues raised locally from property rates and service charges (water, electricity and refuse removal). The 1996 Constitution made provision for 'the equitable division of revenue raised nationally among national, provincial, and local spheres of government'. In 1996/97 the 'equitable share' going to local government amounted to R5.6 billion or 10.8 per cent of municipal budgets. Between 1998/99 and 1999/2000, the local government (in)equitable share actually *fell* from R2.3 billion to R1.7 billion – at precisely the point that conglomerates were listing on the London Stock Exchange and pumping resources out, and Mbeki was navigating the R30 billion (now R60 billion) arms deal.[1]

The contradictory imperatives of local government in the post-apartheid era were clearly evident in the Local Government White Paper published in 1998, a document that drew sharp critical responses from both the liberal right and the left.[2] Both underscored the escalating demands being placed on local government in the face of fiscal austerity. The response from the Centre for

Development and Enterprise – a corporate-funded think tank that intervenes vigorously in policy debates – made abundantly clear that 'the needs of the poor and the demands for an investment-friendly environment with world-class infrastructure are very different' (Bernstein 1998: 300):

> [W]hile any local authority in the new dispensation must be concerned about redress of the disadvantages suffered by poor areas as a consequence of Group Areas and other discrimination from the apartheid period, this must not in any way lead to a deterioration in the quality of administration and services as they impact on wealthier neighbourhoods. While this balance cannot be justified on a moral basis, it is a practical imperative and an essential precondition for the investment and employment creation which will eventually benefit the poor much more in the longer run than administratively-driven redistribution in the short run (CDE 1998: 28).

Underscoring the severity of the crisis of local government, the Centre for Development and Enterprise went on to note that, to the extent that the White Paper is concerned with ensuring the prerogatives of majority-based power, it fails 'to reassure potential investors that some kind of populist deviation in local government, with associated protests from other interest groups, can be ruled out' (1998: 29). In practice, of course, the Centre for Development and Enterprise's insistent emphasis on maintaining predominantly white class privilege in the face of fierce fiscal austerity helped to propel the very protests that they feared. In addition, by the turn of the millennium 'poor areas' had come to pose a biopolitical threat to those whom the Centre for Development and Enterprise sought to protect.

Outright privatisation of municipal services has in fact been quite limited, as we shall see later, but post-apartheid local governments quickly came under heavy pressure to implement principles of cost recovery, often resulting in sharply higher prices for water and electricity and falling payment rates. By 2000 some

250 of the 843 urban and peri-urban municipalities were effectively bankrupt, many others were under severe financial strain, and most of the Regional (i.e., rural) Councils were 'financially nonviable'.[3] To punish residents for non-payment, many municipalities disconnected water and electricity. While the number of cutoffs and reconnections is heavily disputed, there is no question that taps ran dry, toilets failed to flush and the lights went out in many urban households – and that these cutoffs coincided with sharply increasing incidences of HIV/AIDS infections, as well as escalating unemployment. Angry protests against water and electricity cutoffs first erupted in 1997 and, as we saw in Chapter 2, they propelled the initial round of new social movements. Following several disastrous experiments with water privatisation in the 1990s, the ANC government in the 2000s started giving active support to alternative models of corporatisation without privatisation.[4] The Uthukela Water Company described below is one such experiment in a public-public partnership that has, as we shall see, failed spectacularly.

Another set of pressures came from a severe cholera epidemic that raged through southern Africa following heavy floods in southeastern regions in August 2000. By May 2001 cholera had killed 176 people, and infected well over 80 000 – most of them in the province of KwaZulu-Natal. In an essay entitled 'Love in the Time of Cholera', Sitas observed:

> Cholera is following a neat stratification pattern, based on a water-related neo-apartheid, attacking the vulnerable and spreading panic among the wealthy [although none were actually infected]. The assault on the vulnerable needs further amplification – it is not only that the poor, 'subaltern people', overwhelmingly black, are dying prematurely; *that* occurs with impunity . . . It is also about the fact that an area like Umhlanga [on the KwaZulu-Natal coast], a playground of the wealthy, compares with the best of Canada and the West on all socio-economic indicators (2010: 154).

Ironically, it was in the provisioning of water to informal settlements and rural areas that the Mandela administration claimed its greatest redistributive successes in the 1990s. Yet in 1999 Ronnie Kasrils, then Minister of Water Affairs, received the revelation that poor people are unable to pay for water. On a visit to the village of Lutsheko in the Eastern Cape, he was shocked to discover a young mother scooping water out of a hole in a riverbed because she could not afford R10 ($1) a month to pay for water from a communal tap. When the cholera epidemic struck it became clear that large numbers of people were in a similar position – and that providing free water would have been considerably cheaper than the costly official effort to contain the epidemic.

In 2001 the government instituted a policy of providing a minimal allocation of free water to each household, followed by electricity and sanitation, all of which are administered by municipalities. As I will discuss more fully later, the national free basic water policy took its cue from an experiment in Durban in the late 1990s, and so-called free basic services have since morphed into a full-blown municipal indigent policy. Especially in relation to water, this ostensibly protective 'pro-poor' policy is at the same time profoundly punitive through its tight links with 'credit control' – i.e., debt collection – and the crisis of municipal indebtedness. It also turns crucially around meters, a topic that figures prominently in the discussion that follows. Over the course of the decade, municipal indigent policy came to form part of a larger ensemble of 'pro-poor' measures that fall under the rubric of the Second Economy that Thabo Mbeki introduced in July 2003 (Chapter 2).

Initially national-level funding for free basic services remained very limited, with the equitable share hovering around R2–3 billion between 2000 and 2002. From 2003/04 onwards the equitable share grew quite vigorously, along with other transfers to local government.

Table 3.1 Transfers from national to local government.

R million	2002/03	2003/04	2004/05	2005/06	2006/07	2007/08	2008/09	2009/10	2010/11
Equitable share	3 964	6 624	7 678	9 643	11 058	12 631	16 515	21 050	26 676
Conditional grants	4 837	6 048	7 837	7 038	8 443	16 645	18 477	21 111	24 169
Fuel levy sharing (metros)	—	—	—	—	—	—	—	6 800	7 542
Regional Service Council levy replacement grant* (districts)	—	—	—	—	7 000	8 045	9 045	3 306	3 492
Indirect transfers	n.a.	n.a.	n.a.	n.a.	1 436	1 884	2 307	3 017	3 215
Total	8 801	12 672	15 515	16 681	27 937	39 205	46 344	53 163	61 946

Source: Budget Review 2002–2012/13.
* The Regional Service Council replacement grant received by district municipalities since 2006/07 when the Regional Service Council levy was terminated. See Hart (2002a: 247) for an explanation of the Regional Service Council grant.

The local government equitable share is unconditional, in recognition of local government as a constitutionally defined separate sphere of government. A 2008 Local Government Budget and Expenditure Review acknowledged that 'municipalities can exercise discretion in how to channel the equitable share to beneficiaries', while also making clear that 'national free service levels are the main purpose'.[5] In practice many municipalities use the equitable share to fund a far wider array of municipal functions, including salaries for councillors. Calling attention to colossal outstanding consumer debts owed to most municipalities due to unpaid services, the Review notes that 'if municipalities had collected half of these debts, they would have had about 18 percent more revenue with which to fund the delivery of services', and that 'the importance of having sound indigent policies, linked to robust debt collection strategies cannot be over emphasised'.

Growing surveillance by the national Ministry of Finance over municipal finances has accompanied increasing transfers from national to local government. The Municipal Financial Management Act that came into effect in 2004 provides for much tighter central monitoring of municipal finances. At the same time, many senior municipal officials have been placed on performance contracts, and there are reported moves towards establishing a single civil service that will enable far greater central control of local government. Also as part of an effort to exercise central discipline over unruly local governments, the Mbeki administration implemented a system of executive mayors in 2006. Since the mid-2000s, in other words, growing national largesse has gone hand in hand with intensified centralisation of state power. In addition, the ANC began exercising much tighter control over the selection of local ward councillors, often generating considerable resentment. The episode described in Chapter 2 when Mbeki was forced by residents of Ezakheni to rip off his shirt was emblematic of this resentment – but, as we shall see below, this effort at top-down control has far deeper and more systemic reverberations that form an important element of the tensions and contradictions of local government.

Immediately upon assuming power in May 2009, the Zuma administration turned its attention to the generally chaotic state of local government, mindful no doubt of local government elections scheduled for 2011. The Department of Provincial and Local Government was replaced by a new Department of Co-operative Governance and Traditional Leadership, with what Minister Sicelo Shiceka described in his budget vote on 23 June 2009 as a new and expanded mandate.[6] Shiceka also launched a remarkable attack on his predecessor Sydney Mufamadi, a strong Mbeki supporter, accusing him of a narrow technocratic approach, and failing to play an appropriate 'choir conductor' role among different levels of government. The previous week Shiceka had declared that many of South Africa's 283 municipalities were in a 'state of paralysis and dysfunction', citing 'a problematic political/administrative interface, lack of accountability, fraud and corruption, dysfunctional caucuses, weak financial management, poor service delivery, unsatisfactory labour relations and weak public participation structures'.[7] Making clear his intention to wield what he called his choir conductor's stick to keep 'choristers in government and civil society' in line in order to 'protect, guide and direct local government', Shiceka announced a series of initiatives – including Operation Clean Audits aimed at ensuring that all municipalities achieved clean audits by 2014; surveys of all municipalities to identify problems and solutions; halting the outsourcing of services that could be performed by municipal employees; training programmes for councillors; and threats to fire non-performing councillors and officials.

Yet the ongoing chaos of local government was made painfully evident in the run-up to the 2011 local government elections by two highly publicised events: the brutal killing of municipal activist Andries Tatane by police in Ficksburg in April 2011, and the sorry saga of 'open toilets' in several areas.[8] The Tatane murder underscored the resurgence of municipal rebellions – many of them quite violent – that flared up in July 2009, soon after Zuma assumed office, and have shot up still further since then as we saw in Chapter 2.

In the wake of the local government elections, experts within and outside the state issued calls for a Marshall Plan for local government, and a slew of proposals for reform. They include measures to ensure that local government is professionalised and de-politicised by securing the appointment of competent professionals rather than politically influential figures in top management positions; merging unviable municipalities and bringing in 'special purpose vehicles'; and closer monitoring, training and disciplining of councillors, and making them more accountable.

These and other proposals rest first and foremost on the assumption of incompetent, uncaring municipal officials and lazy, corrupt councillors. Yet, as we shall now see, my work in Ladysmith and Newcastle suggests much deeper tensions and structural contradictions than 'lack of capacity' and 'democratic deficit'.

'Water is the Burning Issue': Fluid Politics and the Government of Indigence

The phrase 'water is the burning issue' was given to me by a trade unionist in Ladysmith, describing the chaos that followed the takeover of water by the Uthukela Water Company. In South Africa more generally water is only one of many municipal issues that have become the focus of popular discontent – disputes over housing and threats of removal of shack settlements are possibly the chief catalyst of protest confrontation with local authorities. What makes water an enduring and pervasive source of conflict in many regions of the country – as well as a key window into the inner workings of local government – are four key dimensions, all in tension with one another: water as an embodiment of nature and essential to life; as a commodity; and as a key element of what Foucault (2008) called biopolitical government.[9] In addition, as we have just seen, the provision of free basic water and sanitation forms the foundation of municipal indigent policy set in place in the early 2000s.

In many regions of South Africa water is widely seen as a 'gift from God' that should be free, and to which everyone should have access. This view of water far exceeds liberal notions of rights, and is tied instead to histories and meanings of racialised dispossession. The link with dispossession from the land is quite direct in townships such as Ezakheni outside Ladysmith, and Madadeni and Osizweni some 15-20 kilometres from Newcastle. Like many other townships in the former Bantustans, these dense settlements were formed through apartheid-era 'forced removals' of millions of black South Africans from the 'white' countryside and cities. Part of the Faustian bargain through which people moved into the townships was an understanding that they would be provided with housing, water, electricity and other very basic urban services at a low, flat rate. In places like these, moves to install water meters and commodify water represents a direct violation of this understanding, and is widely experienced as another round of dispossession.

Water is also the single most important focus of biopolitical intervention. In addition to the cholera threats outlined earlier, pipes, drains and sewers form an essential part of a strategy of indirect government, 'inducing cleanliness and hence good moral habits not through discipline but simply though the material presence of fast-flowing water in and through each private household' (Osborne 1996: 115). Yet pipes, drains and sewers do not necessarily produce governable subjects – on the contrary, along with meters, they are the focus of intense and deeply racialised conflict in South Africa today.

Rendering these conflicts all the more intense is the way that municipal indigent policy plays out in practice. A large and important body of research documents how restrictions on water to poor households provokes popular anger, especially in townships where residents are accustomed to running water and flush toilets.[10] Most of this work is in the main metropolitan areas, where local authorities have the coercive capacity to install prepaid meters or restrictive devices. In the Ladysmith and Newcastle townships we shall see how local authorities have battled mightily to install water meters – and how, even in those sections of townships where meters have been installed, they are not being read. Battles over water meters and over indigence/credit control diverge sharply in the two places, as do changing relations among municipal officials, local councillors and residents of former white towns and black townships. Yet, taken together, these divergent dynamics reveal how intensifying national efforts to bring unruly local governments and their populations under control are generating new tensions and contradictions.

To understand water wars in Ladysmith and Newcastle, we need first to map the terrain of battle by attending to (a) how municipal indigent policy and free basic services are linked with 'credit control' and debt collection; (b) the urban-rural tensions built into the new system of municipal demarcations outside the six metropolitan areas, central to which is control over water; and (c) the fate of the Uthukela Water Company, the public-public partnership that provoked the protest march described at the start of this chapter.

Water Wars: The Terrain of Battle
(a) The Logics of Indigence

In 2000, when national policy makers were casting around for an alternative to their insistence on narrow cost recovery, they latched onto the Durban model that Alex Loftus describes as follows:

> [O]ne of the key moments in the beginning of Durban's journey to free water policy was the development of a ground tank system in informal areas. This allowed a fixed amount of water (200 litres per household per day) to be delivered at a relatively low cost to shack areas in the municipality. Initially, residents were charged for the service but the municipality soon realized that the cost of charging individual households outweighed the revenue generated. It was therefore cheaper to provide the service for free. Looking at the rest of the municipality and the costs involved in disconnecting households, it was judged on the grounds of both economic efficiency and universal fairness that the service should be extended to all consumers within the municipality (2005: 191).

The 200 litres per day translates into 6 kilolitres per household per month, regardless of household size. According to the elegant logic of this model, a system of 'stepped tariffs' above the free basic minimum of 6 kilolitres means that high-volume users will cross-subsidise low-volume users, and also encourage conservation (Muller 2008: 78).[11] Loftus paints a far murkier picture of how the 'Durban model' has operated in practice. He shows how for many of those living in shack settlements, it meant the ability to access free clean water for the first time in their lives.[12] For households in established townships accustomed to a flat service fee, however, the Durban model meant 'the escalation of bills, a closer surveillance of the amount consumed and the restriction of supplies to a level barely enough to survive on' (Loftus 2005: 201). How this metering was accomplished and the very different strategies that Johannesburg officials pursued are discussed more fully below.

A key feature of this model of universal free basic water is that it does not entail setting up an indigent register. At the same time, its logic in relation to credit control demands that households in full service areas using more than the 6 kilolitres minimum who fail to pay their bills have to be punished either with the installation of a prepaid meter that only delivers the 6 kilolitres minimum, or a device attached to a regular meter that restricts water supply to the minimum. Especially for households with water-borne sanitation, the 6 kilolitres minimum is brutal – one toilet flush consumes 10 litres. More generally, the inadequacy of 6 kilolitres – and its failure to take account of household size – is a huge point of contention, as well as a lawsuit in Johannesburg (discussed later).

The Durban model was initially very influential in Ladysmith. I vividly recall the municipal manager at the time describing the beauties of the system in the late 1990s and, as we shall see, a version was set in place in the town (but not Ezakheni) in 2001. What quickly became evident in Ladysmith and other places is that the cross-subsidies require a relatively high proportion of large-scale consumers, and that in smaller towns and cities – most of them heavily cash-strapped – the Durban model simply increases costs.

More generally, architects of free basic water soon recognised that the Durban model cannot work in towns outside the metros, and came up with a targeting model in which only households defined as 'indigent' receive free water. While municipalities have some discretion in defining the qualifications for indigence, they are required by the Department of Provincial and Local Government to maintain an accurate indigent register. They must also, obviously, set in place a system of metering to measure and restrict consumption – either a prepaid meter or a restrictive device. The logic of the targeting model is clear: it entails sorting out the 'can't pays' from the 'won't pays', and making things sufficiently unpleasant for the latter to force them to pay up. In effect, towns and small cities with far more limited financial and administrative resources than the metros are being called on to engage in an enormously complex, costly and conflictual exercise of dividing and disciplining the population.[13]

Official directives also advise local government officials to draw on ward councillors to assist in this exercise. This scenario envisages ward councillors, elected by their constituents and supposed to represent them, as instruments in the campaign to identify and cordon off the deserving poor, and ensure that the rest of the population is exposed to the whip of market discipline. In practice, of course, these idealised models are subverted at every turn.

(b) Reconfiguring the Terrain of Local Government: Urban-Rural Tensions

The new system of municipal demarcations, inaugurated with the local elections held in December 2000, entailed a fundamental restructuring of local government. In addition to six metropolitan areas (Category A municipalities), the Demarcation Board identified 232 so-called Category B municipalities that encompass towns and small cities and adjacent rural areas, as well as predominantly rural areas with no urban centre. Outside the metros, groups of Category

B municipalities in turn form part of a set of 46 Category C or district municipalities.

In addition to a fundamental administrative restructuring, the new demarcations redrew the map of electoral politics at the local level by defining wall-to-wall wards of roughly equal size in terms of population. In effect, for the first time in the country's history, each vote at the local level counts equally and, in principle at least, traditional leaders in former Bantustan settlements excluded from the first phase of local government restructuring were replaced by elected representatives. While this process has been extremely contentious, the new system of demarcations and equal weighting of votes has intensified pressures for redistribution of resources to these formerly excluded settlements from former white towns and formal black townships.

The map on p. 112 shows how the new demarcations expanded the boundaries of Ladysmith (now Ladysmith/Emnambithi) and Newcastle to incorporate surrounding rural areas.[14] Each became part of a larger district municipality, which also includes newly formed predominantly 'rural' local municipalities. Thus Newcastle is part of Amajuba district municipality (DC 25), while Ladysmith is included in Uthukela district municipality (DC 23).[15]

In terms of demography, Newcastle is larger and more urban than Ladysmith/Emnambithi – but the Uthukela district is considerably larger than the Amajuba district:[16]

Table 3.2   Population.

Ladysmith/Emnambithi local municipality	225 459	Newcastle local municipality	332 981
Other local municipalities in DC 23	431 527	Other local municipalities in DC 25	135 056
Total Uthukela district	656 986	**Total Amajuba district**	468 037

Source: 2001 Census data.

Newcastle and Ladysmith as part of the Amajuba district municipality and the Uthukela district municipality respectively.

Although Newcastle is larger and more industrialised, the two former white towns and adjacent black townships are structurally quite similar (Hart 2002a). Both were the focus of industrial decentralisation policies during the apartheid era, and the formal townships (Ezakheni outside Ladysmith, and Madadeni and Osizweni outside Newcastle) were formed through forced removals of black South Africans from the surrounding 'white' countryside. Yet my research during the 1990s made clear powerful differences in political dynamics in the two places. Ladysmith/Ezakheni had a long history of political organisation and mobilisation, whereas politics in Newcastle/Madadeni/Osizweni was generally chaotic. These differences reflected the political coherence and strength of the ANC in Ladysmith in contrast to Newcastle, where the ANC was divided and relatively weak in relation to the IFP.

An immediate consequence of the new demarcations was the weakening of the ANC in the newly demarcated municipality of Ladysmith/Emnambithi. In the December 2000 local government elections the ANC won a resounding victory in Ezakheni with very high turnout rates – but lost most of the rural wards to the IFP. An especially bitter loss was St Chads, a densely populated informal settlement immediately adjacent to Ezakheni that had been excluded from the Ladysmith municipality in the interim demarcations. Other than a few boreholes and pumps, residents of St Chads received very little in the way of material improvements, despite the fact that pipes bringing water to Ezakheni run through St Chads. In the second half of the 1990s, provincial representatives of the ANC argued that local resources should be deployed to provide running water to residents of St Chads, but were stymied by ward councillors in Ezakheni who were adamantly opposed to resources being diverted from their constituents.

These tensions surfaced dramatically in the fierce fight over the control of water between Ladysmith/Emnambithi and Uthukela district municipality. My first inkling of the scope and intensity of this fight came in June 2001, when Mike Sutcliffe – a fellow geographer and chair of the Demarcation Board at the time – invited me to a meeting between district and local authorities in Ladysmith to discuss which level of government would control water.[17] The meeting turned into a set of heated exchanges between the municipal managers of the local and district municipalities (both white men).

The larger issues and context of this battle are usefully summarised in a paper entitled 'Local Government Powers and Functions' published by the Institute for Democracy in Africa:

> The Water Services Act established the separation of a water services authority (the municipality with statutory responsibility to ensure that water services are provided) from water services provider (the body actually responsible for providing the service). With the coming of two-tier local government in the country this provided a new challenge for the sector, namely to decide whether the local or district municipality should be the water services authority. The Municipal Structures Act implied it should be the latter, but the Minister of Provincial and Local Government has the authority to amend this position and therefore instituted a process to decide where local municipalities should be the authority. This process, completed in 2002, resulted in a non-uniform outcome with 23 district municipalities being the authority in largely underdeveloped areas and 126 local municipalities having this function for the rest of the country (IDASA 2004: 25).

In other words, when this meeting took place in 2001, there was deep ambiguity on the question of powers and functions. On the drive back to Durban, Sutcliffe agreed that the Ladysmith municipality had the technical and administrative capacity to control water, but that in the larger scheme of things district municipalities should, in his view, be empowered. He also mentioned that he envisaged the ANC doing away with provinces in the future, and that beefing up district municipalities would provide the ANC national government with direct access to large municipalities.[18] In the broader debate over powers and functions, opponents of this position pointed out that assigning powers and functions to newly formed district municipalities meant, in effect, that small cities and towns (and their adjacent formal townships) would bear the brunt of redistribution to dense 'rural' settlements.

In 2002 the Minister of Provincial and Local Government designated Newcastle a water services authority, leaving Amajuba district municipality with authority for water over the remaining 30 per cent of the population in the relatively small local municipalities of Utrecht and Dannhauser. Ladysmith/Emnambithi, however, was required to hand over its water functions to Uthukela district municipality. As we shall see, local officials in Ladysmith/Emnambithi waged a fierce and relentless battle to retain control over water, but in July 2004 they were finally forced to relinquish control.

The consequences of these differential divisions of powers and functions in terms of allocations of resources from the national fiscus have been massive. Later we shall see how, particularly after 2004, the volume of national resources going to local government rose rapidly. Most significant is the so-called equitable share that, although technically unconditional, is clearly intended to fund basic services (mainly water) for the poor. Although all municipalities received more generous allocations, increases have been far larger for those designated as water service authorities.

In principle, the Uthukela district municipality could have retained Ladysmith/Emnambithi local municipality as the water services provider. In practice, a much more far-reaching set of plans to take control over water in the region was underway.

(c) The Conception, Birth and Death of a Water Public-Public Partnership

A major figure in the initiative that produced the Uthukela Water Company was the late Willie Schoeman, a former National Party member of parliament under the apartheid regime, and until 1996 chair of the Joint Services Board – the entity in charge of water provision to dense rural settlements in this region of north-western KwaZulu-Natal prior to 2001. Working in conjunction with a water engineer in Newcastle, Schoeman envisaged a water utility for the whole of the Thukela Basin, and raised funds from an Australian aid agency in the late 1990s to demonstrate its feasibility.

Table 3.3 Equitable share allocations between local and district municipalities.

R thousand	2002/03	2003/04	2004/05	2005/06	2006/07	2007/08	2008/09	2009/10	2010/11
Ladysmith/Emnambithi local municipality	12 191	12 397	18 537	28 473	31 316	40 115	49 193	64 822	83 304
Uthukela district municipality	11 791	21 573	32 937	57 320	63 286	104 886	128 819	159 193	198 196
Newcastle local municipality	20 559	28 178	39 663	75 432	83 900	110 311	135 603	178 204	255 777
Amajuba district municipality	3 256	5 858	6 452	11 263	12 509	48 135	57 718	66 487	78 331

Sources: 2002/03: Government Gazette, Vol. 442, No. 23330; 2003/04–2009/10: Division of Revenue Bills.

When I met with Schoeman in 2005, he talked about his anticipating the incorporation of rural areas and the imperative for a water utility that could realise economies of scale in this relatively well-watered region. At the same time, he was insistent that municipalities should retain control over water, rather than water boards that report to national government, as in the main metropolitan areas. In September 2001, as deputy mayor of Amajuba district, Schoeman presided over the formation of the Thukela Water Partnership.[19] The signatories were the three newly demarcated district municipalities in the Thukela catchment area – Amajuba, Uthukela and Umzinyathi. The partnership agreement unequivocally asserted the jurisdiction of the district municipalities over component local municipalities, and defined the district municipalities as the water service authorities responsible for 'effective and sustainable delivery of water'.[20] The Thukela Water Partnership was designated a multi-jurisdictional water services provider – in effect, a public-public partnership – which evolved into the Uthukela Water Company, launched in Newcastle on 28 June 2004.

When Schoeman forged ahead with the Thukela Water Partnership and designated the district municipalities as water service authorities in 2001, he was effectively riding roughshod over the Newcastle and Ladysmith local municipalities – both of which expected to retain control over water. While Newcastle was successful in its bid to remain a water service authority, municipal officials and DA councillors tried to prevent Uthukela Water Company from becoming the water service provider. In fact, it was only in May 2004 – a month before the launch – that the Newcastle council finally agreed to Uthukela Water Company becoming the water services provider for the town.

Ladysmith municipal officials also fought tooth and nail to retain control over water. The municipal archives are filled with complaints to national government departments about the unfairness of handing over the water services authority to the Uthukela district municipality, and the dire consequences likely to follow. There are also bitter exchanges with district officials, and minutes of meetings in which Ladysmith officials walked out on their district counterparts.

Local politicians in Ladysmith were in a more complex position than municipal officials. ANC councillors, now in a minority, found themselves treading a difficult path between directives from their ANC superiors in national government to support the handover of water to the district municipality as well as the Uthukela Water Company; their antagonism towards the IFP; and the imperative to appeal to rural constituents demanding water. The alliance between the IFP and the DA/NNP that had taken over the council after the 2000 elections also came under pressure. IFP local councillors were heavily under the sway of a powerful IFP mayor in Uthukela district. He was pushing very hard for the district to wrest control of water from the local municipality, and envisaged a key position for himself in the new water utility. As captains of commerce and industry in the town, DA/NNP councillors were deeply apprehensive at the prospect of losing control over water.

These tensions exploded in late 2003, when two NNP councillors broke with the DA/IFP and crossed the floor to join the ANC. The move came following a meeting with the national Minister of Provincial and Local Government, which was also attended by the IFP mayor of Uthukela district municipality. He had, according to the NNP councillors, promised to support their bid for the Ladysmith/Emnambithi municipality to determine water tariffs in the town – but then reneged on this promise at the meeting. The floor-crossing resulted in the ANC's taking back control of the council. DA councillors found themselves confronting the worst possible situation, effectively losing control of everything. This political realignment helps to explain the political unity between the ANC and NNP displayed in the march described at the start of this chapter – and it also explains why the DA was notably missing from the list of signatories to the memorandum of demands handed over to the IFP district mayor.

Newcastle politics also became deeply entangled in the process leading up to the formation of the Uthukela Water Company – but in dramatically different ways. Following the formation of the Thukela Water Partnership in 2001, Schoeman hired Ceenex, an engineering consulting firm based in Pretoria (with offices in Washington, D.C.), to drive the process forward. Headed by its CEO Johan Wagner, Ceenex quickly came to play a major role. In the process, Wagner and Schoeman came into headlong conflict with one another. In the course of this conflict, key figures in the ANC in Newcastle became involved in the project, and Schoeman pulled out. One key result was that ferocious Newcastle politics within and between the IFP and ANC became incorporated in the formation of the Uthukela Water Company, amplifying the already contentious politics that accompanied its conception. This is also why the ANC Alliance in Newcastle refused to collaborate with the Ladysmith march in October 2004.

Uthukela Water (Pty) Ltd was launched on 28 June 2004 at the Newcastle Showgrounds amid great fanfare and with national Minister of Water Affairs Buyelwa Sonjica and IFP Chief Gatsha Buthelezi in attendance. Minister Sonjica's speech was fascinating for its emphasis on how this was a highly innovative public-public partnership – implicitly, at least, contrasting it with the public-private partnerships in water delivery that had proven so problematic in other parts of the country. What became clear was that the ANC government saw the public-public partnership model as a potential solution to the disastrous experiments with public-private experiments elsewhere in South Africa in the late 1990s.[21] Other speakers picked up this theme, with the Managing Director Bheki Khumalo promising to 'marry corporate governance with cooperative government'. What was not clear from the speeches or the glossy brochures was the role that Ceenex would play in this public-public partnership – although in fact it turned out to be substantial and deeply problematic.

Sonjica also drew direct links between indigent policy, credit control and financial sustainability: '[T]he indigent policy needs to be implemented to ensure that poor people who cannot afford to pay for services are assisted while those who can pay should be encouraged to pay... This particular challenge calls for the municipality to develop an effective credit control and debt collection policy to ensure financial sustainability.'

Several speakers waxed lyrical about how poor rural people, deprived for so long in a region rich in water (much of it piped to Gauteng), would reap the benefits of economies of scale and high-tech solutions – such as billing via cellphones. Laurence Sithole, Chief Director of Water Affairs at the Department of Water Affairs and Forestry, sounded a more cautious note: 'It is fitting that the Minister should launch Uthukela Water in her second month. It is innovative and novel – but full of bugs. Our request as the Department is please accept it in its shapelessness and ambiguity. Build on it – don't break it down.'

In less than four years Uthukela Water Company did break down in a rather spectacular fashion. The first major crack appeared in December 2004, when Uthukela district municipality withdrew – some say it was expelled – from the company, leaving behind huge debts. In March 2008, the Provincial Department of Local Government and Traditional Affairs essentially took over Uthukela Water Company. Citing allegations of maladministration, fraud and corruption, provincial officials suspended the directors of the company; appointed an administrator and technical staff to ensure water delivery; took over water service authority functions from the constituent municipalities; and ordered a forensic investigation and comprehensive assessment of the operations of the company.[22] In short, Schoeman's dream of municipalities joining together to ensure control over water died an ignominious death – but its brief life is central to understanding ongoing but dramatically different battles in Ladysmith and Newcastle.

Divergent Water Wars in Newcastle and Ladysmith

The sharply divergent forms of opposition that the Uthukela Water Company provoked in Newcastle and Ladysmith and their adjacent formal townships are linked with the very different ways in which indigent policy and credit control/debt collection have operated in the two places. We shall now see how Newcastle local officials outsourced debt collection and indigence control to a private company that used threats of confiscating property to force payment – and how this coercive strategy was made possible by a history of chaotic politics, while in turn intensifying political turbulence. Ladysmith in contrast emerged as a 'model municipality' in terms of administrative efficiency. Yet over the course of the decade of the 2000s, the capacity of councillors to respond to their constituents eroded significantly.

(a) Newcastle
Reservoirs of Discontent, Torrents of Fury
On 10 August 2004 the Newcastle Ratepayers Association and the Chamber of Commerce called a meeting to protest against Uthukela Water Company service and rising tariffs. The turnout was huge – and, to the surprise of the organisers, extended well beyond the predominantly white membership of these organisations. The *Newcastle Advertiser* on 13 August 2004 carried a front-page banner headline 'ENOUGH! FAT CATS PICKPOCKET US!' along with the following report:

> All races, religions and political affiliates stood united in one common goal – to take on local council for passing what they believe is a crippling new water tariff. The new water service came under fire as one after another ratepayer slammed the salaries of uThukela officials, saying they were lining their pockets at ratepayers' expense.

The report also calls attention to another key concern discussed at the meeting: 'the subsidisation of Newcastle East by Newcastle West and the non-payment factor in Newcastle East'.

A note on the racialised geographies of Newcastle is necessary here. When the former white and Indian town and black townships were amalgamated in the mid-1990s, white power-brokers dubbed the former 'Newcastle West' and the latter 'Newcastle East'. This simultaneously de- and re-racialised discourse enabled geographically bounded contrasts between virtuous (mainly white) Westerners imbued with a 'pay culture' and profligate (black) Easterners defined by a 'culture of non-payment'.

What the racially mixed composition of the meeting made clear was that growing numbers of Africans had moved into 'Newcastle West' – and, like their white and Indian neighbours, were alarmed by rising water tariffs and deteriorating services, as well as by high levels of non-payment in the townships. Organised protest very quickly assumed a racialised form, however. Headed by Sibusiso Lukhele, a teacher who had moved from Madadeni to 'Newcastle West', a group calling itself the Newcastle West Concerned Residents Association (NWCRA) was elected at the 10 August meeting to confront the executive committee (EXCO). A few months later they removed the 'West' from their title as they joined forces with the townships. George Adamson, the convenor of the meeting who was not elected, refused an invitation to join the NWCRA and formed the Newcastle West Development Forum.[23] He and others accused members of the NWCRA of being a front for the ANC, positioning themselves in anticipation of local government elections.

When I met with representatives of the NWCRA in 2005, they insisted that the 'Concerneds' was an apolitical organisation, but alluded to incipient power of the 'Concerneds', which, they claimed, derived from their expertise:

> At first we were accused of being a wing of the DA. But when things heated up, the DA said they don't want anything to do with us – we are babies of the ANC. The DA disowned us. The ANC said we are loose cannons and political toddlers. The IFP also called us immature. They are all scared that we will run away with the wards. If the Concerneds are calling a meeting, there are at least 300–500 people. If we ran in the elections we would take 3 wards in Madadeni, 6 in Osizweni and 5 in town – with 14 wards we would be the power broker in council. But Newcastle Concerneds want to stand as a

watchdog, not to contest elections. In the Concerneds, people get education about the political parties. We attend all the meetings, get the documents and point out the problems.

By late 2005 the Concerneds seemed to have run out of steam, and they did not in fact contest the 2006 local government elections. What is significant, though, is the popular anger in the townships that they tapped into – and that found expression in a series of protests in September 2004. Let me start with reports from the *Newcastle Advertiser*:

17 September 2004: 'Rebellion'
An angry mob gathered outside town hall to protest among other things the hike in tariffs . . . Some threatened to kill the local sheriff who, on instructions from the local court, had attached certain household goods due to non-payment of municipal services. It appears the local council is getting hammered by ratepayers from all sides, with Newcastle West ratepayers demanding more stringent measures be taken against their non-paying counterparts in Newcastle East, and Newcastle East residents protesting against the action the municipality has taken against them for non-payment.

24 September 2004: 'In hiding: Terrified council barricades
building in defence against irate residents'
Extra security personnel were posted in and around the municipal building on Tuesday and local police were alerted after a rumour surfaced that Newcastle East residents planned to storm the building. By 1pm on Wednesday, however, this had not taken place but locals were still being barred access to the building unless they were there to pay their municipal accounts. The protest action is believed to have been sparked by non-paying residents' attachment of household goods and high municipal tariffs.

In fact, the invasion took place the following week – and the invaders took over council chambers, not the municipal building.

In conversation with NWCRA representatives, I noted that, from the pictures, most of the protestors were older women. The response was:

> When you organise a march, you run a risk. Youngsters are angry and unemployed, and they can end up looting. You have to strategise, and bring in elderly people who are mature and can see right from wrong. Women are more manageable. That makes us unpopular with the youth. We told the council we don't want to see this town burning. We protest in an orderly fashion. We recruit leaders and have a plenary session with them. They identify people they know. When people get into the buses or taxis, we make sure they understand.

In further conversation, though, it emerged that it was, in fact, a group of infuriated older women who suggested the hostage taking: 'They said let's barricade the council. We are prepared to stay for four days if necessary.' When asked what they were so angry about, the response was:

> This indigent thing. They are not giving a clear story – there is confusion between R800 and R1 500 to qualify as indigent. Also – some properties are being attached. People are saying, 'How can I pay when I am unemployed? Why can't they write off the debt?' They are also upset that pension grants are counted as income, but child grants are not. This is illegal. Also, the indigent are said to be owing a lot of money. But the council receives money it can use to write off the debt, and they are not doing that – they are just sending the money back. They are also angry that people have to keep applying to retain indigence. When they are senior citizens, why can't they just stay, why do they have to keep reapplying? They are also very angry about the 6 kilolitres of water – it is not enough.

When I pointed out that, in fact, water was not being restricted in the townships, the NWCRA representative responded that people were apprehensive that the council would put in restrictive devices along with meters. Popular anger in the townships, in other words, was directed not just at Uthukela Water Company, but at the combined indigence and credit control measures in the town, to which we now turn.

Outsourcing Indigence

In 2002 the Newcastle municipality outsourced municipal indigent policy and debt collection (known in South Africa as 'credit control') to a private company named Zader Municipal Services. Zader set up offices in the municipal building, and moved quickly to set up an indigent register along with a system of debt collection.

When Zader took over, very few households in the townships were in fact paying the flat fee for water, sanitation and refuse removal.[24] The Zader representative with whom we met in 2005 started out saying that 'in Newcastle West everything is in place; it's the East that's a huge problem'. Zader started out doing a survey of the townships, which, she maintained, made clear that most of the existing information was incorrect. Between October 2002 and March 2003 Zader processed the first batch of indigents. The cutoff to qualify as indigent was R800 total household income, as opposed to R1 100 in the same period in Ladysmith. Those who qualified had their arrears written off and the flat service fee reduced by about 40 per cent.[25]

Zader was immediately flooded with indigent applications – somewhere between 18 000 and 19 000 households.[26] According to the representative they had to close the indigent register, and get people to reapply using far more stringent surveillance systems. 'We operate like detectives,' the representative declared, describing how they now link to a credit bureau and check all claims about residence, jobs and so forth. People also have to provide their identity documents. Yet she also admitted the utter impossibility of nailing down precise information. When I suggested that perhaps 'households' are moving targets, she agreed vigorously. 'That's exactly right!' she declared. 'They're changing all the time. Just when we think we've got it, something shifts – I'm constantly having to change my database.'

Zader's strategy of linking indigence and 'credit control' turned around the threat of attaching household goods. There was a three-step process. Households who failed to pay received a final demand. If they did not respond to that, they received a summons. Zader then handed the case to municipal lawyers to attach possessions. By mid-2005, the Zader representative explained with clinical precision, they had issued 31 698 final demands; 12 000 summonses; and 3 809 households had had their possessions attached.

The intensity of resentment provoked by this blitzkrieg crack-down on debt collection needs to be situated historically. Townships like Madadeni and Osizweni in Newcastle and Ezakheni in Ladysmith are the product of apartheid-era forced removals through which millions of Africans living in areas designated part of 'white' South Africa were uprooted and moved into townships located in Bantustans. Especially for owners and tenants removed from so-called 'black spots' (densely settled areas where black landowners had freehold rights), dispossession and forced removals resulted in radically commodified livelihoods. This was also the case for workers and tenants expelled from white-owned farms. Essentially the apartheid state struck a Faustian bargain through which people who moved into these sorts of townships were promised water, electricity, sanitation and refuse removal at very low, flat fees that were heavily state-subsidised.

In *Disabling Globalization* I describe how, shortly after the 1996 local government elections, newly elected Newcastle councillors (including ANC representatives with 44 per cent of the seats) came under heavy pressure from municipal officials to approve a budget that increased monthly service charges in the townships from R17 to R76. The townships exploded with rage, and the ANC mayor had to take refuge at a police station as Madadeni residents pelted him with stones around which they had wrapped their municipal accounts.[27] Since then, payment rates in the Newcastle townships remained extremely low.

In 1996, as in 2004–05, a Concerned Residents Association of ambiguous political provenance rose up and subsided, leaving behind little if any enduring organisation.[28] Yet the Concerneds in both periods tapped into very deep reservoirs of anger. In the first phase of my research (1994–2000) I spoke with many residents of Madadeni and Osizweni, mostly women, who described the terrible suffering they endured when they were first moved into the townships – and who saw the low, flat rates in effect as reparations. Although I did not meet with participants in the 2004 protests, I have no doubt that their militance was fired in part by memories of dispossession and broken promises by the post-apartheid dispensation – memories that cross generational lines, and endure through ongoing recollections of a past that is decidedly not dead.

Other threads of continuity from the 1990s are evident in the hostile relations between and among ANC and IFP councillors, white municipal officials and strident Newcastle West ratepayers. Municipal officials see Zader as protecting them from the chaotic politics of the townships as well as pressures from residents of 'Newcastle West' – providing the closest they can get to a 'controlled environment' (a term used repeatedly by municipal officials): 'Zader keeps us afloat – politicians can't intimidate a contractor,' one official remarked. In fact, Zader became a political football that in-tensified conflicts within and between political party representatives, as well as the terms on which they engage with powerful municipal officials.

Zader's strategy in the Newcastle townships combined indigent policy and credit control *without* the use of meters to monitor and restrict consumption – the threat of attaching household goods was the enforcement mechanism. It was only in 2005 that meters were installed in the townships by Uthukela Water Company, amid intense conflict and death threats. In 2010, these meters were still not used to restrict consumption.

On the face of it, the situation in the Ladysmith/Emnambithi township of Ezakheni was quite similar – meters have been installed in most (though not all) sections of the township, but they were neither being read nor used to restrict consumption prior to the 2011 local government election. Yet the processes through which indigent policy and credit control came together are, as we shall see, dramatically different. Under pressure from angry and fearful constituents, ANC ward councillors engaged local officials in two key battles in the period leading up to the formation of Uthukela Water Company in 2004. First, in areas where meters were already in place, they increased the minimum allocation from 6 kilolitres to 18 kilolitres. Second, they fiercely opposed the installation of water meters in Ezakheni – forcing a process of negotiation and compromise very different from that in Newcastle. Especially since 2006/07, Ladysmith municipality emerged as a model of efficiency and fiscal probity. Over the same period, however, the capacity of councillors to respond to their constituents has eroded dramatically.

(b) Ladysmith
Opening the Taps, (In)stalling the Meters
Following the 2000 local government election, an alliance between the DA/NNP and the IFP took over the Ladysmith/Emnambithi local council, united primarily by their mutual antagonism towards the ANC-dominated townships – and determined to make township residents pay (and pay more) for services. It is also important that in the period immediately following that election, the municipality was severely cash-strapped. Despite the increase in population through the expanded municipal boundaries, the equitable share had not increased at that point – and, like most other local municipalities, Ladysmith/Emnambithi was quite heavily indebted.

The new alliance moved quickly to tighten debt collection for electricity and water in areas where there were already meters, and to install meters in Ezakheni where there were none. In 2001 local authorities set in place a partial version of the Durban model described earlier in the relatively affluent former white and Indian suburbs, as well as in Acaciaville, an Indian working-class area, and in Steadville, the black township immediately adjacent to the town where meters had been in place for some time. In accordance with the logic of the Durban model, all households received the first 6 kilolitres free, and were charged according to a stepped tariff for additional consumption.

It soon became evident that the municipality could not afford the Durban model, and it was abandoned within a year for the targeting model. Households with incomes below R1 100 a month were eligible to apply for indigent status. In return for having municipal debts written off, they had to have a prepaid electricity meter installed, along with a restrictive device attached to the water meter that reduced water flow to 200 litres a day – in effect, producing a tiny trickle. A municipal engineer described how, if anyone tampered with the restrictive device, the municipality shut down running water inside the house and put a standpipe in the yard.

Municipal officials were very clear that, in accordance with the targeting model, their aim was to sort out the 'can't pays' from the 'won't pays' – and to make life sufficiently unpleasant for the latter group to force payment. At the end of 2002, when the policy had been in effect for six months, the municipal manager remarked that people were scared – and that ward councillors were also afraid of losing their popularity.

In fact, the ANC ward councillors from Steadville and Acaciaville were enraged. They pointed to the terrible hardships imposed on women struggling to nurse family members suffering from HIV/AIDS; to the indignity of not being able to hold weddings and funerals; and to the utter inadequacy of the drips of water coming out of the taps and the horror of clogged toilets even in households not experiencing health crises or ceremonial obligations. 'This is a total nightmare – the municipality is turning us into social workers!' declared one councillor, explaining how she spent most of her time trying to organise water tankers to supplement totally inadequate water supplies in her ward. Although there was no sustained uprising in Steadville and Acaciaville, there were sporadic outbursts of protest.

In 2003, ANC ward councillors launched a concerted campaign to increase the minimum allocation of water from 6 kilolitres to 18 kilolitres a month. As we shall see later, this was also the period in which municipal engineers were struggling to install water meters in Ezakheni, and councillors linked the two issues. In the face of

growing pressure, water engineers described how they engaged in a
surreptitious strategy to increase the flow. One of them showed me
how the restrictive device attached to the meter has three settings –
on, off and 200 litres a day. He and his colleagues figured out how
to file the key to increase the flow. Another explained how 'we
quietly started opening the meters to let through a bit more water.
We read every meter and found that most were using 10–12 kilolitres
per month.' He went on to say that 'some people are genuinely
poor, and we had to do it on compassionate grounds – 6 kilolitres
is really horrendous, especially when you have a flush toilet. It's
just not hygienic.' Yet he and his colleagues readily conceded that
the move to 'open the taps' was driven by ANC ward councillors.

This initiative to increase the minimum allocation was quite at
odds with directives emanating from the DA/IFP-controlled council.
In September 2003, for example, the EXCO of the council resolved
that 'the National policy regarding the 6 kilolitres of free water be
adhered to and that the restrictive devices deliver only 6 kilolitres
as per the policy'.[29] A few months later the ANC took over the
council as a consequence of the floor-crossing described earlier,
and quickly passed a resolution that 'the volume of water dispensed
by the trickle flow device be increased from 200 litres to 600 litres
per day; noting . . . that this would be more acceptable to the
indigent/non-paying community; further noting that there are [sic]
water borne sewerage in Ladysmith, Steadville and Ezakheni which
could become a health hazard should there not be sufficient water'.[30]

Ladysmith/Emnambithi is, to the best of my knowledge, the
first municipality in which an activist council pushed through this
sort of increase in the minimum allocation – in effect, subverting
the logic of the targeting model.

Let me turn now to the struggle over the installation of water
meters in Ezakheni. Municipal officials in Ladysmith/Emnambithi
devoted huge amounts of time and energy to meter technology. In
principle, they said, prepaid meters are tremendously attractive in
providing 'a very controlled environment' – a term invoked
repeatedly by officials in both Ladysmith and Newcastle. In practice,

they decided, prepaid meters were simply not feasible – in addition to being far more expensive. Here is how one of the water engineers explained the decision to install standard meters in Ezakheni:

> There are no successful prepaid meters. They are very open to tampering. We went to Cape Town and the guy said don't do it. Joburg Water has been using prepaids in Kathlehong, and they have had endless battles. We did a huge amount of research. We also took the advice of Stewart Scott [an engineering firm in Pietermaritzburg]. They recommended against prepaids. When the Municipal Manager went to China, he went two days earlier to do research on a new type of meter that runs on a swipe card. We looked at it and it seemed interesting, but they couldn't give any guarantees. In the end we went with standard Kent meters, with a specially engineered restrictive device that is much harder to tamper with.

The first meters were installed in the largely middle-class area (A Section) of Ezakheni towards the end of 2002, although households were still billed the flat service charges.[31] At the time, it was generally understood that households would not be billed for actual water use until meters had been installed throughout Ezakheni. While meter installations in A Section went fairly smoothly, efforts to install meters in other parts of the township met with fierce opposition. 'The meter story has been driven by politics,' declared one of the engineers. 'People were saying, "We will not let you into our property – we will kill you." ' People in Ezakheni described their anger and fear when installation teams arrived in their neighbourhoods. Their rage was compounded when they discovered that workers employed to dig trenches had been brought in from rural areas, and were allegedly linked to IFP councillors. A relatively affluent resident of C Section described how she drove around shouting for women to come and join her to fight the workers and meter installers: 'Women are much more militant,' she declared. 'They will have to deal with the consequences of this meter thing.' She also mentioned how the IFP workers were reminiscent of violence in the late 1980s and early 1990s when an IFP warlord bused troops of heavily armed young men into Ezakheni.[32]

ANC ward councillors in Ezakheni were fiercely opposed to the meters. Under pressure from their angry constituents – and painfully aware of the water restrictions in Steadville and Acaciaville – they fought hard to have the meter installation project in Ezakheni halted. In the face of this fierce opposition municipal officials tried desperately to manufacture consent. One of the water engineers explained:

> We really workshopped the meters. We held meetings every Monday with the councillors and the ward committees, and everyone from the borough engineers office would come. The councillors would hold meetings and let people know what was going to happen before we got there. We also bought a PA [public address] system, and went around explaining before we went in to install meters. And we distributed flyers in each section.

Yet, he conceded, most of the community meetings ended up in a shambles and had to be abandoned, and meter installations remained a constant struggle.

A memo from the borough engineer in February 2004 noted that councillors demanded to know 'how we could be installing meters in Ezakheni when over weekends certain sections of Ezakheni experienced low pressure and in some cases residents did not receive any water', and demanding that 'EXCO address the community with regard to the installation of water meters'. The report concludes that 'at this stage no meters are being installed in Ezakheni' and urges that EXCO members address the community to explain the meter installation project. In short, ward councillors – themselves under fire from angry constituents – were holding EXCO members' feet to the very same fire.

In addition to the sharp contrast with Newcastle, these struggles exemplify the subversion of bureaucratic logic through a sort of popular democracy in action. As I show in *Disabling Globalization* this popular democracy has a much longer history, dramatically exemplified in a series of open budget meetings in the late 1990s. These were extraordinary events in which township residents critically engaged municipal officials and ward councillors, voicing demands and laying out priorities. Open budget meetings came to an end when the ANC lost its majority in the council in the 2000 elections – but they were not reinstated when the ANC regained control at the end of 2003. Several councillors confessed that these meetings were extremely stressful, and that the more perfunctory consultations now required by municipal legislation are far easier. Yet the activism of ward councillors around minimum water allocations and meter installations embodies vestiges of this earlier history.

By 2008 ward councillors had been sidelined from the exercise of bureaucratic power. At the same time, national government hailed Ladysmith/Emnambithi as a model municipality in fiscal terms – one of only about 20 per cent to receive a clean audit. In other words, fiscal probity and the consolidation of bureaucratic power have gone hand in hand with the sharp curtailment of popular democracy in Ladysmith. The process through which this happened helps to pinpoint the deep tensions and contradictions through which municipal indigence operates in practice.

The Political Maelstrom of Indigence

> A **maelstrom** (or **malström/malstrøm** in the Scandinavian languages) is a very powerful *whirlpool*; a large, swirling body of water. A *free vortex*, it has considerable *downdraft* (http://en.wikipedia.org; emphasis in original).

When I returned to Ladysmith in mid-2005, the big story was how efforts to register households as indigent were spreading very rapidly. Early in 2005, at the start of the surge, some 5 000 households in Ladysmith/Emnambithi were registered as indigent – approximately 12 per cent of the roughly 40 000 urban and township households in the municipality. By 2007, the number of 'indigent' households had climbed to around 20 000. This was, of course, a period in which the equitable share was also increasing significantly (Table 3.1).

Mindful of the earlier experiment with indigence in Ladysmith, reports from other parts of the country and theoretical pre-conceptions, my immediate reaction was that being defined as indigent must be a belittling and demeaning source of shame. When I tried to probe this issue with ANC councillors, they immediately responded in terms such as 'actually it's a wonderful thing' and 'oh no, people love it!' The newly defined 'indigents' with whom I spoke confirmed this view, conveying a sense that the government was at last providing some of the support to which they were entitled. What also became clear was that the connotations of 'indigence' in English – a sort of Dickensian image of the cringing poor in nineteenth-century London – has no cognate in isiZulu, and that indigence was being defined and understood in terms such as 'giving to people who don't have enough' and 'restoring our dignity'.

The initial impetus came from municipal officials. Until 2004/05 they had relied on an intricate, administratively costly and time-consuming questionnaire to assess indigence that was focused mainly on households in Acaciaville and Steadville. In 2005, partly in an effort to incorporate Ezakheni households in a comprehensive indigent register in the most efficient way possible, they instituted a system of automatic indigence that the chief financial officer described as follows: 'Where a house value is equal to or less than the national housing subsidy – R36 720 – we give them everything for free. We will rebate 100 per cent of houses in that category. It takes out poor people – you can't expect them to pay.'

He went on to say that this is much more efficient than chasing them up with bills that they can never pay, and estimated some 7 000–8 000 households fell in this category. Those who qualified had their arrears written off, paid no rates and received free refuse removal. The only downside was having to accept a prepaid electricity meter.[33]

The crucial point is that there were no restrictions on water in Ezakheni. In December 2004, following its withdrawal from

Uthukela Water Company, Uthukela district municipality took responsibility for water service provision. While residents of Ladysmith town complained that the provision of water and sanitation was every bit as bad – if not worse – than when the company was in charge, it was clear that things were (and still are) infinitely worse in Ezakheni. In what appears as a sort of quid pro quo, the district municipality did not pursue the meter installation project. Although the supply of water continues to be highly erratic, most Ezakheni residents have, for some time, been getting it for free – or, more accurately, subsidised by the surge in the equitable share going to the district municipality (Table 3.1).[34] There is also a political quid pro quo: while the ANC in Ladysmith/Emnambithi can blame the IFP-led district municipality for poor water services, the latter can claim to be giving away water for free.

For ward councillors, the new system of indigence translated into a rich source of patronage. They had to approve each application and, as one municipal official later observed, 'each signature was a guaranteed vote'. This was also a period in which, as one ward councillor put it, 'we are afraid of people toyi-toying in the street'.

Mid-2005 was a crucial political turning point in South African politics, ushering in a period of intense turbulence. In June 2005, as we saw in Chapter 2, then-President Thabo Mbeki dismissed Jacob Zuma as deputy president of the country, following the conviction of Zuma's financial adviser on fraud and corruption charges in which Zuma was allegedly involved. At the ANC's National General Council meeting held shortly thereafter, deep schisms within the ANC became evident, accompanied by an upsurge in popular support for Zuma and powerful anti-Mbeki sentiment.

In addition, as we have seen, municipal uprisings all over the country intensified in 2005, resulting in the postponement of local government elections originally scheduled for late 2005 to March 2006. This was also a period in which the ANC sought to deal with popular insurrection and the problems of local government by exercising tight control over the selection of ward councillors. During this time, I was able to observe several spectacular expressions of popular anger in Ladysmith directed at the Mbeki ruling bloc – and indeed at the figure of Mbeki himself, when he ripped off his T-shirt to placate an angry crowd at the pre-election rally in D Section in Ezakheni described in Chapter 2. What so infuriated the residents was that national and provincial officials of the ANC had replaced the candidate for ward councillor elected by the ANC branch in that ward.

Contrary to widespread expectations of massive boycotts of local government elections in March 2006, the ANC Alliance actually increased its share of the vote from 60 per cent in the 2000 local elections to 66 per cent in the country as a whole, with a very similar turnout rate. In Ladysmith/Emnambithi the ANC won 56 per cent of seats in council, although the IFP held on to Uthukela district municipality by a narrow margin. Despite expectations of victory, the ANC in Newcastle garnered only 44 per cent of the seats and went into alliance with the National Democratic Convention, a small party that split off from the IFP. By May 2007 this alliance had fallen apart, and an alliance of the IFP and other small parties took over the Newcastle council.[35] Zader remained a key bone of contention; relations between councillors and municipal officials became increasingly fractious; and the capacity of ward councillors to represent their constituents remained as attenuated as ever.

In contrast, the bureaucracy in Ladysmith/Emnambithi increasingly came to operate like a well-oiled machine, conforming closely to national directives for greater discipline in local government. Senior white municipal officials died or retired, and former ANC councillors took over the top positions in municipal government since 2006. Their appointments coincided with progressively more stringent surveillance and control by national government, along with generous remuneration packages. Senior municipal officials were rendered subject to performance contracts, as were the mayor, deputy mayor and speaker of council.

Since the 2006 local government elections, councillors have found themselves in an anomalous position. On the one hand, their remuneration escalated according to a scale defined by national

government – although salaries come out of local budgets. According
to the municipal manager, the salaries of ordinary councillors in
Ladysmith/Emnambithi increased by 52 per cent after the election
to R168 000 a year, and by 2010 averaged R180 000 a year – a
colossal income in relation to that of most township residents. On
the other hand, they were becoming subject to more rigorous
discipline and scrutiny, as a consequence of the tightening national
control and its transmission through the ANC-controlled municipality.

When I visited Ladysmith in mid-2007, a concerted campaign
to ramp up debt collection and limit indigence was taking shape.
Municipal officials along with members of the council's EXCO
had become deeply critical of the system of automatic indigence,
claiming that the number of indigent households far exceeded the
fiscal capacity of the municipality, and that large numbers of
households (including teachers and nurses) who could afford to
pay for services were taking unfair advantage. An often-repeated
phrase was the need to cut indigence to the bone. A senior official
in the finance department summed up the aggressive new stance
from an administrative point of view, emphasising the imperative
to make indigence as unpleasant as possible so as to 'make it very
difficult for illegal indigents to jump on the wagon'. In a classic re-
statement of the targeting model, he laid out strict and limited
terms to qualify for indigence on the one hand, and the imperative
to meter and restrict water use on the other. The fundamental
problem in sorting out can't pays from won't pays was (and remains)
the district municipality's refusal (or inability) to limit water:

> The district and water is a very dicey situation. Ezakheni is still not
> metered fully – you must have meters to restrict water. We will go to
> the district and threaten to report them to central government if they
> don't restrict. They wanted to set up a separate indigent register, and
> we said this is madness. They have accepted using our indigent register
> because they don't have the resources to do it any other way. Technically
> they should do it, but they can't. We will have them on board with
> indigence.

In relation to the services over which Ladysmith/Emnambithi has control, he outlined the following ideal strategy:

> Those flagged as indigent will receive rates for free. But we will not pay for refuse – if they don't pay, we will force them. They must be on a prepaid restricted electricity meter. We will interface with the financial system. Whenever they purchase electricity we will know, and take 50 per cent of the purchase for refuse collection.

What was striking about this and other discussions with long-serving municipal officials was the sense that, in the past, they had always been constrained by 'political interference' – but that ANC councillors were now being brought under control by the new dispensation. As one of them put it: 'Ward councillors have been put on terms – you support this policy or you are out; there is a very strong move to discipline councillors and use performance agreements.' In accordance with the logic of the targeting model, ward councillors were being positioned as frontline troops in the battle to divide and discipline the population. At the same time, ward councillors were painfully aware that moves to limit indigence and apply water restrictions to those who qualified would call forth the wrath of their constituents. As one of them put it in July 2007, 'These days, it's not nice to be a councillor.'

On returning to Ladysmith in December 2007, I discovered that ward councillors had thrown a spanner in the indigence/ credit control machine. The district municipality (under pressure apparently from provincial officials) had accepted the indigent register from Ladysmith/Emnambithi officials and made tentative moves to apply water restrictions to some of the households in Ezakheni. Both the handing over of the lists and moves to apply restrictions called forth an enraged outcry from ward councillors. They focused their wrath on the dilapidated infrastructure that resulted in massive water losses. 'How can you just come with meters only – you must first repair the pipes,' they insisted. In the face of this incontrovertible logic and threats of popular unrest, the district authorities backed off.

It is important to bear in mind that the second half of 2007 was a period of heightened political mobilisation leading up to the ANC conference in Polokwane, and the titanic battle between Mbeki and Zuma. That ward councillors were able to break out of the straitjacket in which they found themselves after the election was, I think, partly made possible by their tapping into powerful anti-Mbeki sentiment.

By the second half of 2008 there was yet another twist in the saga of credit control and indigence in Ladysmith/Emnambithi: municipal officials were forging ahead with constructing a far more limited indigent register – and councillors no longer had any involvement in the process. The councillors with whom I spoke insisted that the initiative to withdraw came from them. One rationale was that 'this way we can put more pressure on the administration' – but what also became evident was that, in the face of the fierce clampdown on indigence, councillors found it politically expedient to distance themselves.

Municipal officials drew a sharp distinction between an idealised model in which councillors help to manufacture consent, and practical reality – in effect, the messy and inconvenient practices of everyday democracy. As one of them put it:

> In principle the ward councillor is the spokesperson for the community. It looks fantastic on paper. In practice it only works if the ward councillor gives you something – the councillors always want to give something away for free. The moment the administration starts to make you pay, they [the councillors] run with complaints . . . We would prefer to share responsibility with the councillors, but it's just not practical. We have now taken a much more scientific route.

This 'scientific route' formally commenced on 1 July 2008 – although information was disseminated from February. The old register based on house valuation was terminated, and aspiring indigents had to apply using a detailed form:

> We learned from our mistakes [i.e., the administratively simpler automatic indigence that drew in huge numbers of applicants]. The new form is much more comprehensive. You must declare your income correctly – you have to prove that you don't have income. We run an ITC [credit bureau] check – the beauty of it is it's so much easier to capture data. We send in a request and four days later we get a response . . . the end result is that we find out that some of those who claim to be unemployed are actually not – we've thrown out about 20 per cent [of the approximately 6 000 new applications].

The official went on to describe how he worked for three hours every night going through the remaining applications on a case-by-case basis – but that 'capture' is far from complete. In a litany strongly reminiscent of the Zader representative in Newcastle, he talked about how people move in and out of households; how there are discrepancies in residential addresses; how 'if you are married in the Zulu way' there is no marriage certificate; how child support is uneven; how he checks bank accounts to track deposits, but deposits can fluctuate – and so on. In other words, the scientific route is slippery and treacherous.

It also proved practically impossible. By 2009 municipal officials had abandoned the scientific route, and gone back to a system of automatic indigence based on house valuation. Those living in houses valued at less than R70 000 pay no rates and have prepaid electricity meters that provide the free basic minimum of 150 kilowatts. In addition, municipal officials instituted 'application indigence' for those living in houses valued at more than R70 000. The latter group has to go through a system of credit checks and accept a prepaid electricity meter. By mid-2010 officials estimated that about 8 000 households qualified for automatic indigence, and another 500 were 'application indigents'.

Yet this apparent solution is a political minefield waiting to explode if and when water restrictions go into effect – especially if the level is set at 6 kilolitres. As one official put it: 'The moment you exercise restrictions, you will lose 40 per cent of the indigency;

no one can be happy with 6 kilolitres – it's impossible.' Simultaneously he made clear the impossible situation in which he and his colleagues found themselves: 'We don't have the tools; but if we do have the tools, we sit with resistance.'

At the same time, the councillors find themselves in an increasingly precarious position in relation to their constituents. They have, as Sitas (2010: 190) puts it, become a petty bourgeoisie 'on their road to class power' – and, simultaneously, their capacity to respond to their constituents on this most crucial of issues is eroding rapidly. Even the most diligent and accountable councillors are effectively being sidelined through the logics built into the way municipal indigence operates in practice.

What makes these reconfigurations of relations among councillors, municipal officials and residents all the more significant and ironic is that, in fiscal and administrative terms, Ladysmith/ Emnambithi features as a model municipality on the larger canvas of South African local government.

When we consider the dynamics unfolding in Ladysmith in relation to those in Newcastle, what is important is not just that these are divergent 'path-dependent' processes rooted in specific historical geographies. Of far greater significance is that both places exemplify how interconnected tensions and contradictions around water provision, indigence and debt collection are tearing apart the fabric of local government, albeit in locally specific ways – and how national interventions aimed at imposing order and discipline are contributing to this unravelling. Let me turn now to suggesting how our excursions to Ladysmith and Newcastle shed light on the escalating tensions of local government in South Africa today.

The Contradictions of Local Government

In zooming out to the broader canvass, it is important to recall the intensified and increasingly anxious interventionism through which successive waves of ANC administrations have sought to bring unruly local governments under control – only to be confronted by escalating conflict. For instance, just as the newly elected Zuma administration was gearing up to play a far more interventionist role in local government in 2009, a resurgence of rebellions directed at local government in many parts of the country flared up – some of them quite violent.[36] Almost every night television screens beamed images reminiscent of apartheid-era popular fury and state violence – angry crowds toyi-toying in the streets, burning tyres and on occasion municipal buildings; the cameras then swivel to police in riot gear firing rubber bullets, stun grenades and tear gas, and pushing screaming people into armoured vehicles.

In comparison with these often brutal confrontations, the protests over water described earlier seem remarkably tame. On the surface, at least, Ladysmith and even Newcastle appear as relatively quiescent and well governed, especially when located on the larger canvas of municipal dysfunction and urban rebellion. While water (and water restriction) is a burning issue in many municipalities, there are many other triggers of protest and confrontation with local authorities. In addition, even in those areas where struggles over water have figured prominently, many of these protests have turned around the imposition of prepaid water meters. So how, then, can battles over water in these two seemingly mundane towns and adjacent townships shed light on the generally parlous state of local government in South Africa today?

Most immediately, they point to the limits of widely held views that the problems with local government derive from 'poor service delivery' that can be laid at the feet of incompetent, uncaring officials and lazy, corrupt councillors. Without question rotten councillors and officials are enormously problematic in many areas; and, no doubt, bringing in more efficient and accountable replacements would produce some improvements in municipal services. Yet I argue that, beneath the surface of contestations over water in north-western KwaZulu-Natal, there are deeper systemic tensions and contradictions than 'lack of capacity' or a 'democratic deficit'.

Broadly speaking, local government is the impossible terrain of official efforts to manage poverty and deprivation in a racially inflected capitalist society marked by vicious inequalities, which, since 1994, have become simultaneously de- and re-racialised. Close attention to Ladysmith and Newcastle since 1994 helps to highlight several related dimensions of this turbulent and shifting terrain that have intensified over the decade of the 2000s. First is the pernicious logic of indigence, linked in turn with debt collection, which seeks to render technical that which is inherently political. Second is the simultaneous growth of opportunity and inequality at local level over the decade of the 2000s, which is generating intense intra-party conflict and eroding the position of councillors.

The Government of Indigence: Techno-Fixing Poverty
We have seen how, in Ladysmith and Newcastle, municipal indigent policy has embroiled municipal officials in ongoing conflicts with councillors and township residents, along with endless battles to sort out the 'can't pays' from the 'won't pays'. That these battles have thus far remained relatively muted in comparison with those in many other places has a great deal to do with the inability of officials to impose water restrictions.

There are some instructive comparisons here with the techno-logics and politics of indigence in large metropolitan municipalities that have far greater coercive capacity than that in many smaller cities and towns, as well as more resources with which to cross-subsidise services. As we saw earlier, well-resourced municipalities can in principle sidestep the morass of means-testing and indigence registers by providing a free basic minimum to all households, cross-subsidised through a stepped-tariff system. According to the logic of the Durban model, indebted households 'self-select' by accepting water restriction in return for debt write-offs, thus minimising bureaucratic intervention. At the same time, the 'can't pays' in principle take responsibility for disciplining themselves. A great deal of critical attention has focused on prepaid meters as the quite literal technology of rule through which neoliberal governmentality operates. In fact, eThekwini (Durban) authorities use flow restrictors rather than prepaid meters.[37] While the specific form of the technology is significant for water users and those who govern them, what is most fundamental to the workings of this neoliberal model of government at a distance is the coercive capacity of the state to impose and maintain water restrictions.[38]

To residents of established townships, the installation of water meters represents a form of dispossession from the most basic means of life that is, at the same time, deeply racialised. In relocation townships like Ezakheni and Madadeni, we have seen how meters represent a double dispossession – a violation of the quid pro quo through which residents (or their forebears) were forcibly removed from land in 'white' South Africa. More generally, the installation of meters in urban townships that have historically had access to water, electricity and other urban services at relatively low, flat rates amounts to ongoing warfare that takes a variety of forms.

From a comparative perspective, what is significant about the Durban model is that meter installation combined with water restriction appeared as a swift surgical strike at a relatively early point. Neil MacLeod, the head of eThekwini Water Services, is reported as having described the rapid installation of replacement meters in townships throughout the city in 1998 as a 'military operation' (cited by Loftus 2006: 1032) that quickly incorporated township residents within new infrastructures of discipline while, at the same time, replacing decaying water pipes that accounted for massive water losses.

Johannesburg authorities have wielded much clunkier weapons and more openly aggressive strategies in their battles to deal with debt and impose water restrictions. In the late 1990s, just as Durban authorities were gearing up for their blitzkrieg, Johannesburg officials ruthlessly disconnected those who did not pay for water and electricity – with the backing of none other than Sicelo Shiceka, then provincial member of the Executive Council for Local Government in Gauteng province, who declared in August 1997 that 'persuasion hasn't been taken seriously, so we are now at the stage of coercion, and it's paying dividends'.[39] Disconnections sparked fierce protests and fed into the formation of oppositional movements that came together under the banner of the APF. They also spawned a veritable army of what have come to be known as struggle plumbers and electricians engaged in reconnecting their neighbours.

While following in the footsteps of their Durban counterparts in providing universal free basic water through a stepped tariff system starting in 2001, Johannesburg authorities have pursued a far cruder strategy that is also more vulnerable to counter-attack. Meter installation in Soweto only began in 2003 – until then, residents still had an unmetered, flat-rate water supply.[40] In that year, Johannesburg Water launched the deeply controversial 'Operation Gcin'amanzi' (Save Water) in the Phiri section of Soweto. In contrast to Durban where township residents received conventional meters (to which flow restrictors could be attached), Soweto residents had to accept either a yard tap or a prepaid water meter that delivers 6 kilolitres of free water a month.[41] In July 2006 five residents of Phiri led by Lindiwe Mazibuko and represented by the Centre for Applied Legal Studies launched a high-profile legal challenge to the adequacy of the minimum water allocation and the constitutionality of prepaid water meters.[42] The Mazibuko case, along with ongoing popular discontent and protest, has exerted tremendous pressure on the City of Johannesburg.

Accompanying these pressures are a series of policy shifts through which the City of Johannesburg has retreated from the Durban model of universal free water and government at a distance, and moved instead towards defining and targeting the indigent. In mid-2006, just as the Mazibuko case was launched, the city made allowance for an additional 4 kilolitres of water per month to households registered as indigent, with an additional annual allocation of 4 kilolitres for emergencies.[43] A fully fledged targeting model made its appearance in mid-2009 when Amos Masondo, the mayor of Johannesburg, announced an entirely new 'Expanded Social Package Policy' dubbed Siyasizana (We are helping one another).[44] Siyasizana figured prominently in efforts by the City of Johannesburg and Johannesburg Water to answer the charges levelled against them in the Mazibuko case, and formed a key element in their appeal to the Constitutional Court in September 2009 – and it appears to have played an important role in the judgment that went against the Phiri applicants.[45]

Like the targeting model with which smaller cities and towns have been grappling for some time, Siyasizana abandons universal free water. In almost every other respect, though, it represents a dramatic departure from existing strategies of dealing with indigence. Instead of identifying households on the basis of income (or house value), Siyasizana trains its sights on the individual – or, more specifically, on individuals with 'special needs' and pathologies rather than those that are simply impoverished. In addition to disease, advanced age, 'very low basic skill level', and residing in a household headed by a child, pensioner or single parent, these include 'history of abuse, history of substance dependency, ex-combatant status and prior incarceration/history of criminal activity'.

To register, individuals have to appear at a customer service centre with a South African identity document, a copy of the city account for the property on which they live and the numbers of their prepaid water and electricity meters. They will then be fingerprinted, and the fingerprint 'will be used as confirmation that the City has permission to verify information about them with other government information systems'.[46] Instead of credit bureau checks and forays into townships to ensure that there are no Mercedes-Benzes parked in the yard, those administering Siyasizana will draw on a comprehensive system of state surveillance through a massive integration of data bases.[47] Applicants will then be assigned 'poverty scores' and placed in one of three bands that determine the level of assistance for which they qualify. In addition to varying levels of water and electricity, the three packages include transport, rental and rates subsidies – as well as registration with the Jobs Pathways programme 'designed to help people become economically self-reliant, and ultimately lift themselves beyond the need of Siyasizana'.

In contrast to the neoliberal logic of government at a distance exemplified by the Durban model, Siyasizana Johannesburg has shifted to an enormously intricate welfarist system of individual poverty scores, backed up by massive combined data systems designed to barcode and stratify the poor, and shepherd them in appropriate directions. Drawing on a revealing interview with Jak Koseff, Director of Social Assistance for the City of Johannesburg, Prishani Naidoo sees Siyasizana as a new set of technologies for governing the poor: 'In the context of growing unemployment and precarity, it could be argued that Siyasizana represents an attempt at the production of a new terrain of subjectification (Foucault), outside that of the discipline of the factory and the wage, in which the emphasis on acceptance of the duty to pay for basic services, and acceptance of the duty to be in a job and/or conducting some kind of entrepreneurial activity "to make a better life for oneself", produces a set of technologies through which poor people are administered to and managed.'[48]

While Siyasizana can usefully be seen as a project of rule, propelled by the legal challenge and ongoing protest, how it plays out in practice is another question altogether. What my work in Ladysmith and Newcastle suggests is that, with this Orwellian strategy of techno-fixing poverty, officials of the City of Johannesburg may well be heading into a far deeper and murkier political quagmire of measuring and monitoring indigence than that in which their counterparts in smaller municipalities have been flailing around for some time. According to a 2011 press report, only 10 per cent of residents estimated to be eligible for Siyasizana had actually applied; and there has been a deafening silence on the numbers enrolled since then.[49]

In the meantime the forces feeding into widespread resentment and discontent continue apace, just as local councillors' positions are becoming increasingly tenuous for reasons that go beyond individual greed and corruption. In her research in Johannesburg, Claire Bénit-Gbaffou found that councillors' powers are attenuated in the face of rising discontent, at the same time as they are presented as being at the forefront of local delivery; in addition, some councillors 'are caught between their possible sympathy for needs expressed at ward level on the one hand, and council policies and policy directions on the other' (2008: 28–9). The chances are high that a de-politicising strategy like Siyasizana will feed into and intensify the corrosion of councillors' relations with their constituents. We have seen how, in Ladysmith/Emnambithi, with its history of intense political mobilisation, councillors are becoming increasingly detached from their constituents – both because of how municipal indigent policy operates in practice to sideline councillors and erode their powers, and because of intensifying intra-party conflicts over access to positions of local power and resources. It is to this latter set of considerations that we now turn.

Petty Bourgeoisies on the Road to Class Power: Local Government as an Arena of Accumulation

An important part of the story I have told in this chapter is the process through which Ladysmith became 'ordinary' over the decade of the 2000s, and the insights this process yields into some of the deeper contradictions of local government.

In 'The Road to Polokwane', Sitas (2010) develops a province-wide argument about how, in KwaZulu-Natal, popular, democratic politics that accompanied the growth of democratic trade union organisations in the 1980s has given way to grassroots populism 'with serious authoritarian undertones'. KwaZulu-Natal, of course, has its own specificities. They include the 'depth of grassroots cultural mobilisation using indigenous forms of expression as a democratic and socialist manifestation in the trade unions and community organisations' (Sitas 2010: 188); intense conflict with Inkatha that erupted in a murderous civil war in the late 1980s and early 1990s; and the peace settlement, followed by democratisation and the incursion of the ANC into IFP strongholds in the 2000s (recall the Bergville meeting described in Chapter 2). The ANC has had to pay for its electoral success through a shift in language, Sitas argues:

Whereas in the 1980s and 1990s the distinguishing language of belonging to one or other movement could show differentiation between democrats and socialists on the one side, and 'traditionalists' on the other, such distinctions were blurred in the interests of peace and 'development' . . . [T]he political culture of mandates, account-ability and participation was given short shrift, so it has begun to be indistinguishable from the other: *uhlonipha* [respect], loyalty and authoritative obedience (2010: 187).

Calling attention to how local councillors are being transformed into a petty bourgeoisie on the road to class power in the context of intensifying struggles over resources flowing into local govern-ment, Sitas observes that 'because of the broader mix of polarising greed and need, each locale (involving branches and councillors and large numbers of expectant people) is animated by class contestations, inclusions and exclusions, crises and differential strains'; and that 'class struggles and competition are rifer *within* branches of the ANC (and Inkatha for that matter) than they are between workers, bosses and the state in broader society' (2010: 187). There are in fact two bourgeoisies: those established through apartheid's Bantustan system, and working-class people who know they can become middle class through the post-apartheid dispensa-tion. Both bourgeoisies have extended patronage networks, but the resources are always too small to accommodate more than a few:

The tragedy being played out is that there is at once too much and too little: enough to enrich some people but not enough for all. Despite the fact that more resources than ever before are being directed to the poorer wards and zones, the need is so high that only a few predominate, and in order to do so, they have to exclude others (Sitas 2010: 191).

Those excluded or 'wronged' become available for mobilisation, and possibilities for collective or co-operative projects are under-mined.

We will return to this analysis in Chapter 5, which situates the contradictions of local government in relation to simultaneous practices and processes of de-nationalisation and re-nationalisation, and traces some keys ways in which they have been changing in and through one another over the decade of the 2000s. Together they enable a fuller understanding of the proliferation of increasingly dangerous populist politics, and the processes through which the ANC's hegemonic project is unravelling. First, though, we need to go back and rethink the transition from apartheid in terms of de-nationalisation and re-nationalisation.

Notes

1. In 1998/99 the Department of Finance devised a formula for allocating the equitable share to municipalities: the bulk was designated as an operating subsidy of R86 ($14) per household earning less than R800 ($133) per month. Data from the Department of Finance Budget Review (1999/2000) and cited in UNDP, South Africa Human Development Report 2000 (Table 3.1: 85), http://hdr.undp.org/en/reports/national/africa/southafrica/south_africa_2000_en.pdf.
2. This paragraph is paraphrased from Hart (2002a: 236).
3. For references and further discussion, see Hart (2002a): 275.
4. See the Introduction to *The Age of Commodity* (McDonald and Ruiters 2005) for a useful discussion.
5. http://www.info.gov.za/view/DownloadFileAction?id=87397?.
6. Following the toppling of Thabo Mbeki in September 2008 and the resignation of Minister of Provincial and Local Government Sydney Mufamadi, then-President Kgalema Motlanthe appointed Sicelo Shiceka to the position. Shiceka moved quickly to appoint task teams to address municipal problems.
7. Article entitled 'SA's muncipalities in "state of paralysis"', *Mail & Guardian Online*, 10 June 2009.
8. See the article on open toilets available at http://www.scielo.org.za/scielo.php?pid=S0018-229X2012000100005&script=sci_arttext.
9. See Lemke (2011) for the different senses in which Foucault used the term, and Chari (2010) for an illuminating deployment of the concept of biopolitics.
10. In addition to the excellent collection of studies in McDonald and Ruiters (2005), these include among others Bond (2004), Bond and Dugard (2008), Loftus (2005, 2006) and Naidoo (2010).

11. Mike Muller was the Director General of the Department of Water Affairs and Forestry from 1997–2005.

12. It should also be noted that the provision of free basic water is far from universal. The Durban (now known as eThekwini) municipality has denied access to water, sanitation and electricity to extensive areas of shack settlements that officials are trying to move to peripheries far from work, schools and other services (see the website of the Durban shack dwellers' movement, Abahlali baseMjondolo, http://www.abahlali.org/).

13. The nightmarish quality of indigent registers is made painfully evident in a report issued by the Directorate of Free Basic Services in the Department of Provincial and Local Government in 2005 entitled 'Study to Determine Progress with and Challenges Faces by Municipalities in the Provision of Free Basic Services and Supporting those Municipalities Struggling with Implementation'.

14. Between 1996 and 2000 Ladysmith municipality included only the former white town and Ezakheni, and Newcastle included only Madadeni and Osizweni.

15. The map includes the largely rural Umzinyathi district municipality to the east, which, as we shall see, joined with Amajuba and Uthukela to form the Uthukela Water Company.

16. See Table 7.2 (Hart 2002a: 278), which contains demographic data from the 1996 population census that were used as the basis of the new demarcations. These data show Ladysmith/Emnambithi with a population of 178 551 and Newcastle with 287 550; 60 per cent of households in Ladysmith/Emnambithi are classified as urban, compared with 81 per cent in Newcastle. Municipal officials insist that census data vastly underestimate the number of people living within their boundaries.

17. For information about the Demarcation Board, see Cameron (2006).

18. Following the 2009 election, less than a decade later, the possibility of doing away with provinces has become the focus of intense political debate.

19. Funding for this initial stage came from the Municipal Infrastructure Investment Unit, the Development Bank of South Africa and the European Union.

20. 'Each Partner is a water services authority and will remain the water services authority in its respective area of jurisdiction with the functions and power as stipulated in terms of Section 84 of the [Municipal] Structures Act as well as Section 11 of the Water Services Act.' Partnership Agreement of the uThukela Water Services Provider Partnership, 18 September 2001: 5.

21. See McDonald and Ruiters (2005) for an eloquent analysis of these problems.

22. 'Provincial Interventions: Report to the Select Committee on Local Government', Department of Local Government and Traditional Affairs, KwaZulu-Natal Provincial Government, March 2008.
23. A heated exchange of letters between Adamson and Lukhele appeared in the *Newcastle Advertiser*, 12 November 2004, in which Adamson expressed his disdain for NWCRA, and Lukhele asserted that only nine people attended the annual general meeting of the Newcastle West Development Forum, of whom five were observers.
24. The fee varied between R248 and R72, according to whether there was a tarred road and sanitation. For a discussion of diverse conditions in the Newcastle townships, see Hart (2002a).
25. The flat rate depended on the area – if there is a tar road and sanitation it was R248 – indigents get R95 deducted. The lowest rate was R72, and the intermediate R130.
26. This represents approximately 50 per cent of township households, which municipal officials estimate at around 37 000.
27. That the ANC won the largest bloc of votes in this election had a great deal to do with the fact that a controversial Taiwanese industrialist ran for the IFP. He has since joined the ANC as a national parliamentary representative.
28. These processes are described in Hart (2002a: 250–4).
29. EXCO Resolution EC16/9/2003, 11 September 2003.
30. EXCO Resolution, 18 January 2004.
31. In 2002, monthly service charges were as follows: R23 for water; R18 for refuse; R11 for sanitation; and rates in A section averaged R76.
32. For a fuller description, see Hart (2002a: Chapter 3).
33. Although prepaid electricity meters can be topped up, they supply limited amounts at any one time. The most succinct description of what this means in practice was from an Ezakheni resident who described how 'with 60 square metres you can cook, have a bath, watch TV and iron. With 20 square metres you can only do one thing at a time.'
34. In principle, residents are still supposed to pay a flat fee for water. In practice, according to Ladysmith officials, a very small proportion of households actually pay. District officials, all of whom were beholden to the IFP, did not respond to my requests for information.
35. In what seems like an ongoing political game of musical chairs, the ANC managed to wrest control of the Newcastle council from the IFP in mid-2009 through going into alliance with a splinter group from the National Democratic Convention.
36. For an incisive analysis of the problems of attaching the label 'service delivery' to these protests, see Richard Pithouse, 'The Service Delivery Myth', http://sacsis.org.za/site/article/610.1. In 2009 researchers at the University of

the Witwatersrand conducted studies in communities where violent protests had taken place; for an overview of the findings and an interesting analysis, see Von Holdt (2011).

37. Installation of the flow restrictor is accompanied by a 15-minute training session that 'makes customers aware of how to manage with 200 litres a day', according to the city's water policy statement, which goes on to note that any tampering with the flow-restricting device will result in permanent disconnection until the amount owing has been paid in full. For a description of debt and disconnection policies, see http://www.durban.gov.za/durban/services/water_and_sanitation.

38. Indeed, one could argue that flow restrictors are more oppressive than prepaid meters in that they do not allow for the option to purchase additional water.

39. 'Gauteng authorities recoup R500 million in service arrears', South African Press Association, 13 August 1997. I am grateful to Patrick Bond for this reference.

40. I am drawing here on a chronology laid out in the Founding Affidavit of the Leave to Appeal *Mazibuko v City of Johannesburg* (2009/08/035) assembled by the Centre for Applied Legal Studies, http://web.wits.ac.za/Academic/Centres/CALS/.

41. According to the Founding Affidavit (paragraph 74), 'regardless of whether they had any arrears, no Phiri residents were ever given the option of a conventional metered supply such as is available in the richer suburbs of Johannesburg'. Critical literature on prepaid meters in the Johannesburg townships includes Bond and Dugard (2008), Harvey (2005), Naidoo (2010), Ruiters (2007) and Von Schnitzler (2008). Muller (2008) articulates a defensive position.

42. Detailed documentation of the Mazibuko case can be found on the website of the Centre for Applied Legal Studies, http://web.wits.ac.za/Academic/Centres/CALS/.

43. Johannesburg authorities instituted an indigent register in 1998 and in 2001 estimated about half a million households in the city to be indigent – yet in 2005 only 118 000 households were registered, and this number fell to 108 000 in 2008 according to figures supplied to CALS (CALS comment on City of Johannesburg proposed tariffs, 25 April 2008), http://web.wits.ac.za/Academic/Centres/CALS/.

44. City of Johannesburg, 'Expanded Social Package Programme', 24 June 2009, http://www.joburg.org.za.

45. See Pierre de Vos, 'Water is Life but Life is Cheap', http://constitutionallyspeaking.co.za/water-is-life-but-life-is-cheap/.

46. City of Johannesburg, 'Expanded Social Package Programme', http://www. joburg.org.za/index.php?option=com_content&task=view&id=4012& Itemid=114.

47. 'This Expanded Social Package system is a national pilot for Social Development's National Integrated Social Information System, which combines data from the Unemployment Insurance Fund, the South African Social Security Administration, the Department of Housing and the Department of Home Affairs. This will allow us to verify people's eligibility for benefits without the poor having to produce any documents to prove their own level of poverty.' In his illuminating account of biometric government in South Africa, Breckenridge notes that the 'poorest of the poor' are far more directly affected by cutting-edge technologies and database systems than their middle-class contemporaries (2005: 282).

48. 'Technologies for Knowing and Managing the Poor in South Africa: The Case of Johannesburg Post-Apartheid'. Paper delivered at a seminar in the Sociology Department, University of Johannesburg, 1 August 2012.

49. http://www.bdlive.co.za/articles/2011/06/20/poor-not-taking-up-city-rebate-offer. When the programme was first announced the Centre for Applied Legal Studies was deeply critical, pointing to the chronic under-representation of low-income households in registration-based endeavours, the demeaning character of the application process, and the lack of public consultation. See Jackie Dugard, 'Phiri: Lawfare rather than warfare', *Mail & Guardian*, 24–30 July 2009: 33.

4

Revisiting the Transition

De-Nationalisation and Re-Nationalisation

LET ME START this chapter with a passage from my book *Disabling Globalization*. Writing in 2001, I was trying to reconcile the ANC's hegemonic power and popular appeal with its embrace of neoliberal economic policies that, by the late 1990s, were hitting the working classes very hard:

> [T]he post-apartheid state coalition has not only constructed a populist unity, articulating 'the people' into a political subject . . . with – not against – the power bloc; it has also accomplished this apparent unity in the face of escalating material inequality and poverty, and economic policies that are patently unpopular with a large segment of its support base. In the mid-1990s discourses of non-racial national unity were ascendant, exemplified in the language of the 'rainbow nation', and the towering moral authority of Nelson Mandela. Since the late 1990s the picture has become far more complex, as the power bloc led by Thabo Mbeki has shifted images from rainbows to the African Renaissance, positioning the ANC at the forefront of battles against racism. These and other discourses not only resonate with everyday experiences of racism by large numbers of black South Africans; they have also called forth overtly racist responses from the white liberal opposition that validate charges against them, and consolidate anew the ANC's populist unity. Through all of this, the power bloc centered around Thabo Mbeki consistently invokes 'globalization' to circumvent any questioning of neoliberal nostrums and policies, or of their alignment with capital . . . Shot through with contradictions, this

apparent populist unity co-exists with powerful currents of discontent and critique from within the alliance; from segments of the NGO community; and, most importantly, from the interstices of everyday life where large numbers of South Africans navigate between the emancipatory promises of official discourses and the glamour of the mass consumption economy on the one hand, and harsh material deprivation on the other (Hart 2002a: 32–3).

In retrospect, as argued throughout the present book, I have come to see 2001 as a key turning point, unleashing the dialectics of protests and containment outlined in Chapters 2 and 3 that demand a new set of analytical lenses.

In this chapter I want to elaborate on the argument that, in order to comprehend the mounting crisis in South Africa since the early 2000s, we need to go back and rethink the transition from apartheid. Rather than *just* an elite pact – although it was in part that – the transition is more usefully understood in terms of simultaneous processes of de-nationalisation and re-nationalisation that have been playing out in relation to one another in increasingly conflictual ways.

Instead of focusing primarily on the ANC's adoption of conservative neoliberal macro-economic policies in 1996, I am using the term de-nationalisation to encompass the terms on which heavily concentrated corporate capital re-engaged with the increasingly financialised global economy starting in the early 1990s, and the ways in which these forces are driving increasing inequality and the generation of surplus populations. While successive ANC administrations have moved in more interventionist directions since the early 2000s and now declare themselves strongly anti-neoliberal and passionately pro-poor, the ravages wrought by processes of de-nationalisation continue apace.

Re-nationalisation engages what is most obviously missing from my earlier analysis – namely crucial questions about how the post-apartheid 'nation' came to be produced, as well as the ongoing importance of articulations of the 'nation' to the ANC's hegemonic project. Despite focusing on race, racism and histories of racialised dispossession in my earlier work, I was inattentive to the 'national question' – a profoundly evocative term that for many South Africans conjures up struggles against colonialism and imperialism, the indignities and violence of racial injustice and dispossession, the sacrifices and suffering embodied in movements for national liberation, and the visions of social and economic justice for which many fought and died. I also failed to take seriously a key phrase of the ANC Alliance – the NDR – the meanings and ownership of which, as we shall see, have become an increasingly contentious site of struggle within the ANC Alliance over the decade of the 2000s.

In the first part of this chapter I lay out the main contours of de-nationalisation and re-nationalisation. Then I revisit the first phase of the post-apartheid order (1994–2000) and suggest how we might set de- and re-nationalisation in motion in relation to one another by using the concept of 'articulation' discussed in Chapter 1. As mentioned there, this concept has a long history in South African race/class debates, and has been put to work in some very different ways. I will propose how, with the modifications suggested in Chapter 1, it is a powerful analytical tool, enabling new angles of vision on some of the key forces at play during the initial post-apartheid period. In turn, these insights are directly relevant to delving more deeply into the dialectics of protest and containment since 2001, which we shall be doing in Chapter 5.

Dimensions of De-Nationalisation

South Africa remains an extreme case within the configurations of uneven and combined development: an advanced industrial economy and first-world lifestyles exist with abject poverty and unequal social relationships and resource distribution of all kinds. The picture of slow growth, declining investment, rising un-employment, rural degradation, and income and wealth inequality that characterised the economy towards the end of the 1990s remains little changed over a decade later (Ashman, Fine and Newman 2011: 15).

South Africa is now 'officially' the most unequal society in the world, the authors point out, with the poorest 20 per cent of South Africans receiving 1.6 per cent of total income, while the richest 20 per cent garner a whopping 70 per cent of total income.

Before elaborating on what I mean by de-nationalisation as a defining feature of the post-apartheid era, let me call attention to two key issues. First is the question of 'neoliberalism' that, in the first part of the decade of the 2000s, operated as a hugely important popular category for crystallising and condensing multiple expressions of discontent, especially in the first round of so-called 'new social movements'. It also came to function as a term of abuse, particularly in relation to Thabo Mbeki. His identification with GEAR, the conservative package of macro-economic policies unilaterally imposed in 1996, played powerfully into his deep unpopularity with a large segment of the population. Since the ousting of Mbeki in 2008, the Motlanthe and Zuma administrations have emphatically distanced themselves from neoliberalism – even though it was Mbeki who initially drove significantly increased government spending on social welfare and a series of 'develop-mental state' initiatives after 2004, in important part as a strategy of containment of popular discontent (Chapter 2). As a con-sequence, 'neoliberalism' as an oppositional category has lost much of the traction it once had. Indeed, for many on the liberal right, the economy is being strangled by over-regulation, militant unions ramping up wages and excessive spending on welfare that is bleeding 'responsible' (read white) taxpayers dry. This rhetoric further bolsters ANC claims that 'we are not neoliberals', and that the global economy is fully to blame for economic woes and the terrifying escalation of unemployment. As Marais (2011: 137) astutely points out: 'Paradoxically, in singling out and demonising GEAR as the grand moment of rupture and betrayal, the left helped government and corporate South Africa script their claims of a qualitative break [with conservative Mbeki-ite economic policies].'

Second, instead of debating whether or not South Africa is 'neoliberal', it is more useful to go back to debates over the long-standing political-economic crisis, and focus on the historically specific forms and dynamics of capital accumulation in relation to changing global political-economic forces. In their analysis of the crisis in South Africa, Saul and Gelb (1986) argued that the 'apartheid boom' was running out of steam in the early 1970s. Deep structural problems in the economy – skilled labour shortages, the limits of the white consumer market and the high black unemployment rate – were compounded by balance of payments deficits, high inflation and volatile gold prices. These economic imperatives were playing out on a terrain on which '"political" factors cut across any presumed "logic of capital" in extremely complex ways' (1986: 85) – including growing militancy of black workers and the Soweto uprising of 1976. A somewhat different analysis focuses on a longer-term crisis of over-accumulation that predates the political upheavals of the 1970s. In this view, 'the crisis was fundamentally economic – a crisis of profitability – and not merely political' (Legassick 2007: 442; see also Bond 2005). This analysis has become part of a critique of Gelb (1991) and others who turned to regulation theory in the 1990s.

While I cannot do justice here to complex and wide-ranging debates over South African political economy, the approach that I find most useful turns around what Fine and Rustomjee (1996) call the minerals energy complex (MEC), a cluster of heavy industries around mining and energy that have dominated the economy since mineral discoveries in the late nineteenth century.[1] Strongly linked to one another but weakly linked to other industrial sectors, the MEC continues to play a central role in shaping the course of capitalist accumulation in South Africa in and through relations between capital and the state. Understood as a system of accumulation, the MEC 'provides a bridge between the abstract tendencies of the capitalist mode of production and . . . how the political economy of capitalism is put together [in specific times and places] and the critical role played by the state in the process' (Ashman, Fine and Newman 2010: 180).

With the crisis of apartheid in the 1980s, the combination of sanctions and exchange controls, 'gave rise both to conglomeration across the economy . . . and the expansion of a huge and sophisticated financial system as cause and consequence of the internationally confined, but domestically spread, reach of South African conglomerates with Anglo-American in the lead' (Fine 2008: 2).[2] In 1990 when the ANC was unbanned, five colossal conglomerates – encompassing mining and related manufacturing, banking, retail and insurance operations – controlled 84 per cent of the capitalisation of the JSE (Chabane, Goldstein and Roberts 2006: 553).

A number of analysts have pointed to how, at the moment of its unbanning, the ANC had no economic policy, and have documented the process through which corporate capital, the Bretton Woods institutions and foreign governments quickly heeded an injunction by the *Financial Mail* to 'patiently and systematically educate blacks into the economic realities of the world'.[3] Some significant new insights emerge from recently published books by two University of Stellenbosch academics, Sampie Terreblanche (2012) and Willie Esterhuyse (2012), both members of a group of Afrikaner academics who called for negotiations with the ANC in the mid-1980s. Terreblanche (2012: 62) describes how he participated in six clandestine meetings with ANC leaders in Britain from 1987 onwards, financed by Consolidated Goldfields, and goes on to explain how:

> From 1990 Nelson Mandela and Harry Oppenheimer (CEO of the Anglo-American Corporation) met regularly for lunch or dinner and from early in the 1990s the MEC met regularly with a leadership core of the ANC at Little Brenthurst, Oppenheimer's estate. When other corporate leaders joined the secret negotiations on the future of the economic policy of South Africa, the meetings were shifted to the

Development Bank of Southern Africa, where secret meetings took place during the night (2012: 63).

Ronnie Kasrils, at the time a member of the NEC of the ANC and directly engaged in the negotiations to end apartheid, has recently stated that neither he nor other senior members of the NEC or SACP were aware of these meetings:

> Agreement at the level of secret negotiating and endorsement in very broad terms later by an ANC-SACP leadership eager to assume political office (myself no less than others) sealed our Faustian moment. Those late-night deliberations were never revealed to the ANC's collective leadership at NEC level nor to the SACP for that matter. Joe Slovo, SACP chairman and leading theoretician, engrossed with the 'sunset clause' golden-handshake pension pay-off for the racist old guard, knew nothing to my knowledge of the night-time shenanigans and certainly did not raise any alarm bells. We readily accepted the devil's pact and are damned in the process. It has bequeathed to our country an economy so tied in to the neo-liberal global formula and market fundamentalism that there is very little room to alleviate the dire plight of the masses of our people. Little wonder that their patience is running out; that their anguished protests increase as they wrestle with deteriorating conditions of life; that those in power have no way of finding solutions (Kasrils 2013: xxvi).

The negotiations may have been secret, but their effects were evident. By November 1993, one observer noted, 'the language and tone [of ANC and business policy documents] are so similar that at times they appear interchangeable' (cited by Marais 1998: 154). While the Bretton Woods institutions, global corporations and foreign governments (especially the US) played a role in these negotiations with the ANC, Terreblanche points to the dominant role played by representatives of the MEC.

In this context I am using the term 'de-nationalisation' to encompass an array of moves by South African conglomerates intent on reconnecting with the increasingly financialised global economy, from which they were partially excluded during the 1980s. In addition to maintaining property ownership, 'they wanted the freedom to move their capital *out*' as Bassett (2008: 194) put it. A largely ignored aspect of South African macro-economic policy, Fine (2008: 4) points out, is the extent to which it enabled South African conglomerates to disinvest from the economy. In addition to managed liberalisation of exchange controls, conglomerates successfully pushed for permission to move their primary listings to London in the 1990s on the grounds that it would allow South African firms to raise capital more cheaply in international markets and encourage inward foreign direct investment. In practice, 'Rather than London listings enabling conglomerates to raise capital to fund investments in South Africa, there has been a much more striking pattern of outward acquisition and investments' (Chabane, Goldstein and Roberts 2006: 559).

The large-scale unbundling of conglomerates in the late 1990s also played into de-nationalisation. It coincided with the South African government's raising the limits on the amounts companies could invest abroad, prompting a spate of mergers and acquisitions between South African and off-shore companies (Fine 2010: 32). Despite corporate unbundling, high levels of concentration *within* sectors have continued as a consequence of vertical mergers that increased the control of dominant firms (Chabane, Goldstein and Roberts 2006: 557). In addition, production has remained concentrated in increasingly capital-intensive core MEC sectors where high levels of resource and monopoly rents continue to be extracted from the economy, and diversification out of the MEC has been minimal (Mohamed 2010).[4] At the same time, liberalisation of exchange controls and high interest rates have encouraged destabilising and unproductive inflows of short-term capital that have promoted bubbles in real estate and financial asset markets, as well as rising consumer debt. They have also led to volatility of the currency, providing an additional impetus to outward investment and increased consumption of imports, as well as shrinking the industrial base.

Exemplary of what I am calling 'de-nationalisation' – and largely missing from much of the debate over whether or not South Africa is still neoliberal – is massive and escalating capital flight, and how government officials are trying to deal with it. Ashman, Fine and Newman (2011: 9) report estimates of capital flight as a proportion of gross domestic product (GDP) increasing from an average of 5.4 per cent a year between 1980–93 to 9.2 per cent of GDP per year from 1994–2000, and averaging 12 per cent a year between 2001 and 2007. In 2007, it shot up to 20 per cent of GDP. At this point, capital flight from South Africa was more than double the already low level of domestic investment: 'The impact has been to intensify falling domestic investment in productive activities, declining capital stock across almost all productive sectors, macro-economic austerity and vulnerability, and de-industrialisation of the economy, further entrenching unemployment, poverty and extremely inequality in the provision of basic services' (2011: 7).

The authors point as well to a plan announced by the South African Reserve Bank in 2010 to provide amnesty for illegal capital flight, while also further easing exchange controls in an effort to 'regularise' formerly illegal expatriation of wealth. The reason why South Africa has turned a blind eye to (illegal) capital flight in the past and is seeking to regularise it in the future, they argue, 'is to be found in the extent to which the interests of conglomerate capital have managed to exert continuing influence over economic policy in the post-apartheid period, not least as such domestic conglomerates have both adjusted to the imperatives of globalisation that were constrained under apartheid, whilst fully embracing over the past twenty years the processes of financialisation that have so obviously accelerated with such disastrous consequences for the world economy' (Ashman, Fine and Newman 2011: 10). Official moves to relax capital controls still further are all the more ironic in light of the International Monetary Fund's volte-face in 2010, recognising capital controls as legitimate policy tools (2011: 21).

Later in this chapter I discuss the re-articulations of class and race within and through which corporate capital restructuring has taken place in relation to the state – a key dimension of which is BEE that has produced a small, extremely wealthy black business class elite, many of them rentier capitalists.[5] For purposes of the present discussion, the key point is that many BEE deals also have a de-nationalising dimension through public-private partnerships with foreign capital and government at different levels.

Over the decade of the 2000s we have witnessed successive ANC administrations chasing after the chimera of 'decent jobs' while working in alliance with corporate capital to facilitate the giant sucking sound through which resources are siphoned to other regions of the world. A closely related irony to which Franco Barchiesi vividly calls attention is that 'the deeper waged employment has decayed into a condition of precariousness and immiseration, the more prominent work and job creation have become as governmental responses to social problems' (2011: 93). Another governmental response has turned around calls to 'empower' the so-called 'Second Economy' and/or link it more fully to the 'First Economy'. Yet, as several researchers have pointed out, for very large numbers of people rendered 'surplus' to the needs of capital, spatial and structural inequality is such that the problem is not one of exclusion from the core economy, but adverse inclusion within it (Du Toit and Neves 2007: Philip 2010).

Even before the global economic crisis hit in late 2008, the combined result of these forces was a jobless form of growth and the persistence of mass poverty for the majority of the black population, alongside increasing – albeit partially de-racialised – concentrations of wealth. By the same token, 'levels of investment within the domestic economy have remained limited, not primarily because of the lack of attraction to inward investment [unions, regulation, crime, etc.] but because of the external orientation of domestic conglomerates and their failure to invest in the domestic economy' (Fine 2010: 31). Developments since 2009 – including ongoing massive job losses, escalating consumer debt, increasing capital flight and short-term inflows strengthening the currency and undermining exports – are not simply the predictable impact of the global financial crisis, but have been mediated through the political economy of the MEC and its de-nationalising dynamic.

Before turning to consider post-apartheid processes of re-nationalisation, it is important to reflect on another aspect of de-nationalisation – namely the absence, by and large, of white corporate capital from the power bloc. In a 2011 article in the *London Review of Books* on Lula's Brazil, Perry Anderson observed:

> What it [the Lula regime or Lulismo] had achieved was a kind of inverted hegemony. Where, for Gramsci, hegemony in a capitalist social order had been the moral ascendancy of the possessing over the labouring classes, securing the consent of the dominated to their own domination, in Lulismo it was as if the dominated had reversed the formula, achieving the consent of the dominant to their leadership of society, only to ratify the structures of their own exploitation. A more appropriate analogy was not the United States of the New Deal, but the South Africa of Mandela and Mbeki, where the iniquities of apartheid had been overthrown and the masters of society were black, but the rule of capital and its miseries was as implacable as ever. The fate of the poor in Brazil had been a kind of apartheid, and Lula had ended that. But equitable or inclusive progress remained out of reach.[6]

The lens of de-nationalisation lets us see how, in post-apartheid South Africa, the apparent consent of white corporate capital to leadership by the black majority represents a bourgeois project of a special type.

Through practices and processes of de-nationalisation, white South African corporate capital has on one level succeeded spectacularly in securing the conditions for accumulation. Yet, at the same time, these very same practices and processes have systematically eroded livelihoods and fed into undermining the capacity of the ANC to fulfil its role of securing the consent of those whom it governs. To grasp how and why this is the case, we need to understand de-nationalisation in relation to the other dimension of South Africa's passive revolution – that of re-nationalisation.

Remaking the 'Nation' after Apartheid: Projects and Practices of Re-Nationalisation

In a 1988 discussion pamphlet on 'The South African Working Class and the National Democratic Revolution', Joe Slovo – then general secretary of the still-banned SACP – posed the following question:

> The existence of cultural and ethnic diversity side by side with unifying processes, has aroused friendly queries on our approach to the national question. *Do we believe that our peoples already constitute one nation? If not, are they (or should they be) moving towards single or separate nationhood?* What is the future of the cultural and linguistic diversity and how do we cater for this diversity within the framework of a unitary state? (Slovo 1988: 2; emphasis in original)

He was responding, inter alia, to pressures from the Soviet Academy of Sciences for a multinational solution to the issue of minority rights in a post-apartheid order[7] – a position that echoed strongly with pressures from the liberal right for a consociational form of government along these lines.[8] Slovo's answer was unequivocal:

> *Despite the existence of cultural and racial diversity, South Africa is not a multi-national country. It is a nation in the making; a process which is increasingly being advanced in struggle and one which can only be finally completed after the racist tyranny is defeated. The concept of one united nation, embracing all our ethnic communities, remains the virtually undisputed liberation objective* (1988: 25; emphasis in original).

Along with his insistence on national unity as a key weapon in the battle against racist tyranny, Slovo underscored its centrality to the doctrine of the NDR, and the vanguard role of the working class in the march towards socialism:

> *The winning of the objectives of the national democratic revolution will, in turn, lay the basis for a steady advance in the direction of deepening our national unity on all fronts – economic, political and cultural – and towards a socialist transformation. For our working class nation-building means, among other things, unifying themselves nationally as the leading class whose developing culture, aspirations and economic interests become increasingly those of the overwhelming majority of our people* (Slovo 1988: 30; emphasis in original).

In retrospect, of course, it is easy to dismiss this document as an archaic remnant of an era about to be tossed into the dustbin of history – especially when one recalls that it was at precisely this moment that South African corporate capital was paving the way for rapprochement with the ANC with the assistance of key Afrikaner academics as noted earlier. Yet Slovo's 1988 engagement with pressures from the Soviet Union serves as an important reminder of the problematic and ambiguous status of the South African nation at the moment the liberation movements were unbanned in 1990. It also underscores the powerful forces that came together in 1989/90: the collapse of the Soviet Union, and with it the apartheid regime's claims as the bulwark against communism in Africa; and the global triumph of increasingly financialised market capitalism and liberal democracy.

As we shall see, Slovo's insistence on the NDR as central to reconstitution of the South African nation has remained a consistent theme of the post-apartheid order, at the same time that the meanings and ownership of the NDR have become a veritable battleground within the ANC Alliance, especially since the late 1990s. First, though, we need to attend to two other dimensions of official projects of re-nationalisation that, on the face of it at least, appear in sharp tension with one another: the practices and meanings that conjured up the rainbow nation, alongside the ANC government's embrace of punitive, coercive immigration laws and practices.

Conjuring the Rainbow Nation

The most incisive analysis of the rainbow nation in my view is by Sitas, who draws on a marvellous poem by the worker poet Alfred Temba Qabula written in 1995 entitled 'Of Land, Bones and Money' (Sitas 2010: 25). In the opening lines, Qabula offers a powerful provocation about the negotiations that ended apartheid:

> They talked, they talked a lot
> about this and about that
> ignoring that the real talk
> was about land,
> about bones
> about money
> in this country without a proper name
> in this camp of the restless dead . . .

Framing his argument around Qabula's poem, Sitas insists that analyses of the transition have been too narrowly focused on the pragmatics and compromises of the negotiated settlement, while paying insufficient attention to the affective, cultural and ideological shifts that made it possible. Concurring that the negotiated settlement was indeed about land, bones and money, Sitas focuses as well on 'this country without a proper name'. Qabula makes clear that 'South Africa is not a nation, it is a functional camp, a space that lacks a collective meaning' (Sitas 2010: 27). Accordingly, the transition required discursive shifts – a process of scripting the 'nation' through what Sitas calls 'conflicting and competing narratives of commonality and indigenerality' (2010: 27). Corporate interests did indeed lead a 'revolution within the revolution' that was decisively influential, but 'the shift in the "national ontology" came from the robe and the cross, across denominations, from above and from below':

> [T]he 'epiphany' that was achieved went something like this: the children of God, bounded by the territory called South Africa, no

matter what their histories, share this land and its future. The follies of the past must be forgiven and confessed, faced. The horrors of the present must be stopped. Humility has to define all competing sides, apartheid was a mistake, using God to justify apartheid, was a regrettable sin, but now look at Mandela; despite the past, his imprisonment and his suffering, he is ready to forgive and reconcile; look at de Klerk; despite his past, he is ready to atone (Sitas 2010: 31).

The key to this national ontology of indigenerality lay in its 'ecclesiastical abstraction from historicity' and its status as a transcendent 'third space': 'as long as religious atonement was ever-present . . . the negotiations could lead to the pragmatics of compromise over "land, bones and money"' (Sitas 2010: 31). Turning again to Qabula as well as to Jacques Derrida who visited South Africa in 1996, Sitas reminds us that the erasures and repressions entailed in the production of this national ontology – its 'restless dead' – would continue to haunt it.

There are some interesting tensions here with some of Chipkin's (2007) key claims. For Chipkin, the move to constitute South Africa as a nation took place *after* the transition from white minority rule and the first democratic election. It was the Truth and Reconciliation Commission (TRC), he argues, that sought to establish the ontological grounds for the existence of the South African nation: 'the challenge of the TRC was to overcome the worry that the South African people did not exist' (Chipkin 2007: 174). Established in 1995 by the Promotion of National Unity and Reconciliation Act, the TRC was not just about 'truth-telling' by perpetrators of human rights abuses; it was also about establishing relations of national identity, Chipkin insists, pointing inter alia to Desmond Tutu's observation that 'we were a useful paradigm for our nation, for if we could eventually be welded into a reasonably coherent, united and reconciled group then there would be hope for South Africa'. Yet what the TRC produced, he argues, was not the 'South African people' but rather humanity as a whole – a 'rainbow people of God', as Tutu put it, united in their diversity. For Chipkin this failure of the TRC as a nation-building project lay in its casting the effects of apartheid in terms of human rights (2007: 183). Yet the project of nation-building is inherently paradoxical, he argues, because it is driven to suppose that the nation already exists in itself (2007: 181).

Writing in the same year that the TRC was established, Qabula foresaw with great clarity the limits and fragilities of the rainbow nation (cited in Sitas 2010: 25):

> But Tutu and the dominees[9] saw rainbows
> and they agreed
> and we agreed:
> a fence on this plot, no fence on that
> a skeleton here and a skeleton there
> give a black cent and take a white rand
> in this nameless country
> but we prayed together in this camp
> what we did not say in our prayer
> was that the seasons of drought have no rainbows

For Sitas, the limits of Mandela's non-racialism and reasons for the failure of rainbowism as a narrative for nation-building and unity, went far beyond the discursive impossibility of the TRC:

> Its failure can be attributed to white intransigence and to whites' self-serving indifference to the 'new' South Africa. The straps of racism were too close to white hearts. The refusal of the white population to own the past frightened and angered Mandela. The backlash from the African intelligentsia and the emerging black middle classes brought back the rain clouds; there was no space in their status scripts for such a notion (Sitas 2010: 22).

In other words, 'indigenerality' and the 'rainbow nation' helped make possible the transition – but were fatally undermined by the 'grand ideological cleavages of class and race' (Sitas 2010: 38) that they papered over.

In a related analysis of the weaknesses of the TRC in relation to nation-building and reconciliation, Neville Alexander (2002: 128) noted that they were the direct result of the political compromises of which the TRC was the offspring: 'This is the main reason why it [the TRC] could not and did not undertake any in-depth analysis of the system of apartheid and especially not of the role of big business in sustaining, if not actually initiating, that system.' The TRC's inability to require reparations of course also undermined its moral authority. The final report of the TRC recommended that the government pay some \$375 million in reparations, and that businesses that had benefited from apartheid policies make reparations through a special wealth tax. Then-President Thabo Mbeki rejected these recommendations, authorising a modest one-time payment of R30 000 (less than \$4 000) to each of about 22 000 people defined as victims of apartheid, and refusing to impose a tax on businesses. In retrospect, we can see these tensions as an early manifestation of the conflictual relations between de- and re-nationalisation.

While rainbowism has largely dissipated, there are moments when this inclusive non-racial nationalism springs forth – the 2010 Soccer World Cup being one such instance. Yet, as we saw in Chapter 2, this moment of romantic rainbowism was accompanied by a powerful undertow of xenophobic threats that are ongoing, and that need to be understood, at least in part, in relation to a second key dimension of official re-nationalising practices and process.

'Fortress South Africa'

Coinciding with its embrace of the rainbow nation and indigenerality, the newly formed ANC government moved quickly to adopt one of the 'dying acts of apartheid' – the harshly punitive Aliens Control Act of 1991. 'Rooted in racism' (Peberdy and Crush 1998), the Act consolidated immigration legislation dating back to the formation of the Union of South Africa, and was described by its primary author as 'a negative piece of legislation . . . [that] says who must be removed, who is not wanted in South Africa' (cited by Peberdy 2009: 144).[10]

'Fortress South Africa' (Crush 1999a) has become entrenched in the post-apartheid landscape. The new government amended the Aliens Control Act in 1995 'to improve control over immigration', as then ANC Deputy Minister of Home Affairs Lindiwe Sisulu put it. The amended act placed heavier emphasis on the skills of potential immigrants, and the number of approved applications for permanent residence fell steadily over the 1990s (Peberdy 2009: 148). It was only in 2002 that the Aliens Control Act was replaced by the Immigration Amendment Act, with the explicit objective of 'meeting South Africa's skills and investment needs' while forbidding entry to those who lacked them.

Despite some legislative easing of immigration requirements for those with requisite skills after 2002, the post-apartheid era has been marked by systematic tightening of border patrols and a sharp reduction of designated border posts and airports receiving international flights. Internal policing of undocumented migrants has also been ramped up. Such migrants have no right to challenge their arrest, detention or repatriation in a court of law, and many are held in appalling conditions in Lindela, a privately operated detention centre outside Johannesburg in which the ANC Women's League is a shareholder.[11] Between 1990 and 2002, 1.7 million migrants were deported, with the numbers doubling between 1994 and 1999 from 90 000 to over 180 000 per annum (Crush and Dodson 2007: 446). Reports of police brutality and corruption in the treatment of migrants are legion. The full force of official measures have been directed at Africans from other parts of the continent, and the policies and practices of rebounding the nation have played directly into antagonistic popular sentiments and xenophobic (or Afrophobic) attacks.

Academics have also fed the flames of xenophobic sentiment. Crush (1999: 3) calls attention to a study by the state-sponsored

Human Sciences Research Council (HSRC), which claimed that there were 9.5 million non-South Africans in the country in 1995, of which 4.1 million were there 'illegally' (Minnaar, Hough and De Kock 1996). The study came under heavy fire for its flawed methodology and absurd overestimates, and in 2001 the new CEO of the HSRC admitted to the fallacious claims and withdrew all HSRC estimates. Yet these estimates bolstered official and popular understandings of South Africans being engulfed by 'tidal waves' of illegal immigrants pouring into the country.

Most observers point to the disjunctures between South Africa's liberal democratic ethos and ugly realities of Fortress South Africa. Michael Neocosmos (2010) stakes out a sharply contrary position: that in South Africa xenophobia is not antagonistic to human rights discourse but congruent with it:

> Xenophobia and the authoritarianism of which it is but an example, are a product of liberalism, liberal democracy, and Human Rights Discourse. It is not an irrational aberration brought about from outside the liberal realm (for example from an authoritarian or irrational 'other', from a 'backward tradition') but rather it is made possible/ enabled by liberalism itself. It must be understood and can only coherently be understood as a result of a form of politics where the state is seen as the sole definer of citizenship and where, given the absence of prescriptive politics among the people, passivity prevails (2010: 115).

At the core of this argument is the claim that 'state politics has sytematically de-politicised the people with emphasis being exclusively placed on managerialism (to deliver "human rights"), juridical expertise (to protect "human rights") and education (to alter xenophobic attitudes)' – in other words, that 'technicism has replaced active politics' (Neocosmos 2010: 115). Chapter 3 provides detailed evidence on projects to render technical that which is political, showing how they play into the contradictions of local government and growing popular discontent. In Chapter 5, I will locate these processes in relation to the contradictory forces unleashed by the unravelling of ANC hegemony – but this requires our paying close attention to questions of African nationalism.

Articulations of African Nationalism: The National Question and the NDR

An important key to forging connections between de-nationalisation and re-nationalisation lies in grasping changing articulations of the 'national question' and the NDR. Writing in 1997, Pallo Jordan – one of the key intellectuals of the liberation movement – asked:

> Is there a national question in post Apartheid South Africa? The easy answer is: not in the form in which it is conventionally understood! Racism is no longer institutionalised; all South Africans now have the franchise; racial restrictions on property rights and on access to the professions, trades, forms of work have been abolished; the instruments of labour coercion have been done away with; and a democratic constitution has put an end to legal repression.[12]

Yet, Jordan went on to observe, South Africa remains a deeply racialised society – conceding as well that '[t]here were also compromises forced upon us because we could ill-afford to jeopardise the larger prize – majority rule – in pursuance of a few uncertainties'.

As Alexander (2002, 2010) and others have argued, the NDR played a major mediating role in enabling these 'compromises' with corporate capital – thus playing directly into the processes I am calling de-nationalisation that significantly reduced the uncertainties confronting capital. Such compromises have also meant that the NDR shows no signs of giving way to socialism, as some of its proponents confidently predicted. In addition, as we shall see, it has become a vociferous site of struggle in the post-apartheid order. At the same time, it is important to recognise the discursive power of the NDR – how it articulates in flexible ways three key ideological threads of the liberation movement:[13]

[D]iscourses of the national liberation movement were characterised by the intersection of nationalist, liberal-democratic and broadly socialist paradigms . . . [T]he particularity of one or other political tendency was determined by the way its exponents blended or interpreted these three discursive strategies, each of which, of course, derived from and reinforced specific class interests, whether or not the social actors involved were conscious of these (Alexander 2010: 3).

The language of the NDR and its closely linked acronym Colonialism of a Special Type (CST) originates from *The Road to South African Freedom*, an SACP document authored by Michael Harmel (writing under the pseudonym Lerumo) in 1962 at a moment when the party was underground, and enmeshed in the turn to armed struggle in the wake of the Sharpeville massacre in 1960. Following an analysis of South Africa in terms of CST, the document lays out the imperative for a NDR under the leadership of the ANC:

The immediate and imperative interests of all sections of the South African people demand the carrying out of . . . a national democratic revolution which will overthrow the colonialist state of White supremacy and establish an independent state of National Democracy in South Africa.

The main content of this revolution is the national liberation of the African people. Its fulfilment is, at the same time, in the deepest interests of the other non-White groups, for in achieving their liberty the African people will at the same time put an end to all forms of racial discrimination. It is in the interests of the White workers, middle class and professional groups to whom the establishment of genuine democracy and the elimination of fascism and monopoly rule offers the only prospect of a decent and stable future.

The main aims and lines of the South African democratic revolution have been defined in the Freedom Charter, which has been endorsed by the African National Congress and the other partners in the national liberation alliance. The Freedom Charter is not a programme for socialism. It is a common programme for a free, democratic South Africa, agreed on by socialists and non-socialists.[14]

To guarantee the 'abolition of racial oppression and White minority domination' the document underscores the need for redistribution of land, nationalisation of key industries, and radical improvements in the living conditions of working people – all of which have of course been stymied by processes of de-nationalisation in the post-apartheid era. Yet there is repeated insistence that these are not proposals for a socialist state, but for the building of a national democratic state within the framework of the Freedom Charter of 1955.[15] At the same time the document asserts that in addition to expunging racial oppression and addressing the pressing and immediate needs of the people, the NDR will 'lay the indispensable basis for the advance of our country along non-capitalist lines to a communist and socialist future'. This notion of a two-stage revolution has its origins in the Third Comintern in the 1920s, and was neither peculiar nor new to South Africa. In 1928 Stalin handed down an enormously controversial directive for the (then) Communist Party of South Africa 'to advance the slogan of an independent native South African republic as a stage towards a workers and peasants republic with full equal rights for all races, black, coloured and white'.[16]

The ANC adopted the principles of the NDR and CST at its conference in Morogoro in Tanzania in 1969 that marked an important turning point in the liberation struggle. Delegates voted to open membership in the ANC to all racial groups for the first time in its history, although only black people were eligible for membership of the NEC. Control of the army (Umkhonto we Sizwe, or MK) was, however, vested in a Revolutionary Council that was open to minority groups – and on which Joe Slovo and other leading SACP members served. Stephen Ellis remarks that '[t]he Party [SACP] had effectively restored the guiding role it had established in regard to the ANC in the months between the SACP's 1960 decision to create MK and the Rivonia arrests two and a half years later, but now on a higher level of sophistication' (Ellis 2012: 81).[17] Ndebele and Nieftagodien (2004) describe how the 'Strategy and Tactics' document prepared for the Morogoro conference built directly on *The Road to South African Freedom*, and also forged a close relationship between political struggle and military force. The point of departure of the 'Strategy and Tactics' was that '[t]he primacy of political leadership is unchallenged and supreme, and all revolutionary formations and levels (whether armed or not) are subordinate to this leadership' (cited by Ndebele and Nieftagodien 2004: 593).

At Morogoro, the NDR facilitated a re-articulation of race in the liberation movement that enabled the 'non-racial' articulations of nationalism embodied in the anti-apartheid struggle and the rainbow nation. At the same time Morogoro made clear how the NDR is linked to a militarised and masculinist articulation of nationalism – one that reappeared with a vengeance in Zuma's deployment of 'Bring me my machine gun' in 2005, and discussed more fully in Chapter 5.

Unquestioned adherence to the NDR and CST has remained de rigueur within the liberation movement. Yet both principles have long been subject to profound criticism from the left within and as well as outside the ANC/SACP – and form an important focus of a series of fierce debates over class, race and nationalism. From within the alliance, the most fully developed critique was by Wolpe who pointed out that the 'internal colonialism thesis' (in other words CST) 'purports to rest on class relations of capitalist exploitation'. In practice, however, it treats class relations as residual, and it conceives of relations of domination and exploitation as 'occurring between "racial", "ethnic" and "national" categories' – thus converging with the conventional liberal race relations theory of plural society (1975: 230). In a 1978 article in the *Review of African Political Economy*, Ruth First expressed her adamant opposition to the two-stage revolution approach:

I agree with those who argue against the conception of a revolution having to pass through a national-democratic before a socialist stage. This is because I do not see any such things as 'pure' national or 'pure' class oppression/exploitation. The national and the class struggle are not part of some natural order of succession, but take place coterminously. This is because workers are exploited as workers and also as members of a nationally oppressed group, and not even their national demands can be met without the destruction of the capitalist order. It is because national demands cannot be met under capitalism that the proletariat is the essential leader of the SA revolution . . . (1978: 98).

The most consistent and fiercest critic of the NDR from outside the alliance during and after the apartheid era was the late Neville Alexander. On his release from Robben Island, Alexander expressed his critique of the SACP/ANC two-stage formulation in *One Azania, One Nation: The National Question in South Africa* (1979) that he published under the nom deplume No Sizwe. Until his death in 2012, Alexander remained relentlessly critical of how, through its NDR/CST formulation, the SACP 'abdicated any pretensions to political leadership of the mass movement and permitted the . . . aspiring black middle-class leadership of the ANC to lead the mass struggle' (Alexander 2002: 25; see also Alexander 1985, 2010).

Today the standard critique by the left outside the alliance is that the NDR operates first and foremost as an instrument of deception:

Left critics . . . argue that the [ANC] alliance, through its National Democratic Revolution (NDR) ideological discourse, fulfils an important legitimating function. It glues together disparate social classes under the hegemony of conservative class interests – a coalition of white and emerging comprador black capital (enmeshed in ever-expanding networks of patronage and corruption), and a professional black middle class that has done rather well out of the post-apartheid dispensation. In other words, the organised working class are [is] being deceived – by their leadership, also implicated in patronage politics – into supporting the ANC against their own class interests, and some believe that the time has come to build a 'left opposition' outside the alliance (Pillay 2011: 31–2).

A related version of this argument is Michael MacDonald's *Why Race Matters in South Africa* (2006), the key claim of which turns around what he calls South Africa's formula for stable democratic capitalism: 'racial nationalism legitimates "non-racial" democracy; "non-racial" democracy legitimates capitalism; and capitalism, building an African bourgeoisie along with black middle classes in conjunction with the democratic state, gives material substance to and sustains the salience of racial nationalism' (MacDonald 2012: 4). Hence, MacDonald goes on to note, racial nationalism is bending to the needs of political economy – not for the first time in South African history.

Yet 'South Africa's formula' linking racial nationalism, non-racial democracy and capitalism is, in practice, far from stable. On the contrary, it is shot through with tensions and contradictions that cry out for closer attention – especially in light of a dynamic of capitalist accumulation through which the organised working class is shrinking relative to the growing population of black South Africans consigned to conditions of 'wageless life'.

In *Do South Africans Exist?* (2007), Chipkin advances a different critique. The theory of the NDR was, he recognises, the pre-eminent expression of nationalist resistance and organisation in South Africa.[18] What made it specifically nationalist was that it 'posited the citizen as a bearer of marks of population' (2007: 12) – in other words, distinctions defined in terms of race. Marks of population for Chipkin 'produce the effect of a frontier within and between populations', designating 'those who are properly regarded as members of "the people"'; moreover, 'the measure of the nation – these marks – is produced by the nationalist movement' (2007: 222), and is sharply at odds with democracy. In a piece entitled 'The Curse of African Nationalism' provoked by the xenophobic violence in May–June 2008, Chipkin observes that the ANC leadership's claims of a 'third force' as responsible for the xenophobic violence exemplify their refusal to come to terms with the racist nationalism of those committing ethnic cleansing.[19] Asking what the way out of this impasse of African nationalism might be, he suggests:

> It does not necessarily mean a return to the non-racialism of Mandela. It is necessary to follow Mbeki's lead and pursue policies to reduce or eliminate white dominance in South African institutional life. Yet this must be done in the name of post-nationalist politics – one that affirms that South Africa is not an African country or black state.[20]

Yet articulations of the nation and liberation – including the national question, the NDR, the Freedom Charter and other allusions to the history of suffering and struggles against apartheid – cannot just be swept aside or wished away. They remain central to how ANC hegemony operates in the post-apartheid era – with hegemony understood neither as manipulation nor simply as consent, but rather as an ongoing process of struggle discussed more fully in Chapter 5.

What needs to be grasped more fully is how and why meanings of the NDR have become a site of increasingly vociferous struggle and contestation within the ANC Alliance. Also of great importance are how invocations of the 'nation' and 'liberation' reverberate powerfully with grassroots politics, often through their appeals to racialised suffering, dispossession and struggles against apartheid. In Chapter 5, I will show how liberation-linked articulations of nationalism remain crucial to the capacity of successive ruling blocs within the ANC to define the terms on which wide arrays of struggle and contestation take place, and how since the early 2000s such articulations have become an intensifying source of vulnerability. I will also try to demonstrate how these ongoing processes of re-nationalisation, which can only be properly grasped in relation to those of de-nationalisation, are driving forces behind the unravelling of ANC hegemony since 2001 and the intensification of the South African crisis.

As I have been arguing throughout this chapter, such an analysis requires rethinking the transition from apartheid. Having outlined the key dimensions of de-nationalisation and re-nationalisation, let me now set them in motion in relation to one another to suggest how, together, they shed new light on the first phase of the post-apartheid order (1994–2000).

Rethinking the First Phase of the Post-Apartheid Order, 1994–2000

In many critical narratives of the transition, 1996 functions as a key turning point. This was the moment, according to such accounts, when the ANC government cast aside the benevolent neo-Keynesian Reconstruction and Development Programme (RDP), and unilaterally imposed neoliberal structural adjustment in the guise of GEAR. Viewing 'neoliberalism' as the prime enemy, many see GEAR as representing the inauguration of Mbeki's '1996 class project', as well as a shift from 'racial to class apartheid' (Bond 2005: 253–308). In addition to acting as the driving force behind GEAR, Mbeki was responsible for murderous AIDS denialism. Thus 1996 is also widely seen as the moment when the evil Mbeki effectively took over from the saintly Mandela, representing as well a shift from Mandela's inclusive liberal rainbow nationalism to Mbeki's narrow, racially inflected Africanist nationalism.

As noted earlier, part of the problem with this view of GEAR as the key moment of rupture is that it enables both the present ANC government and some fractions of corporate capital to claim a decisive break with deeply unpopular economic policies in the 2000s. As Marais goes on to point out in his critique of this claim, 'GEAR no doubt was a profound intervention, but it was a dramatic element of a longer narrative of restructuring that dates back to the halting efforts of the apartheid regime in the early 1980s and which now arcs forward beyond GEAR' (2011: 137) – and has not yet run its course. The portrayal of a sharp shift from the 'good' (or initially good) RDP to 'bad' GEAR also downplays the extent to which alliances between corporate capital and a powerful fraction of the

ANC had sidelined alternatives such as the Macro-Economic Research Group report in the early 1990s (Fine and Padayachee 2000), while also guaranteeing the ongoing dominance of a system of capital accumulation centered on the MEC and its repositioning in relation to the global economy. In addition, it is important to attend to the relations between these de-nationalising forces and processes of re-nationalisation. Far from just a shift from neo-Keynesianism to neoliberalism, both the RDP and GEAR entailed redefinitions of the NDR that took shape in relation to forces unleashed by de-nationalising processes.

In a prescient article published in 1994, Asghar Adelzadeh and Vishnu Padayachee documented the process through which the RDP – originally proposed by COSATU – had been systematically watered down, especially in the White Paper through which the RDP was 'translated into a programme of government' following the 1994 election.[21]

> An essentially neo-liberal RDP strategy, which is what we are left with, may well generate some level of economic growth; should this happen, the existing mainly white and Indian bourgeoisie will be consolidated and strengthened; the black bourgeoisie will grow rapidly; a black middle class and some members of the black urban working class will become incorporated into the magic circle of insiders; but for the remaining 60–70 per cent of our society this growth path, we venture to predict, will deliver little or nothing for many years to come (Adelzadeh and Padayachee 1994: 16).

What is at stake in the RDP for the ANC and its allies, Wolpe noted in the last paper he published before his death in 1995, is the completion of the NDR: 'That is to say, the establishment of a democratic electoral and parliamentary system and the electoral victory of the ANC are considered to provide the principal enabling condition and instrument for, in the words of the [RDP] *White Paper*, a "fundamental transformation" of the social and economic order' (1995: 89). Yet, he noted, citing the passage above from

Adelzadeh and Padayachee (1994), the framing of the RDP and the White Paper submerged crucial political issues. While operating on a deeply contested terrain, the RDP eradicated sources of contradiction and conflict by asserting harmony and a consensual model of society; and, on the basis of this premise, it conceptualises the state as the unproblematic instrument of the RDP (Wolpe 1995: 91). Accordingly, he concluded, conceptions of 'fundamental transformation' central to the NDR were likely to become a major source of contestation in the future.

In effect, Wolpe was reviving an older debate about the limits of the notion of two-stage revolution of which the NDR is a part. As noted earlier, he was an early and fierce critic in the 1970s of the principles of the NDR and CST. By the late 1980s he seems to have taken a far more reconciliatory position, declaring that 'what is absolutely clear in the contemporary period is that no section of the national liberation movement is committed to or struggles for, what may be termed, a bourgeois national democratic revolution' (Wolpe 1988: 33). Pillay (2007) has taken me to task for pointing to this shift in Wolpe's position (in Hart 2007), noting his marginalisation within the SACP for his earlier critique; his having to accept the 'two-stage' perspective in order to enter debate; and his giving this perspective 'a different, more nuanced content' (Pillay 2007: 178). While I agree that Wolpe's analysis of two-stage revolution in his 1988 book *Race, Class and the Apartheid State* was far more nuanced than many others, what is revealing is his having to toe the party line in order to enter debate. This disciplining makes all the more significant his analysis of the tensions built into the RDP, and his prediction – fully borne out – that the NDR would become a major site of contestation. One can add as well that the instrumental conception of the state to which he pointed in this article persists to this day in the ANC Alliance.

This more complex view of the RDP enables us to see how the unilateral declaration of GEAR in 1996 was more than just a shift from relatively benign neo-Keynesianism to harsh neoliberalism. GEAR was not simply a roll-back of the state; nor was it just the final victory of class over race apartheid. Instead, I suggest, GEAR represented a *redefinition* of the NDR in terms of a re-articulation of race, class and nationalism, along with the assertion of new technologies of rule. These include the consolidation of conservative forces bent on working in alliance with white corporate capital to create a black bourgeoisie nominally more responsive to 'development'; creating the conditions in which the state can hold not only its agencies but also non-state bodies to its principles; inciting not only the black bourgeoisie but the population more generally to become 'entrepreneurs of themselves'; and making social support conditional on the correct attitudes and aspirations.

In other words GEAR was not *just* about macro-economic policy – it was also part of much deeper reconfigurations of state power. As I have argued more fully elsewhere (Hart 2008), such reconfigurations are only very partially captured by concepts of neoliberalism as governmentality or a rationality of rule. An important part of what is missing from the governmentality approach is the political economy of the state and its attempts at managing contradictions within a particular form of hegemony.

This redefinition of the NDR embodied a powerful drive to contain working-class pressures, along with a sharp disciplining of the left within the ANC Alliance. An initial manifesto of this broader state project was an ANC discussion document issued in 1996 entitled 'The State and Social Transformation', widely believed to have been authored by Thabo Mbeki. The manifesto asserts the imperative for containing 'the instinct towards "economism" on the part of the ordinary workers' in the following terms: 'If the democratic movement allowed that the subjective approach to socio-economic development represented by "economism" should overwhelm the scientific approach of the democratic movement towards such development, it could easily create the conditions for the possible counter-revolutionary defeat of the democratic revolution' (paragraph 6.11). From one perspective, then, GEAR can be seen as part of a vanguardist project to exercise a new *form* of activism defined in technocratic and hierarchical terms, and to assert the dominance of a transnationally connected technocratic elite over mass mobilisation and action.[22] Yet as we saw in Chapters 2 and 3, it is one thing to define a project of de-politicisation, and quite another to presume that it is accomplished in practice.

Understanding GEAR as in part a redefinition of the NDR is crucial to grasping both the battles within the ANC Alliance that exploded over the decade of the 2000s, and the contradictions embodied in the hegemonic projects of successive ruling blocs within the ANC that form the focus of Chapter 5.

Beyond GEAR, Mbeki's nationalism was far more complex than just a retreat to a narrow Africanism, Marais has convincingly argued: 'It formed part of more ambitious confrontation with the politics of identity and terms of belonging . . . that updated the African nationalism of the late 1940s and early 1950s, establishing perimeters for inclusion that were not strictly racial, while at the same time pivoting on the interests and histories of the African majority' (2011: 417). More recently Marais has suggested how Mbeki's HIV/AIDS denialism 'was paraded as a form of nationalist defiance' – but a defiance that avoided a critique of corporate capital: 'It was as if the embrace of economic and technocratic orthodoxy in post-apartheid South Africa demanded . . . resistance [that took the form of] anti-imperial posturing – for which AIDS became the stage'.[23] Marais' arguments, in conjunction with analyses of denialism by Posel (2005) and Gevisser (2007), make clear how articulations of sexuality and race were crucial and deeply contentious dimensions of re-nationalising practices and processes during the Mbeki era. At the same time, they cannot be understood apart from the dynamics of de-nationalisation.[24]

In 2008 researchers at Harvard estimated that the AIDS stance of the Mbeki regime was responsible for avoidable deaths of more than a third of a million people in South Africa.[25] For the majority of those affected by the ravages of HIV/AIDS this un-speakable suffering came on the back of shrinking and increasingly precarious employment, and fiscal austerity that hit local government especially hard (Chapter 3). Much of the burden of what many call 'the crisis of social reproduction' falls on women, as Fakier and Cock (2009) and others have documented. There have also been fundamental reconfigurations of intimacy (Hunter 2010; Mosoetsa 2011; Xulu 2012), and the four crises that Sitas identifies:

> The spread of HIV/AIDS that has exploded the intimacies of gender and kinship-based powers; the imponderable crisis in livelihood which has shamed easy correlations between economic growth and prosperity. There has been economic growth; there has been a radical loss of access to livelihood; all institutions designed to equalise voices and participation to co-determine decisions have failed; the crisis of protocols and institutions that attempted to proscribe 'otherings', racism and derogation within new value systems . . . They are crises because ordinary people's cultural formations can neither recoil nor refract them into coherent practices and, in the process, cultural formations have lost their capacity for steering and navigating social action as such . . . What emerges is not a vibrant civil society, but a spasmodic and turbulent reconfiguration (Sitas 2010: 171).

At the same time he issued a reminder that 'people are not spasmodic reflect-responders to social pressures' and that the radical deterioration of life chances does not necessarily translate into resistance (2010: 183).

It is important here to recall that, for all the pressures that were building up in the late 1990s, they were produced and manifest in locally specific (but spatially interconnected) ways as discussed in Chapter 3. In Chapter 5 I will show how the contradictions of local government need to be understood in relation to processes of de-nationalisation and re-nationalisation, that are linked in turn to the contradictions built into the ANC's hegemonic project and how it has played out in practice.

Notes

1. Fine and Rustomjee vigorously (and in my view correctly) call into question the prevailing view that South African industrialisation had followed a failed import substitution model, analogous to that in much of Latin America. For a discussion of the political and policy stakes at the time, see Fine (2010).
2. See Ashman et al. (2011: 12) for a fuller discussion of this process.
3. See Marais (1998, 2011) and Bond (2000).
4. For example, between 1990 and 2008, mining as a proportion of exports rose from 15 to 38 per cent (Southall 2010).
5. One of the fiercest critics of BEE from a social democratic perspective is Moeletsi Mbeki, author of *Architects of Poverty* (2009) and brother of former-President Thabo Mbeki.
6. http://www.lrb.co.uk/v33/n07/perry-anderson/lulas-brazil.
7. 'Dr Gleb Starushenko, a member of the Soviet Academy of Sciences, told the 1986 Soviet-African conference that, in his personal opinion, a parliament which accommodated group rights should be considered for the post-apartheid period. This parliament would consist of two chambers; one on the basis of proportional representation and the other "*possessing the right of minority veto*", which could operate on the basis of "equal representation of the four communities". Dr Starushenko (whose pro-liberation intentions are not in dispute) would also like to see the ANC work out "*comprehensive guarantees for the white population*" and "programmes" which give our "bourgeoisie the . . . guarantee" that there will be no broad nationalisation of capitalist property' (Slovo 1988: 29; emphasis in original).
8. In the second half of the 1980s, the consociational solution laid out by Lijphart (1985) found widespread support among strategically placed groups of white South African intellectuals.
9. Clergy of the Dutch Reformed Church.
10. Peberdy (2009) provides an extremely useful historical overview of immigration legislation in South Africa, reminding us that 'at those moments when the South African state has been reinvented – for instance in 1910, 1948, and 1961 – it has also reinvented its national identity and nation-building project and immigration anxieties, although in different ways and for different reasons' (2009: 162).
11. For an example of many reports on horrendous conditions in Lindela, see http://www.timeslive.co.za/thetimes/2012/06/08/lindela-hell-ignored.
12. Pallo Z. Jordan, 'The National Question in Post 1994 South Africa', 1997, http://www.marxists.org/subject/africa/anc/1997/national-question.htm.
13. See Marks and Trapido (1987) for a useful discussion of the history of these strands in relation to one another.

14. http://amadlandawonye.wikispaces.com/1962,+SACP,+The+Road+to+ South+African+Freedom.
15. See Chipkin (2007) for a useful discussion of the Freedom Charter, although, as I argue in Chapter 6, it is important to recognise the very different conditions and processes that gave rise to the Freedom Charter and the NDR.
16. For a deeply critical account by Baruch Hirson, see http://www.marxists.org/ archive/hirson/1989/native-republic.htm.
17. Rivonia refers to the suburb north of Johannesburg where Nelson Mandela and 18 other senior members of the ANC and SACP were arrested in 1963.
18. Chipkin is careful to make clear that his is not a conventional historical account, but rather a genealogical analysis focused on the question, 'What was nationalist about the discourse of the NDR?' (2007: 64).
19. http://mg.co.za/article/2008-06-05-the-curse-of-african-nationalism.
20. http://mg.co.za/article/2008-06-05-the-cure-of-african-nationalism.
21. See also Bond (2000) for an argument about how the RDP White Paper effectively evacuated the progressive elements in the original framing of the RDP.
22. Johnson (2003) argues that Mbeki and his followers have found the re-organisation of the state along conventional (neo)liberal lines quite compatible with their Leninist understanding of the primacy of vanguard party leadership over mass action.
23. http://mg.co.za/article/2012-04-05-making-sense-of-the-indefensible.
24. I will develop these arguments more fully in a forthcoming paper that engages as well with re-articulations of race, sex and nation in the time of Zuma.
25. http://www.guardian.co.uk/world/2008/nov/26/aids-south-africa.

5

The Unravelling of ANC Hegemony

Generations of Populist Politics

Insofar as the proletariat perforce begins the construction of its
hegemonic project from a subaltern position, its theoretical
comprehension must ascend along the same path, beginning from
the theoretical dissection of the solidified integral state of
bourgeois passive revolution, in order to dismantle it in reality
. . . [For Gramsci] the concept of a future and possible proletarian
hegemony emerges from a more exact appreciation of the nature
of the actual and effective bourgeois hegemony against which it
must struggle (Thomas 2009a: 223).

BUILDING ON THE discussion of de-nationalisation and re-
nationalisation in Chapter 4, this chapter turns the spotlight on
questions of hegemony. I will argue that articulations of the nation,
liberation and the NDR are central to the ANC's hegemonic project.
Far from just a matter of false consciousness or manipulations from
above, these articulations tap into and draw upon popular
understandings, memories and meanings of racial oppression,
racialised dispossession and struggles for freedom. While articulations of the nation and liberation are vitally important to the
ANC's hegemonic power, they are simultaneously a source of
weakness and instability because they are vulnerable to counter-
claims of betrayal – a vulnerability intensified by how processes of
de-nationalisation play out in practice. These instabilities and
fragilities are evident in the increasingly dangerous populist politics
that have developed over the long decade of the 2000s (2001–12).

This chapter will support these arguments by returning to Chapter 2, and re-interpreting the dialectics of protest and containment in relation to de-nationalisation and re-nationalisation.

Implicit in this chapter is that de-nationalisation and re-nationalisation constitute the specific form of South Africa's passive revolution – an argument that I elaborate on in Chapter 6 along with its wider implications. By focusing on hegemony, I am working with a different conception of passive revolution than one which posits a sharp distinction between domination and hegemony.[1] Like populism, hegemony is a slippery and contentious term. Accordingly, let me start by laying out the understandings of hegemony and populism that I will be using in this chapter.

Hegemony, Populism, Nationalism: Engaging Debates

Hegemony is often used simply as a synonym for state power or leadership. In discussions that invoke Gramsci, hegemony frequently refers to consent as opposed to coercion and domination. Both of these understandings of hegemony are problematic. So, too, are related concepts of civil society understood as NGOs and other organisations located between the state and the market (or economy), and counter-hegemony as springing up from civil society, similarly understood as outside or beyond the state.

A more general difficulty lies in views of Gramsci as a Western Marxist that was used to bolster Eurocommunist projects in the 1970s and into the 1980s, and that have also informed some of the ways Gramsci has been deployed in South Africa. According to these interpretations, Gramsci drew a sharp distinction between the East (Russia) and the West (Western Europe). The East, in this reading, is characterised by coercion and the domination of the state over civil society, whereas in the West consent and hegemony are culturally rooted in civil society, which has preponderance over the state. Accordingly, while in the East it was possible to overthrow the state by a frontal attack (war of manoeuvre), revolutionary strategy in the West requires a protracted war of position (or attrition) fought in the trenches of civil society.

In 'The Antinomies of Antonio Gramsci', a hugely influential essay written at the height of Eurocommunism in the 1970s, Perry Anderson (1976a) launched a searing critique of reformist and Eurocommunist appropriations of Gramsci – while also pointing to the slippages and ambiguities in Gramsci's prison writings that lent themselves to such appropriations. Gramsci was, of course, aware that capitalist class rule necessarily comprised coercion as well as consent, Anderson argued, but 'his use of hegemony often tended to imply that the structure of capitalist power in the West essentially rested on culture and consent' (1976a: 76). Likewise, his use of the idea of war of position suggested that the work of a Marxist party was simply that of ideological conversion. 'In both cases, the role of coercion-repression by the bourgeois State, insurrection by the working class – tends to drop out' (1976a: 76), thus opening the way to reformist appropriations of Gramsci.

In *The Gramscian Moment*, Peter Thomas (2009a) develops an extended critique of Anderson, insisting that '[i]t is the dialectical unity of East and West, and not their antinomian opposition [as Anderson would have it], that constitutes "the essential terms of [Gramsci's] theoretical universe"' (Thomas 2009a: 220).[2] For Gramsci (as opposed to Anderson), 'West and East are comparable, just as variations in the West itself, because both participate in the dynamic of an expansive political and economic order that is fundamentally and essentially internationalist in character' (2009a: 203). This alternative reading of Gramsci is grounded in a broader body of recent scholarship.[3] Moving beyond a conception of Gramsci as a Western Marxist has important implications for thinking about and with passive revolution, I will suggest later, because it underscores the profoundly comparative character of his work.

For purposes of the present discussion, what is important is that Thomas corrects several misconceptions of Gramsci's use of hegemony cast in terms of Anderson's antinomies. The first misconception is that bourgeois hegemony is a strategy aimed at producing consent as opposed to coercion, along with an understanding of hegemony/consent as the opposite of domination/coercion.[4] Thomas shows that this is a misreading, and that Gramsci's true starting point was 'the dialectical integration of hegemony with domination, of consent with coercion, united in their distinction' (Thomas 2009b: 164). Rather than a logic of either/or, 'one emerged from the other and vice-versa, depending upon the specific conditions of the conjuncture' (2009a: 166).

It is also not the case that for Gramsci 'hegemony (direction) pertains to civil society, and coercion (domination) to the State', as Anderson (1976a: 21) asserts. Gramsci did indeed use the term 'State' to denote both what he called the 'integral State' (a dialectical unity of political society and civil society) and political society (or the state in its narrow sense), but this was not the result of confusion. It was instead 'an attempt to specify that the identity-distinction between civil society and political society occurs under the hegemony of the state. It resulted not in a blurring of the boundaries of the state, but in a clearer delineation of the specific efficacy of the bourgeois state as both a social and political relation . . .' (Thomas 2009a: 191).

In other words, far from being 'located' in civil society, hegemony traverses political and civil society – but it is political society that predominantly sets the terms of traversal. The bourgeois state will remain the 'truth' of civil society, Thomas goes on to note, until subaltern classes become aware of their own capacity for self-organisation and self-regulation.[5] This is not a matter of counter-hegemony – a term that Gramsci never used. Instead, Gramsci was concerned with the formation of an alternative proletarian hegemony grounded in the philosophy of praxis. Nor was 'philosophy of praxis' a code word for Marxism that Gramsci used to evade his prison censors. Rather, it was crucial to his profoundly anti-vanguardist concern to 'rethink the concrete forms in which the materialist conception of history and the critique of political economy can move from being the preserve of small groups of people to becoming the base for a genuine mass culture and civilization' (Thomas 2012: 19). Philosophy of praxis thus embodies understanding philosophy and ideas as practical activities, and of recognising that 'everyone is a philosopher'. As discussed more fully in Chapter 6, Gramsci's concepts of hegemony and philosophy of praxis were heavily dependent upon language and translation.

In a useful exposition of this understanding of Gramsci, William Roseberry proposed that we think of hegemony *not* as consent, but rather as a *process* of contention and struggle in which 'the words, images, symbols, forms, organizations, institutions, and movements used by subordinate populations to talk about, understand, confront, accommodate themselves to, or resist their domination are shaped by the process of domination itself' (1994: 361). What hegemony constructs, then, is not a shared ideology, but rather 'a common material and meaningful framework for living through, talking about, and acting upon social orders characterized by domination' (1994: 361). To the extent that a dominant order is able to establish 'not consent but the prescribed form for expressing both acceptance and discontent, it has established a common discursive framework' (1994: 364) – one in which 'forms and languages of protest and resistance *must* adopt the forms and languages of domination in order to be heard'.

In this sense, ANC hegemony is crucially contingent on official and popular articulations of the nation, liberation and the NDR. The meaning and ownership of the NDR, however, is also a key site of struggle within the ANC Alliance, intensified by the dynamics of de-nationalisation. Questions of populism burst on to the public stage in the mid-2000s with the rapid rise of Zuma to political prominence.

Populism is, of course, anathema for many on the left in South Africa and elsewhere in the world. According to many left critiques, populism glorifies the role of the authoritarian, anti-intellectual leader as the protector of the masses, and stands sharply opposed to a progressive politics grounded in class conflict. Ironically, much of the critique of Zuma from the liberal right is also cast in terms of populism. In much recent commentary, 'populism' is widely used to contrast Zuma and his followers to an idealised model of 'normal', 'civilised', 'mature', 'rational' liberal democracy. In short, both the left and the liberal right have converged on a model of populism underpinned by an unquestioned notion of the 'manipulated mindless masses'.

In his book entitled *On Populist Reason*, Ernesto Laclau proposed a different understanding. Instead of starting with a model of political rationality that sees populism in terms of what it lacks, Laclau maintains that '[p]opulism is the royal road to understanding something about the ontological constitution of the political as such' (2005: 67) – an argument that has sparked intense debate.[6] My own position in this debate is that Laclau ends up endorsing a deeply problematic conception of populism that counterposes an all-knowing theorist to the ignorant masses (Hart 2013). In effect, he reinvents the manipulated mindless masses model.

A more useful approach, I suggest, is to go back to Laclau's earlier essay 'Towards a Theory of Populism' in *Politics and Ideology in Marxist Theory* (1977), drawing on some aspects of his analysis of populism and reworking others. The core of Laclau's argument is that populism is most usefully understood in terms of its *form* rather than its *content*. What is distinctive about populism as a political form is its appeal to the 'people' versus the 'power bloc' – but in itself this says nothing about its political content. Indeed, it is possible to call Adolf Hitler, Mao Zedong and Juan Peron simultaneously populist '[n]ot because the social bases of their movements were similar; not because their ideologies expressed the same class interests, but because popular interpellations appear in the ideological discourses of all of them, presented in the form of antagonism and not just of difference' (Laclau 1977: 174). The term interpellation conveys the idea that individuals are 'hailed' or constituted as subjects through ideological apparatuses.[7]

Contrary to the standard left position, populism for Laclau is not about an appeal to the 'people' over and above class divisions. Instead, populism – along with other non-class ideologies like nationalism with which it is often linked – are elements that only exist in *articulation* with class discourses and hegemonic projects, with articulation understood here both as 'joining together' and 'giving expression to' as discussed in Chapter 1. Widely divergent examples of populism – from the extreme right to the left – thus depend on specific articulations of populist and class politics. 'Popular traditions', he argued, often carry greater stability and strength than class ideologies because they represent the 'ideological crystallisation of resistance to oppression in general' (Laclau 1977: 167). Yet they can only be grasped in relation to class – which is why the most divergent political movements often appeal to the same ideological symbols:

> The figure of Tupac Amaru can be invoked by various guerrilla movements and by the present military government in Peru; the symbols of Chinese nationalism were conjured up by Chiang-Kai-Shek and Mao Tse Tung; those of German nationalism by Hitler and by Thälmann. But even though they constitute mere elements, popular traditions are far from being arbitrary and they cannot be modified at will. They are the residue of a unique and irreducible historical experience and, as such, constitute a more solid and durable structure of meanings than the social structure itself (Laclau 1977: 167).

In developing this argument, Laclau drew a sharp distinction between the populism of the dominant classes and a populism of the dominated classes: 'When the dominant bloc experiences a profound crisis because a new fraction seeks to impose its hegemony but is unable to do so within the existing structure of the power bloc, one solution can be a direct appeal by this fraction to the masses to develop their antagonism towards the State' (Laclau 1977: 173). Laclau goes on to note that the populism of a fraction of the dominant class is always repressive because it attempts a more dangerous experiment than an existing parliamentary regime: whilst the latter seeks to *neutralise* the revolutionary potential of popular interpellations, the former tries to *develop* that antagonism but to keep it within certain limits. Yet, for Laclau, populism in the sense of articulations of 'the people versus the power bloc' is also crucial to the hegemonic ambitions of dominated sectors. 'Socialist-populism' is not an expression of the ideological backwardness of a dominated class, he insisted. It is, on the contrary, 'an expression of the moment when the articulating power of this class imposes itself hegemonically on the rest of society' (1977: 196). Hence, *'classes cannot assert their hegemony without articulating the people in their discourse; and the specific form of this articulation, in the case of a class which seeks to confront the power bloc as a whole, in order to assert its hegemony, will be populism'* (1977: 196; emphasis in original).

The strength of Laclau's (1977) analysis is his insistence on understanding populism in relation to articulations of class and nationalism. His analysis of bourgeois populism provides a useful starting point for analysing the proliferation of populist politics in South Africa in the decade of the 2000s, although it needs to be qualified. A key limitation of this approach is its reliance on conception of 'interpellation'. These limits are made clear in an essay by Sitas entitled 'Class, Nation, Ethnicity in Natal's Black Working Class' (1990) that was, in effect, an intervention in the heated workerist/populist debate that dominated oppositional politics during much of the 1980s, and to which we shall return in the concluding section of this chapter. While acknowledging Laclau's (1977) understanding of class in relation to non-class elements, Sitas launched a sustained critique of Laclau's uncritical conception of interpellation. Specifically calling into question the way Laclau was being used in the 1980s in South Africa to analyse Zulu ethnic nationalism as the product of ideological interpellations from above, Sitas insisted that the black working class in Natal is not a *tabula rasa*, but bears its own traditions: '"Zulu-ness" must be viewed as a negotiated identity between ordinary people's attempts to create effective and reciprocal bonds (or functioning cultural formations) out of their social and material conditions of life *and* political ideologies that seek to mobilize them in non-class ways' (Sitas 1990: 266) – and each sets limits on the other.

What this critique points to are the imperatives for grasping the interconnections between populist politics 'from above' and popular understandings arising from the social and material conditions of everyday life. It also points towards a more fully Gramscian analysis of hegemony as process outlined above, in which issues of language are crucial. Gramsci's understanding of philosophy of praxis also helps us to see the limits of Laclau's theory of socialist populism (Hart 2013).

In the discussion that follows I draw on a revised version of Laclau's theory of bourgeois populism to argue that Mbeki sought to neutralise the revolutionary potential of popular antagonisms; Zuma sought to develop them, but contain them within limits – which is always a dangerous experiment, as Laclau pointed out; and that Malema sought to capture and amplify the revolutionary potential of popular antagonisms, generating a dynamic that, the SACP maintains, has tended towards fascism. I am going to flesh out these arguments by revisiting the turbulent 'long decade' of the 2000s (2001–12) laid out in Chapter 2, and reinterpreting the amplifying tensions and contradictions through these lenses. In the process, I will show how it is not just a matter of bourgeois populism 'from above' and socialist populism 'from below', but a dialectical process through which popular antagonisms in the arenas of everyday life and struggles within the ANC Alliance are deeply interconnected, and have been inflected through simultaneous processes of de-nationalisation and re-nationalisation.

The Dialectics of Protest and Containment Revisited
Phase I (2000–05/06): Neutralising Popular Antagonisms
Any effort to grasp how hegemonic processes have transformed over the decade of the 2000s must start with the Bredell land occupation, and the swift eviction of shack dwellers in July 2001. As we saw in Chapter 2, Bredell represented the moment when the coercive face of the post-apartheid state made its first widely publicised appearance. It did so in a guise powerfully reminiscent of its apartheid predecessor, with images of police with attack dogs

bundling people into the notorious armoured vehicles known as hippos, and demolition crews pulling down shacks. New to the picture were the well-dressed ANC officials fleeing in their Mercedes-Benzes under police protection – solid embodiments, as it were, of the willingness of the post-apartheid state to deploy coercion to protect private property rights, and of the political hazards that accompanied this project. While the overt violence of Bredell was relatively brief and contained, the fallout in terms of erosion of the ANC's moral authority was massive.

A second key marker of the new millennium was the rapid rise of new social movements in the period immediately following Bredell, representing concerted expressions of popular antagonism directed at the ANC. Framing their antagonism in terms of anti-neoliberalism, these movements made dramatically clear the Faustian bargain through which the ANC and corporate capital had brought an end to apartheid. Coinciding with two major global conferences, the new social movements were of course intensely humiliating for the ANC, as were the transnational connections and support they elicited.

Mbeki's immediate response, as we saw in Chapter 2, was a coercive crackdown against new social movements, especially the LPM – a move facilitated by the internal disorganisation of the movements themselves. What also happened in the latter part of 2002 was a further re-articulation of the NDR. Having redefined the NDR in terms of creation of a black bourgeoisie in the 1990s (Chapter 4), he now deployed the NDR as a disciplinary weapon against new social movements and left opponents within the alliance. It became, in effect, a means of beating opponents into submission. Going back to Chapter 2 we can see how, in the flood of documents and statements emanating from Mbeki and his henchmen, those who oppose him are accused of 'conduct[ing] a campaign of terror against the revolution [NDR]'. What is significant here is how the NDR takes on a new and threatening position in what Roseberry (1994) calls the languages of contention through which hegemonic processes operate.

In the post-apartheid period Mbeki's disciplinary deployment of the NDR represented a novel and significant re-articulation of nationalism. There is, however, a startling continuity with the early 1980s, when some members of the SACP in exile lashed out fiercely against the independent Federation of South African Trade Unions.[8] The terms of critique are so similar – including linking the 'ultra-left' to the (neo)liberal right – that one is led to wonder whether Mbeki and his loyal assistants hauled out dusty old copies of the *African Communist* in which many of these critiques appeared.

Following this offensive against those with the temerity to challenge its accommodation with corporate capital, the ruling bloc headed by Mbeki changed tack in 2003 with the discovery of the 'Second Economy' and invocation of the 'developmental state' (Chapter 2). This was also the moment at which the stringent fiscal austerity of the 1990s started to give way to rather more generous allocations from national to local government – although, as we have seen, municipal indigent policy was tightly linked with 'credit control' and separating the 'can't pays' from the 'won't pays' (Chapter 3).

It is, of course, very easy to discern the technocratic, de-politicising thrust of these and other initiatives. The key point, though, is that they were not accomplished in practice, even though several of the most militant new social movements quickly fell into disarray. Following the April 2004 election, we witnessed escalating and violent popular protest and municipal rebellions (Chapters 2 and 3) – notwithstanding the trumpeting of Second Economy benevolence by the Mbeki administration and its intellectuals. While many of these uprisings were directed at local government officials and councillors, and framed in terms of failure to deliver basic services and housing, they extended well beyond specific local grievances to encompass much broader and deeper popular antagonisms that the new social movements had failed to mobilise – but that Jacob Zuma was able to capture and re-articulate in a reconstituted hegemonic process, discussed more fully below.

The beginning of the end for the Mbeki-led ruling bloc came in mid-June 2005, at the National General Council meeting in Pretoria (Chapter 2), which followed shortly after Mbeki's dismissal of Zuma as deputy president of the country. The National General Council became, in effect, the crucible in which Wolpe's (1995) prophecy that the meaning of the NDR would become a key site of struggle (Chapter 4) was fully realised. The explosive anger that erupted at the National General Council also underscores the double-edged character of articulations of nationalism as liberation – how they are key elements of the post-colonial hegemonic project, while at the same time deeply vulnerable to charges of betrayal. The National General Council was the moment when the ruling bloc within the ANC lost its grip on articulations of the nation and liberation, and the coalition behind Zuma entered the battle to redefine the hegemonic languages of contention centred on the meaning of the NDR, and augmented by what Gunner (2008) calls the 'unruly power of song'.

Key contours of these battles to re-articulate race, class and nationalism find clear expression in a special edition of *Bua Komanisi!* issued by the Central Committee of the SACP in May 2006 and the furious response on 19 June from the ANC.[9] In a rejoinder entitled 'Is the ANC Leading a National Democratic Revolution or Managing Capitalism?' the SACP reiterated its accusation that the ANC has come to be dominated by 'the narrow self-interest of an emerging black capitalist stratum with close connections to established capital and to our movement' that acts 'not in order to advance the NDR, but for personal self-accumulation purposes'.[10]

From the perspective of Laclau's (1977) theory of populism, the National General Council can be seen as the populist moment, when a new fraction of the dominant bloc seeks to assert its hegemonic power by appealing to the masses to develop popular antagonism against the ruling bloc.

Phase II (2005/06–2009/10): Developing but Containing Popular Antagonisms

In the period following Zuma's victory over Mbeki at Polokwane (Chapter 2), analyses of what has come to be called the 'Zunami' (or Zuma tsunami) often depicted it as a 'rebellion from below', spearheaded by the left within the ANC Alliance (COSATU and the SACP). The alliance left and those associated with it celebrated the triumphal opportunity for working-class leadership of the NDR, while the liberal right predictably viewed what they saw as a 'communist putsch' with fear and trepidation.

In retrospect, this left triumphalism is heavily over-stated. Southall (2009) and others have pointed out that support for Zuma came from a much broader 'coalition of the aggrieved' that included as well the ANC Youth League, Umkhonto we Sizwe veterans and provincial leaders on the losing side of ANC patronage. Butler (2009: 69) also identified 'branch-level discontent about the monopolisation of patronage opportunities by incumbents, poor service delivery, and the general high-handedness and arrogance that characterised the higher reaches – or even the middling one – of Mbeki's administration', and Friedman added to the mix former intelligence operatives who had served under Zuma in exile.[11] Crucially as well, the coalition that lined up behind Zuma included key BEE figures. Southall (2009: 324–5) identifies several key groups of black capitalists who threw their support behind Zuma early on, along with many others who quickly switched allegiances following Polokwane.

Southall points to further reasons why the claim that COSATU and the SACP led a democratic 'rebellion from below' is deeply questionable:

> First, it provides little in the way of evidence of how COSATU and the SACP managed to secure control of the ANC on the ground . . . Second, there is an unwarranted assumption of COSATU and SACP internal unity, when it seems that there was considerable dissonance

within both organisations. Third, there is a failure to elaborate the actual relationship between COSATU and SACP, rendering their distinct roles in the making of the tsunami opaque (Southall 2009: 322–3).

This 'dissonance' included the sidelining and purging of COSATU and SACP members who questioned support for Zuma. Devan Pillay (2011: 37) describes how a 'climate of fear fell over the working-class movement, and few dared to publicly question the suitability of Zuma'. Most significantly, in 'The Road to Polokwane', Sitas (2010: 190) points out that 'some of the most mutinous energy and action occurs in areas and wards where neither COSATU and the SACP, nor the new social movements have any sway'.

The question remains, therefore, of the forces driving massive grassroots support for Zuma. Distaste for Zuma on both the independent left and the liberal right has authorised condescending and at times bizarre assertions of the reasons why millions of ordinary people threw (and many continue to throw) their support behind him.[12] The tendency on much of the independent left has been to regard such support as false consciousness, or as an unpleasant populist resurgence of Zulu ethnic nationalism that the figure of Zuma is somehow capable of interpellating from above – an interpretation that fails to take into account support for him well beyond KwaZulu-Natal and isiZulu-speaking populations.[13] Perhaps the most extravagant claim was that of Achille Mbembe, who likened support for Zuma to a collective suicide impulse akin to the 1856–57 Xhosa cattle killings – 'a populist rhetoric and millenarium form of politics which advocates, uses and legitimises self-destruction, or national suicide, as a means of salvation'.[14] His recommendation was that fractions of the SACP, the trade unions and the ANC Youth League should leave the alliance to form their own political party: 'What should emerge is a new political mainstream committed to a liberal constitution, to an explicitly social democratic agenda and to an Afropolitan cultural project.'

The imperative for a more adequate understanding of popular support for Zuma is not just one of setting the historical record straight; it bears directly on some of the most crucial issues in South Africa today, including the character, contradictions and limits of ANC hegemonic processes, and the proliferation of populist politics. In my initial effort to come to grips with this issue I argued that part of what Zuma represents is a move to seize the mantle of the liberation struggle, and present himself as its rightful heir:

> Positioning himself as the hero of national liberation is the key to Zuma's capacity – at least for the time being – to articulate multiple, often contradictory meanings into a complex unity that appeals powerfully to 'common sense' across a broad spectrum. They include his asserting himself as a man of the left (much to the chagrin of many on the left who point to his support for GEAR, as well as his links to certain fractions of capital); as a traditionalist who dons leopard skins on key occasions (and as one who brought peace to KwaZulu-Natal, helping to end the violent civil war of the early 1990s); and as an anti-elitist (his regular reference to himself as 'not educated' – but, by implication, extremely smart – is a direct attack on the technocratic elite surrounding Mbeki, often portrayed by Zuma supporters as arrogant and self-serving, and as not having served in the trenches of the revolutionary struggle). These re-articulations of race, class, and nationalism are also shot through with gender and sexuality.
>
> Yet these are not simply interpellations from above. The figure of Zuma operates in many ways as a point of condensation for multiple, pre-existing tensions, angers, and discontents that until recently were contained within the hegemonic project of the ruling bloc in the ANC, and have now been diverted into newly opened fields of conflict. How this popular anger will be inflected remains a wide open question. S'bu Zikode, leader of the Durban shackdweller's movement (Abahlali base mjondolo) put it succinctly at a public lecture on June 29 2006, when he urged the audience to understand that 'our desperation and anger can go in many directions' (Hart 2007: 97–8).

This argument grew directly out of the palpable and mounting popular discontent that I was able to observe at close quarters in Ladysmith and Newcastle – and that, especially in Ladysmith, contrasted so dramatically with local political dynamics in the first phase of the post-apartheid order. Starting with the *imbizo* in Bergville in December 2003 (Chapter 2), I also became increasingly aware of Zuma's capacity to give expression to multiple dimensions of discontent and senses of betrayal, to link them together and to draw sharp contrasts between himself and Mbeki – to become, in other words, the 'authoritative other' to which very large numbers of people 'uploaded' hope and leadership, as Sitas (2010: 193) puts it.

Drawing on long-term ethnographic research in another region of KwaZulu-Natal, Mark Hunter (2011) offers additional important insights into how Zuma was able to resonate with the everyday lived experiences of millions of poor black South Africans – including very large numbers of women who enthusiastically embraced him despite his having been charged with rape, and young people who flocked to register and vote for him in the 2009 elections. Hunter shows how the long-term contraction of employment that many label the 'crisis in social reproduction' is deeply entangled with transformations of intimacy – signified by a sharp reduction in marriage, the inability of a large proportion of the younger generation to 'build a home' (*ukwaza umuzi*), and intensifying gender conflict, 'as women deride men for failure to marry them and men deride women for their new independence' (2011: 13). At the time of the rape trial, Hunter argues, women in the settlement where he worked regarded Zuma not as a rapist but as a respectable patriarch, willing and able to support his wives and children, and having offered to pay bride-price (*ilobolo*) to marry the woman who accused him of rape. This analysis accords closely with my own observations in the areas where I work – namely, that the rape trial served, if anything, to consolidate support for Zuma among women, and underscore a sense of his having been betrayed (Chapter 2). More generally, Hunter argues:

It is precisely Zuma's ability to talk to society's tremendous economic and personal upheavals . . . that allowed him partly to transcend generation, ethnicity, and gender. For the youth, he brought hope of work, service delivery, and a re-mooring of gender relations now in turmoil; for the old, he could also stand for a renewed sense of generational respect. If many South Africans felt a strong sense of betrayal towards their political leaders, Zuma somehow stood inside and outside government: he connected in new ways (and quite contrary to the famous feminist slogan) the personal and the political (2011: 20).

Zuma's capacity to connect with and speak to the painful articulations of race, class, gender and sexuality in the everyday lives of many poor black South Africans is closely linked with his wresting ownership of the liberation struggle from the Mbeki fraction – and, in the process, redefining the hegemonic languages of contention. Central to this process was his signature song, 'Awaleth' Umshini Wami' (Bring me my machine gun) and events such as the reburial of Moses Mabhida, along with others like those described in Chapter 2. Gunner's extraordinary article entitled 'Jacob Zuma, the Social Body and the Unruly Power of Song' (2008) points to the dangers of dismissing 'Umshini Wami' as no more than an unpleasant manifestation of Zuma's hypersexualised militant masculinity that he used to mobilise the manipulated mindless masses. With its deep links to liberation songs of the struggle era, Gunner explains, people recognised it as part of a language that they knew:

The song . . . broke into popular public memory by recalling an earlier and more dangerous way of being. It evoked the years of pre-1994 resistance to the apartheid regime, the tense urban gatherings and the mass funerals. It forced back into the public imagination memories and stories of the long marches through the bush, the lost family members, and the camps to the north in the countries which had hosted the freedom fighters. These were all sites marked by song as an expressive tool. Song was a means of capturing and giving expression to the aspirations, the anxieties and the vision of people in that particularly turbulent and painful moment in South Africa's history (2008: 38).

Like many liberation songs, '*Umshini Wami*' is 'embedded in a largely masculinist conception of militarism and nationalism' (Gunner 2008: 40) – one that failed to resolve questions of gender equality as Shireen Hassim (2007) and others have shown. Yet, Gunner argues, it was far more than an ethnic Zulu composition:

> It was a song of the dispossessed and of the citizen-to-come. Perhaps at the heart of the song is the verb '-letha' (bring) suggesting a movement of process, of moving towards something yet to be made; suggesting too that the action is sanctioned by the giver or bringer. The instrument of the machine gun, umshini wami, suggests not so much brute power of war but that of agency, and the ability of the individual sanctioned by the group to bring about change (2008: 43).

Yet the machine gun also 'sent a warning to any complacent settling into a negotiated liberal democracy at the very same time that it gave hope to the longing for social and political change' (Gunner 2008: 40).

Far from contradictory, the militant nationalist masculinity of '*Umshini Wami*' and the respectable, responsible patriarchy described by Hunter are mutually reinforcing. Both resonate deeply with memories, meanings, experiences and practices in the multiple arenas of everyday life, meshing together to solidify a 'common sense' understanding of Zuma as a powerful and compassionate leader.[15] By linking a militant nationalist past to the promise of a secure familial future, Zuma extended the languages of hegemony and, as Gunner (2008: 28) puts it, enabled the participation of multiple publics in national debates. This point was driven home to me very clearly in December 2007, when I was following the Polokwane drama with friends in Ladysmith. As news of Zuma's huge victory over Mbeki broke, a friend turned to me and said, 'You must understand, Gill, that this is about the masses versus the intellectuals.'

The populist turn not only expanded the languages of contestation; it also transformed the dynamic of hegemonic processes. Returning to Laclau's (1977: 161) epigraph at the beginning of the discussion of populism, hegemony is partly about articulating different visions of the world in such a way that potential antagonism in neutralised. To the extent that what Laclau calls bourgeois (as opposed to socialist) populism entails developing but containing popular antagonisms it is, as he pointed out, an inherently dangerous experiment that is likely to call forth increased repression.

Barely five months after Polokwane, the outbreak of xenophobic attacks in May 2008 was a hideous manifestation of how, as S'bu Zikode anticipated in 2006, the anger of the poor can go in many directions. At least some of those who went on these murderous rampages did so singing '*Umshini Wami*' – an ugly reminder of what Gunner calls the 'unruly power of song'. These bloody fields of conflict into which the song was diverted are also a reminder of how the history of militant nationalism evoked by the song were articulated with other dimensions of post-apartheid re-nationalising practices discussed in Chapter 4 under the heading of 'Fortress South Africa'. Also of great significance is the reception Zuma received in shack settlements on the East Rand immediately after the attacks, when a man leapt up and warned him, 'if you are a stumbling block, we are going to kick you away' (Chapter 2).[16]

The rise of Julius Malema and his challenge to Zuma in the post-Polokwane period can be seen as another manifestation of the dangers that accompany strategies to develop but contain popular antagonisms. The Malema challenge also represents an intensification of contradictions built into the ANC's hegemonic project, most usefully understood in terms of how re- and de-nationalising forces are playing out in relation to one another in increasingly conflictual ways.

Phase III (2010–12): Capturing and Amplifying Popular Antagonisms

Writing in the *New York Review of Books* in April 2012 about Malema's 'inflammatory and racially tinged populism', his attacks on Zuma and the bitter splits within the ANC, Joshua Hammer entitled his article 'A New Crisis in South Africa'. This narrative of novelty focused on an oedipal fight to the death between the young upstart Malema and the old patriarch Zuma obscures a much longer, deeper and intensifying crisis marked by some important continuities.

At the core of Malema's challenge was (and may well be again) a re-articulation of nationalism in terms of race and nature – the theft by white colonisers of the land and rich mineral resources of South Africa – and linking that to a powerful appeal for 'economic freedom in our life time' for the youth of South Africa. Underscoring the compromises that the older generation of ANC leaders had made, his calls for nationalisation of the mines and expropriation without compensation of white-owned land expanded the languages of contention well beyond the terms on which Zuma had challenged Mbeki.

One of the ironies of this seemingly radical re-articulation of nationalism was that the main focus of the Youth League attack was not just Zuma, but his close association with the SACP – an attack in which the Youth League had powerful backing from a fraction of black capital headed by billionaire Tokyo Sexwale. Tying this alliance together was a strong thread of anti-communist African nationalism that stretches back into the first part of the twentieth century. Malema and his lieutenants made extensive use of this history, likening themselves to the ANC Youth League of the 1940s. On the eve of the disciplinary hearings on 30 August 2011, for example, Floyd Shivambu (writing on behalf of the ANC Youth League NEC) called attention to 'the noble precedent for the League's actions':

> Mandela, Sisulu and Tambo represent the most outstanding generation of freedom fighters across all liberation movements in Africa and the

world . . . In 1948, this generation of freedom fighters adopted a programme of action, a tool to mobilise society and structures of the ANC behind the call for real freedom from colonial oppression and exploitation. This programme was adopted at the 1949 national conference of the ANC in Mangaung, and those who know the evolution of the ANC will appreciate the impact it had in changing its character into a fighting mass movement for all the people of South Africa. The ultimate mobilisation and adoption of the Freedom Charter was a consequence of the 1949 programme of action . . . These developments were possible because the leadership of the ANC was not intolerant of the leadership of the ANC Youth League. While they were clearly irritated by the new proposals of the league, the leadership of the ANC never resorted to organisational and political mechanisms to silence the voice of the youth.[17]

Notably missing from contemporary invocations of the first Youth League, Forde (2011: 118) notes, is how 'after 1949, the young extreme nationalists were forced to modify their rigid, anti-communist stance'. What is significant is that, far from discarding the past, the Youth League rebellion turned around a shrewdly selective deployment of history and reassertion of a narrow African nationalism.

This reassertion went hand in hand with a redefinition of the NDR, and a move to snatch it away from the alliance left. Forde, for example, reports a discussion with Malema, in which he insisted that his plan is to complete the NDR – which he framed as moving from the first stage of political power to economic and social power – while expunging the language of socialism (and justifying his own lavish consumption) in the following terms:

You see, people are afraid of the word socialism and you must not pronounce it a lot. It will scare them. I might have houses. I might have watches. That's what the economic system dictates now. But when we've got an economic system that says that everything we have we need to bring together and share among ourselves, I will be the first one to surrender. I've got no problem with socialism. I've got a problem with socialists who want to hijack the ANC and without giving this phase of our revolution a chance to unfold. They want to take us immediately to socialism. That will have serious consequences (cited in Forde 2011: 81).

'Throughout his first term [as president of the ANC Youth League],' Forde notes, 'he consistently criticised the communists and started out his second term by piercing a sharp knife into the back of Blade Nzimande, the secretary-general of the SACP' (2011: 83).

The SACP lashed out hard against the Youth League attack, starting with a report to a Special National Congress in December 2009 warning of a proto-fascist tendency emerging from an anti-communist axis 'between BEE elements and alienated youth':

[E]lements of BEE capital have been exploring a class axis between themselves and the great mass of marginalized, alienated, often unemployed black youth. The material glue of this axis is the politics of patronage and messiahs, and its tentative ideological form is a demagogic African chauvinism. Because of its rhetorical militancy the media often portrays it as 'radical' and 'left-wing' – but it is fundamentally right-wing, even proto-fascist. While it is easy to dismiss the buffoonery of some of the leading lieutenants, we should not underestimate the resources made available to them, and the huge challenge we all have when it comes to millions of increasingly alienated, often unemployed youth who are potentially available for all kinds of demagogic mobilization.[18]

These warnings were repeated in 'The Road to South African Socialism', the political report prepared for the SACP's 13th National Congress in July 2012, which reiterated the dangers of proto-fascism and identified 'the right-wing, populist-demagogy of the "new tendency" as the gravest ideological threat to our national democratic revolution'.[19]

At numerous points the document underscores the imperative for 'advancing, deepening and defending the national democratic revolution', and devotes Chapter 4 to expounding on 'The National Democratic Revolution – The South African Road to Socialism' in terms that insistently distinguish the SACP's revolutionary nationalism from 'an elite abuse of nationalism for narrow self-promotion', and invoke the past in relation to the present, as well as the SACP's ownership of the NDR:

> Since the late 1920s, the Communist Party in South Africa has identified the national democratic revolution as the road to socialism. The rich struggle history that this strategic perspective has promoted over many decades speaks for itself. The wisdom of this strategic perspective is even more relevant in our post-1994 South African and global reality.

What this reclamation of history conveniently glosses over, among other things, are the enormous conflicts and opposition to the Native Republic thesis that Stalin handed down to the Communist Party of South Africa in 1928.

In addition to battles conducted on the terrain of the NDR and selective deployments of history, both sides in this conflict embody key continuities with prior struggles in the post-apartheid era. Undoubtedly the 'elements of BEE capital' identified by the SACP latched on to Malema's capacities for mass mobilisation, given the limitations of their own mass base. Yet the SACP is similarly reliant on Zuma. In the period prior to Polokwane, as I argued earlier, the dynamic was not just that of a 'coalition of the disgruntled' shunted aside by Mbeki uniting behind Zuma; of central importance were the complex societal forces propelling widespread popular support for Zuma that has rendered him an essential if ambiguous political asset for the alliance left. Also in the mid-2000s, Mbeki's efforts to contain Zuma enhanced Zuma's capacity to mobilise popular support. What Malema did was to steal the trope of betrayal from Zuma, aided in part by Zuma's moves to contain the threat that he presented by ramping up popular antagonisms.

The apogee of this threat came, of course, in the immediate aftermath of the Marikana massacre, which provided Malema with the most extraordinary opportunity to drive home the 'truth' of his re-articulation of nationalism in terms of race and nature, and to connect it directly with the suffering of black workers; the ongoing control of mining by white capitalists (and a few black compradors exemplified by Cyril Ramaphosa); and the moral bankruptcy of the ruling bloc within the ANC.

If Bredell was the moment when the coercive face of the post-apartheid state became visible, it was at Marikana that its militaristic might was unleashed with full force. Over the decade of the 2000s, the proliferation of populist politics has gone hand in hand with tightening disciplinary measures and heightened official secrecy as securocrats close to Zuma have gained an upper hand.[20]

Exemplified in all of this are the contradictions inherent in ANC hegemony: the process through which articulations of the nation and liberation are crucial to organising popular consent, while simultaneously opening the ruling bloc to charges of betrayal. The ongoing and pervasive imperative to inject selective meanings of the past into the present (part of what I am calling re-nationalising practices and processes) operate in tandem and in escalating conflict with a dynamic of accumulation that produces intensified inequality along with accelerating generations of 'surplus labour' populations.

The Stakes of Theory: Moving Beyond Western Marxism
The erosion of ANC hegemony and the proliferation of populist politics that I have traced in this chapter exemplify the depth and seriousness of the crisis in South Africa. Far from resolving the crisis, the conquest of Malema by the Zuma ruling bloc has prolonged and intensified it, paving the way either for his return, or for the rise of another demagogic figure.

In South Africa today we have a situation in which the SACP positions itself as the vanguard of the subaltern struggles, and custodian of a particularly crude version of a theory of nationalism in relation to capitalism that has increasingly come to function as a disciplinary mechanism within the ANC Alliance. Pillay (2011: 41) provides an example of how COSATU organised a 'civil society' conference in conjunction with the Treatment Action Campaign in October 2010, and did not invite the ANC or SACP. Jeremy Cronin of the SACP came up with a furious response, claiming that COSATU was falling into a 'liberal trap' to upset the NDR.[21] Cronin asserted a counter-definition of 'civil society' as the terrain of anti-state, pro-market liberalism, and claimed that, because the conference made no reference to the NDR, it was effectively 'anti-transformation'. This example of how the NDR continues to function as a disciplinary measure is precisely what Mbeki was doing in 2002 in his ferocious response to new social movements. Another illuminating instance is the address by Zwelinzima Vavi, Secretary General of COSATU, to the SACP Congress in July 2012. Vavi reminded his audience of how, in 1962, the SACP had advanced the theory of Colonialism of a Special Type (CST). He then called on the SACP as the 'revolutionary vanguard' to assist us in 'understanding whether we are well on our way in South Africa to dismantle this diabolical capitalist system', and calling for 'the most penetrating, fiercely scientific, disciplined and accurate theoretic Marxist-Leninist critique of the world and SA capitalism, and the resultant correct revolutionary working class political programme'.[22] While this address can be read as partly tongue-in-cheek, it highlights the official outsourcing of intellectual work to the SACP, and the imperative to toe the CST/NDR line.

For many on the left outside the ANC Alliance, as noted in Chapters 1 and 4, questions of nationalism remain an anathema – understood, at best, as a manifestation of false consciousness. Notably absent from a range of left positions is serious attention to the popular resonances of articulations of nationalism in relation to those that emerge from tensions within the ANC Alliance.

This configuration of forces is deeply dangerous, but far from new. Of direct relevance here is Andrew Nash's (1999, 2009) brilliant analysis of the rise and fall of Western Marxism in South Africa in the 1970s and 1980s, and its relationship to the Soviet Marxism of the SACP.[23] Nash provides a nuanced analysis of the process through which leading figures on the left opposed to the Stalinism of the SACP and committed to a radical critique of capitalism accommodated to the ANC Alliance and the dictates of capital in the late 1980s and early 1990s. He also calls attention to how many of those from the white student movement associated with the independent trade union movement, the Federation of South African Trade Unions, in the 1980s were unable to come to terms with African nationalism, and how these inabilities were accompanied by major organisational limits.

In addition, Nash sheds important light on how the SACP – and, more specifically, Cronin – used a narrow reading of Gramsci as a Western Marxist to clean up its Stalinist image in the late 1980s. He shows how this Marxism presented itself as open to debate, while also setting limits on that debate in the name of the practical necessity for unifying the oppressed: 'To do this, it was necessary also to draw on the past – on its symbols, sacrifices, heroes . . . But it is a struggle only for the recovery of the past, never for its critical interrogation; it seeks inspiration, and never self-knowledge' (Nash 1999: 75).

Thus, he argues, this Marxism filled the gap left by the collapse of the Soviet Union and the discrediting of its Marxism. It did away with the crude dogmatism of Soviet Marxism, while preserving its instrumentalism.

If we are to draw on Gramsci to confront the incredibly difficult present circumstances in South Africa, then I suggest we need to abandon notions of him as a Western Marxist. Even Anderson (1976b), who attached the label in the first place, recognised that it did not really apply in Gramsci's case; and, as Nash (1999) points out, Eurocommunist appropriations of Gramsci in the 1970s and 1980s were even more problematic when they were taken up in South Africa.[24] This is why the more accurate readings of Gramsci in the recent work of Thomas and others outlined at the beginning of this chapter are so important. In addition to emphasising Gramsci's focus on the *relations* between the East (Russia) and the West (Europe) rather than their antinomian distinctions, the work of Thomas, Morton and others provides fresh insights into the concept of passive revolution – a concept that is totally missing from Anderson's (1976a) account of Gramsci's antinomies.[25] By grounding the concept more fully in the conditions out of which it emerged, this work also enables us to think with greater precision about what it means to translate passive revolution in relation to other times and places.

This is the task that I take up in Chapter 6, where I suggest how passive revolution provides potentially useful leverage into the South African crisis – but this requires an exercise of translation that includes incorporating insights from Fanon.

Notes

1. It is indeed the case that in his analysis of the Risorgimento (Italian national unification in 1860), Gramsci speaks of the role of Piedmont as 'one of the cases in which these groups have the function of "domination" without that of "leadership": dictatorship without hegemony' (1971: 105; Q15 §40). Yet, as Carlos Nelson Coutinho (2012: 179) reminds us in his analysis of Brazil, this does not mean that the state acting as a protagonist of passive revolution can do without some degree of consensus – 'otherwise it would have to resort to coercion and only coercion, which in the long run would simply prevent it from functioning'. More generally, as we shall see, hegemony for Gramsci is about the dialectical relations between coercion and consent, which can only be understood concretely. In addition, as we shall see in Chapter 6, as Gramsci extended passive revolution beyond the Risorgimento, hegemony featured as a central element of the analysis.

2. Thomas argues that far from working with abstracted categories of 'East' and 'West', Gramsci was drawing on insights from post-revolutionary Russia to reconstruct understandings of bourgeois class rule in Western Europe in relation to the theory and practice of a democratic proletarian hegemony that the 'last' Lenin was trying to set in place after the Civil War in 1921. The New Economic Policy, he argues, was not simply a retreat or a defensive measure. It represented a political and cultural revolution as much as an

economic programme, embodying 'an attempt at a practical application of the united front, or the attempt to build a class politics on a mass basis that confirmed the proletariat's capacity to transform the specificity of its allied social forces into a political power of a completely different type' (Thomas 2009a: 237). It was this possibility of democratic proletarian hegemonic politics that the Stalinist dictatorship decisively destroyed – and that, Thomas argues, Gramsci was seeking to recuperate in the *Prison Notebooks*.

3. This includes Buttigieg's translation into English and annotation of the first eight prison notebooks (Gramsci 1992, 1996, 2007) and Haug (1999, 2000, 2007, 2010). Ives and Lacorte (2010) make available important Italian scholarship. For an overview of the recent efflorescence of work on Gramsci, see Ekers and Loftus (2013).

4. According to Anderson, Gramsci's starting point is Machiavelli's image of the centaur, half-animal and half-human, from which Gramsci derives an explicit set of oppositions between force and consent, domination and hegemony, violence and civilisation (Anderson 1976a: 20).

5. '[H]egemony in civil society is necessarily comprehended in political society and overdetermined by it. There thus must be an attempt to forge "political hegemony" also *before* seizing state power or domination in political society – for, without such an attempt to transform leadership in civil society into a political hegemony or into nascent forms of a new political society, civil hegemony itself will be disaggregated and subordinated to the . . . existing political hegemony of the ruling class' (Thomas 2009a: 194; emphasis in original).

6. See Hart (2013: 302).

7. For Althusser, who coined the term, 'ideology "acts" or "functions" in such a way that it "recruits" subjects among the individuals . . . or "transforms" the individuals into subjects . . . by that very precise operation which I have called *interpellation* or hailing, and which can be imagined along the lines of the most commonplace everyday police (or other) hailing: "Hey, you there!"' (1971: 48; emphasis in original).

8. See Nash (1999) for documentation of these critiques.

9. SACP, Special Issue of *Bua Komanisi*, 2006, http://www.sacp.org.za/main.php?ID=2339, and ANC, 'Managing National Democratic Transformation', 2006, http://www.anc.org.za/ancdocs/misc/2006/anc_sacp.html.

10. SACP, 'Is the ANC Leading a National Democratic Revolution or Managing Capitalism?', 2006, http://www.sacp.org.za.

11. *Business Day*, 30 January 2008.

12. When I first broached the argument about the need for a deeper understanding of popular support for Zuma at an International Sociological

Association conference in Durban in July 2006, some of my independent left comrades labelled me a '100% Zuma girl' – a reference to a popular T-shirt bearing the image of Zuma and emblazoned with '100% Zulu boy' that many supporters wore to his rape trial.

13. See Hunter (2011).
14. Achille Mbembe, 'South Africa's Second Coming: The Nongqawuse Syndrome', 2006, http://www.opendemocracy.net/democracy-africa_ democracy/southafrica_succession_3649.jsp.
15. With 'common sense' here interpreted in Gramscian terms as *senso commune*, as noted earlier and discussed more fully in Chapter 6.
16. See also Dlamini (2011).
17. http://www.timeslive.co.za/opinion/commentary/2011/08/28/history-on-side-of-the-anc-youth-league.
18. Blade Nzimande, 'Proto-Fascist Tendency Emerging in ANC', 2009, http://www.politicsweb.co.za/politicsweb/view/politicsweb/en/page71646?oid =154300&sn=Detail&pid=71646.
19. http://www.sacp.org.za/docs/docs/2012/drafpol2012.pdf.
20. See http://www.dailymaverick.co.za/article/2011-06-16-jane-duncan-on-the-ever-increasing-menace-of-sas-security-cabal#.UdQUXhUaI5g, and the website of the Right2Know Campaign, http://www.r2k.org.za.
21. Jeremy Cronin, 'Whose Terrain?' *Umsebenzi Online* 9 (22), November 2010.
22. http://www.sacp.org.za/docs/sp/2012/sp0713.html.
23. Following Anderson (1976b), Nash defines Western Marxism as 'the tradition of Marxist thought which developed mainly in Western Europe – from Lukacs, Gramsci and Korsch in the 1920s through the Frankfurt School in the 1930s and 1940s to the work of Marcuse, Sartre and Althusser who in different registers, provided major impulses to the student and workers uprisings of the 1960s' (Nash 1999: 66).
24. See Legassick (2007) for a comprehensive critique.
25. Recent work on passive revolution includes Coutinho (2012); Morton (2007, 2010, 2011, 2013); Thomas (2006, 2009a, 2012); Tugal (2009); and a collection of articles in a special issue of *Capital and Class* (Vol. 34, No. 3, 2010). This issue contains an interesting debate in which Callinicos criticises Gramsci's stretching of the concept, along with a number of recent efforts to deploy it in different contexts. He expresses concern that 'what had originally been conceptualized as a particular path *to* capitalist domination – from above, gradually, and without violent rupture – comes to be understood by Gramsci as a principle means of *maintaining* capitalist domination in an epoch of wars and revolution' (2010: 492; emphasis in original). In response, Morton (2010) points out that Gramsci's extending

and reworking – or as Gramsci would have said 'translating' – the concept in relation to changing conditions is very much part of his historicist (or spatio-historical) method, and a strength rather than a weakness. I agree with Morton's insistence on the value of Gramsci's method, but I think it is also important to hold on to the core meaning of passive revolution as 'socio-political processes in which revolution-inducing strains are at once displaced and partially fulfilled', as Callinicos (2010: 498) puts it, while also attending closely to what it means to translate the concept into different times and places.

6

Through the Lens of Passive Revolution

The South African Crisis Revisited

> Dialectical thought has flourished always in the margins and interstices of society. It seeks to follow the movement of contradictions while the major social institutions are designed to resolve or obscure them. This mode of thought seeks out the hidden cracks in prevailing ideas and conjunctures, anticipates the unexpected, imagines a future vastly different from the present, and examines the potentialities of the present to seek a basis for its realisation. The dialectical tradition in South Africa has been no different from this. But the margins and interstices of South African political and intellectual life are under unprecedented pressure today, as ideas and activities are brought into line with the needs of the market (Nash 2009: 210).

IN THE PREFACE I described how the Marikana massacre erupted on 16 August 2012 just as I was drawing this book to a close, and compelled me to consider a longer lineage of debate around the protracted crisis in South Africa that goes back to Saul and Gelb's (1981, 1986) important intervention.

Marikana exemplified the deep, ongoing, organic crisis that capital's 'revolution within the revolution' sought to resolve.[1] When Peter Bruce of *Business Day* saw Marikana as 'the end of the beginning of the end' (Chapter 1), he was in effect acknowledging that the capacity of the ANC to manage the fallout of capital's revolution was running out of steam. This is not to absolve the ANC government from responsibility; but it is to insist that the persistent (if somewhat indirect) rule of capital and preservation of white privilege must be front and centre of any effort to comprehend the course of the transition.

While I agree with Bassett's (2008) contention in her revised analysis of Saul and Gelb's *The Crisis in South Africa* – namely that white corporate capital has been *too* successful – we also need to recognise that politics cannot be read off the structural conditions of accumulation, and that 'the anger of the poor can go in many directions'. As Gramsci reminded us, economic crises 'can simply create a terrain more favourable to the dissemination of certain modes of thought, and certain ways of posing and resolving questions involving the entire subsequent development of national life' (1971: 184; Q13 §17) – and, went on to note, 'The specific question of economic hardship or well-being as a cause of new historical realities is a partial aspect of the relations of force, at various levels' (1971: 184; Q13 §17).

What I have been driving at throughout this book is precisely the question of relations of force at various levels – an approach which, for Gramsci, was deeply spatial: 'international relations intertwine with these internal relations of nation-states, creating new, unique and historically concrete combinations', and 'this relation between international forces and national forces is further complicated by the existence within every State of several structurally diverse territorial sectors, with diverse relations of force at all levels' (1971: 182; Q13 §17).

In post-apartheid South Africa, a spatial understanding of the processes of de-nationalisation and re-nationalisation is crucial to grasping how hegemonic processes work in and through re-articulations of the nation and liberation. I have also demonstrated the contradictory ways that the hegemonic projects of successive ruling blocs have played into amplifying populist politics, and how we cannot understand these processes simply in terms of domination as opposed to hegemony and manipulated mindless masses. It is important here to recall Julius Malema's insistent deployment of symbols of liberation; and that even though the Zuma-ites seem to have squashed him, the issues and the popular anger that he tapped into are not going away any time soon. A closely related point concerns the inability of much of the left within and outside the ANC Alliance to engage with the proliferating expressions of popular discontent that I am calling 'movement beyond movements'. As argued at the end of Chapter 5, there is a dangerous impasse between the SACP's narrowly vanguardist and disciplinary articulations of nationalism, and the dismissal of nationalism by many on the independent left.

My task in this final chapter is to reflect on the prior chapters and their wider implications through the lens of passive revolution – and to make clear the theoretical and political stakes in thinking about de-nationalisation and re-nationalisation as the specific form of South Africa's passive revolution. The analysis unfolds in two steps: first considering how we need to rethink passive revolution in relation to present circumstances; and second using this revised understanding to bring key aspects of recent South African dynamics into sharper focus.

While Gramsci's analysis of passive revolution offers powerful insights, it is necessarily partial in understanding the forces at play in post-apartheid South Africa. Translating passive revolution in South Africa today turns importantly around the specificities of anti- and post-apartheid nationalisms, and their deep entanglements with racial oppression and racialised dispossession.[2] Here the complementarities between Fanon and Gramsci are essential. As mentioned in Chapter 1, Fanon did not just excoriate post-colonial bourgeois nationalism, he recognised anti- and post-colonial nationalisms as *both* essential *and* dangerous. It is in relation to this imperative for denaturalising nationalisms that the complementarities and convergences between Gramsci and Fanon are so important. They turn around Gramsci's elaboration of the philosophy of praxis, and its close affinities with Fanon's call for a new humanism distinctively different from that of liberalism.

Passive Revolution and Post-Colonial Nationalisms: Gramsci and Fanon

> So strikingly similar are Gramsci's and Fanon's idioms and programs – to say nothing of their supportive concepts – that I am tempted to call Gramsci a precocious Fanonian . . . Without a doubt, the conceptual supports of Fanon's vision of the national, the social and the revolutionary as cognate terms of a new political practice, have an elective affinity with Gramsci's philosophy of praxis and its political implications (Sekyi-Otu 1996: 118–19).

Let me begin with Gramsci. Three dimensions of his concept of passive revolution that emerged from his efforts to analyse fascism in Italy in the 1930s remain salient in South Africa today: (1) passive revolution as a profoundly spatio-historical concept that calls for what in *Disabling Globalization* I termed relational forms of comparison; (2) the deeply dialectical character of passive revolution; and (3) the close connections of passive revolution with philosophy of praxis.

Gramsci used passive revolution to refer both to concrete historical processes and as a comparative method.[3] To understand fascism in Italy in the 1920s and 1930s, Gramsci went back not only to the Risorgimento in 1860 but to the French revolution, and used passive revolution to produce new understandings of European history from the French to the Russian revolution in 1917, as well as reactions to the Russian revolution in the form of fascism in Italy and the New Deal in the US.[4] Elaborating what he meant by fascism as passive revolution, Gramsci pointed to far-reaching changes that were being introduced into the economic structure of Italy through corporative organisation, 'without however touching (or at least not going beyond the regulation and control of) individual and group appropriation of profit' (Gramsci 1971: 120; Q10I §9). From an ideological and political point of view, he argued, fascism creates expectation and hope among 'the great mass of urban and rural petit bourgeois. It thus reinforces the hegemonic system and the forces of military and civil coercion at the disposal of the traditional ruling classes' (1971: 120; Q10I §9).

At the same time Gramsci pointed to the danger of what he called historical defeatism in relation to passive revolution, 'since the whole way of posing the question may induce a belief in some kind of fatalism' (Gramsci 1971: 114; Q15 §62), endowing the bourgeoisie with impregnable power. Yet, he went on to insist, 'the concept remains a dialectical one – in other words, [it] presupposes, indeed postulates as necessary, a vigorous antithesis which can present intransigently all its potentialities for development' (1971: 114; Q15 §62). For Gramsci, passive revolution is not about an iron cage, but a criterion of interpretation requiring a dialectical understanding of contradictions and fragilities.[5]

The 'vigorous antithesis' refers not to 'counter-hegemony' and even less to 'cultural persuasion' as Anderson (1976a) alleges, but to philosophy of praxis. For Gramsci 'philosophy of praxis . . . must be a criticism of "common sense" [*senso commune* or that which is taken for granted], basing itself initially, however, on common sense in order to demonstrate that "everyone" is a philosopher and that it is not a question of introducing from scratch a scientific form of thought into everyone's individual life, but of renovating and making "critical" an already existing activity' (1971: 330–1; Q11 §12). For Gramsci, language and translation were crucial to the collective practices, processes and organisational forms through which 'common sense' can become more critical and coherent.

The imperative for spatio-historical translation underscores what is limited and necessarily partial about Gramsci's concept of passive revolution – namely that, while he was not operating with crude West/East dichotomies as argued in Chapter 5, his focus was on Europe in relation to the Russian revolution.[6] What is crucially missing from Gramsci's alternative history from the French to the Russian revolutions, is the Haitian revolution – that raises both the centrality of race and slavery in the making of the modern world, and the much wider spatio-historical ambit of passive revolution.[7]

More generally, any effort to translate passive revolution has to be situated within an understanding of the spatially uneven dynamics of global capitalism, and must be attentive to specificities as well as to interconnections; to the ongoing reverberations of colonial histories and changing forms of imperialism; and to the constitutive articulations of race, ethnicity, gender and sexuality with class and nationalisms.[8]

The Link with Fanon

Even though Fanon did not use the term passive revolution, his depiction of post-colonial predicaments in the third chapter of *The Wretched of the Earth* (1963, 2004) makes the connections between passive revolution, colonialism and post-colonial nationalisms clearly evident. Widely cited in South Africa today, this chapter delivers a scathing account of how the party 'which during the battle had drawn to itself the whole nation' becomes a means of private advancement of the national bourgeoisie. An 'authentic' national bourgeoisie ought to 'put itself to school with the people'; instead, the national bourgeoisie rapidly becomes 'the transmission line between the nation and capitalism . . . [becoming] quite content with the role of the Western bourgeoisie's business agent' (1963: 150–3). He refers as well to the 'intellectuals who on the eve of independence rallied to the party, now make it clear by their attitude that they gave their support with no other end in view than to secure their slices of the cake of independence', noting that the 'party is becoming a means of private advancement' (1963: 169–71). Fanon is also intent on laying out how forms of bourgeois comprador nationalism that come to predominate in the post-colonial period create the conditions among subaltern classes for the passage from nationalism to 'ultra-nationalism, to chauvinism, and finally to racism' (1963: 156). These and other denouncements of comprador bourgeois nationalism resonate powerfully in contemporary South Africa.

Yet much less attention has been given to Fanon's deeper analysis of anti- and post-colonial nationalisms: that they are *both* essential in the overthrow of colonial power, *and* dangerous in all the ways he lays out so vividly; and *also* that as Sekyi-Otu puts it, Fanon's calumny against the national bourgeoisie 'is not his last word on the matter' (1996: 172). Reflecting on Fanon specifically in relation to South Africa in the immediate post-apartheid period, Sekyi-Otu provides a powerfully illuminating reading of Fanon in relation to Gramsci that spells out most fully Fanon's call to work through and beyond nationalism to a new humanism – what I am calling denaturalising nationalism.

Passive revolution is, I suggest, a useful lens through which to bring this relatively neglected dimension of Fanon's work into sharper focus, and grasp the complementarities between Gramsci's philosophy of praxis and Fanon's efforts to point towards a new humanism in ways directly relevant to South Africa today. The similarities are remarkable.[9] Both Fanon and Gramsci were relentlessly focused on the processes through which subaltern classes might become active participants in the production of new forms of critical understanding and collective action; and both assigned a crucial role to intellectuals who are neither vanguards nor celebrants of subaltern wisdom, but engaged in mutual processes of transformation.

In addition, each defined the challenges of nationalism in relation to the specific forms of passive revolution and to internationalism. For Gramsci, the challenge posed by Italian fascism was how to forge a 'popular-national collective will' – not just an alliance between urban proletarians and peasants, but a *national* bond between subaltern classes alienated from one another by the sharp divide between northern and southern Italy bequeathed by the Risorgimento. Cultural and linguistic as well as economic, this divide 'was often felt, on both sides, as a *racial* difference' (Ahmad 2000: 134). Gramsci was also emphatic that, while 'the point of departure is "national" . . . the perspective is international and cannot be otherwise' (1971: 240; Q5 §127). Since 'it is in the concept of hegemony that those exigencies which are national in character are knotted together', he went on, 'a class that is international in character . . . has to "nationalise" itself in a certain sense' (1971: 241; Q5 §127).

In a move that extends beyond Gramsci, Fanon's emphasis on 'national consciousness' helps to underscore the specificity of anti-colonial nationalism as well as the international vision that they shared. In addition to embodying a critique of imperialism and racism, national consciousness for Fanon was a unifying force, essential to bridging rural-urban, racial, ethnic, regional and other divisions produced or reinforced by colonialism. In other words, national consciousness contains important elements of critical common sense forged in the struggle against colonialism – and that is why it cannot be bypassed in any effort to constitute collective forces capable of superseding post-colonial passive revolution:

> National claims, it is here and there stated, are a phase that humanity has left behind . . . We however consider that the mistake, which may have very serious consequences, lies in wishing to skip the national period . . . National consciousness, which is not nationalism, is the only thing that will give us an international dimension (Fanon 1963: 247).

Yet he also insisted that 'if nationalism is not made explicit, if it is not enriched and deepened by a very rapid transformation into a consciousness of social and political needs, in other words into humanism, it leads up a blind alley' (Fanon 1963: 204).

Coming back to the epigraph at the start of this section, let me expand briefly on Sekyi-Otu's point about the close affinity between Gramsci's philosophy of praxis and Fanon's vision of a new political practice. Philosophy of praxis for Gramsci was profoundly anti-metaphysical, and is usefully thought of as 'coherent, but non-systemic thinking which grasps the world through human activity . . . It is a thinking that indeed addresses the whole, but from below, with patient attention to particularity' (Haug 2000: 11–12). It is grounded as well in spatio-historical as opposed to abstracted understandings. In much the same way, Fanon refused deductive reasoning and 'scholastic abstraction' (Sekyi-Otu 1996: 119). He argued, for example, that in the course of anti-colonial struggle there emerges in practice 'a demystification of the nationalist rhetoric of an undifferentiated people' (1996: 119) as 'some members of the colonialist population prove to be closer, infinitely closer, to the nationalist struggle than certain native sons [*sic*] . . . and the racial and racist dimension is transcended on both sides' (Fanon 2004: 95). Yet, as Sekyi-Otu points out, 'this new reality, these new meanings, are not discrete events but social and semantic formations structurally related to "the old colonial reality" to colonial history' (1996: 119). Thus a key task in any effort to denaturalise nationalism is a relentless focus on 'the contradictions which were camouflaged by this reality' (Fanon 2004: 96) – in other words, a critical interrogation of the past.

A closely related parallel is the central importance that both Gramsci and Fanon accorded to language. For Fanon, as for Gramsci, the possibilities for a new humanism turned crucially around 'the generation of a common vocabulary of disputation and concerted action: universal understandings of contestable claims' (Sekyi-Otu 1996: 180). Trained as a linguist, Gramsci paid close attention to translation as well as to language. For him, 'Translation is the life itself of language and of thought, because it makes new fields of human activity visible and appropriable' (Tosel 2010: 283). Confronting questions of translation in his essay, 'This is the Voice of Algeria', on the changing uses of the radio in the 1950s, Fanon showed how French – the language of colonial coercion and alienation – was converted in practice through a collective process of translation 'to the service of a radically new "world of perception," a new universe of expression and action' (Sekyi-Otu 1996: 191).

Finally, Fanon and Gramsci were both closely attentive to the organisational forms that would enable the realisation of philosophy of praxis. In distinct although related ways, both recognised the need for mediators – for Gramsci organic intellectuals from within the ranks of subaltern classes in Italy; for Fanon dissident members of the national bourgeoisie in post-colonial Africa. Gramsci's metaphor in the *Prison Notebooks* of the 'modern prince' is often used to label him as a vanguardist, if not a closet Stalinist, seeking to reinstate a hierarchical communist party form. An alternative reading, consistent with his emphasis on language and translation, is that he envisaged the modern prince as 'the type of organisation that would allow for debates that need to happen, the points of disagreement, the composition of alliances and new perspectives' (Thomas 2012: 18). Sekyi-Otu 'give[s] Fanon's vision a Gramscian twist' by suggesting the figure of the modern griot, defined by 'transformative and radical democratic commitments . . . as opposed to the commemorative and conservative function of the traditional griot' (1996: 265, see also 203-4). In other words, both Fanon and Gramsci envisaged an ongoing process of democratic and dialectical pedagogy, in which the educator must herself be educated.

Translating Passive Revolution in South Africa Today

My task in this concluding section is to suggest the analytical and political stakes of rethinking the South African crisis through the lens of passive revolution. Following from the preceding discussion of Gramsci and Fanon, I focus on the three key dimensions of the concept of passive revolution – spatio-historical, dialectical and philosophy of praxis (Gramsci) or new humanism (Fanon) – and work through translating the concept in relation to contemporary South Africa. I will also suggest how passive revolution helps extend key arguments developed in *Disabling Globalization* into the present, and point to potentially productive directions for future work.

The Spatio-Historical and Comparative Dimensions of Passive Revolution

The South African transition in the early 1990s took place in the midst of the global triumph of increasingly financialised forms of neoliberal capitalism and liberal democracy, along with resurgent nationalisms in many regions of the world. Chapter 1 alluded to how the spatio-historical character of de-nationalisation and re-nationalisation, understood as the specific form of South Africa's passive revolution, enables us to think about South Africa in relation to the rest of the world as extreme but not exceptional – an argument that I now need to spell out more fully.

Over the course of the South African transition, the 'normal' workings of global political economy have generated conditions and crises across the world that increasingly resemble those in South Africa: widening inequalities, ongoing dispossession in many forms, and the generation of massive populations that are 'surplus' to the needs of capital. In his essay on 'Wageless Life', Michael Denning (2010: 81) insists that 'proletarian' is not 'a synonym for "wage labourer" but for dispossession, expropriation and radical dependence on the market'. The historical extent and depth of racialised dispossession makes South Africa extreme, but increasingly unexceptional in the face of ongoing – if not accelerating – dispossession elsewhere. At the same time, the corporate restructuring enabled by the transition and the spatially extraverted forms of accumulation under the aegis of the ANC government have ensured South Africa's position at the head of the pack in the global inequality stakes.

While South Africa is often described as the protest capital of the world, we are now witnessing escalating and massive protests across the globe – in Turkey, Brazil, Sweden, Egypt, Greece, and the list goes on. Calling attention to the promises and the dilemmas of these uprisings in a June 2013 article in the *London Review of Books*, Slavoj Zizek notes:

> [T]he US has consistently pursued a strategy of damage control in its foreign policy by re-channelling popular uprisings into acceptable parliamentary-capitalist forms: in South Africa after apartheid, in the Philippines after the fall of Marcos, in Indonesia after Suharto etc. This is where politics proper begins: the question is how to push further once the first, exciting wave of change is over, how to take the next step without succumbing to the 'totalitarian' temptation, how to move beyond Mandela without becoming Mugabe.[10]

While one might question the puppet-master role that Zizek assigns so exclusively to the US, what he is describing here can be seen as a series of passive revolutions that could well proliferate in the face of escalating popular anger around the world. Indeed, there have already been several recent efforts to analyse the aftermaths of the 2011 protests in Egypt and Tunisia in these terms.[11]

The problem, however, with the question of 'how to move beyond Mandela without becoming Mugabe' is who is to decide where 'politics proper' begins, and what form will it take. Clearly, there has been considerable movement beyond Mandela's brand of liberalism, but it has gone in different directions. A key implication of taking passive revolution seriously is that any political strategy to confront the brutalities of the present and construct a different future has to begin with actually existing practices and meanings in the arenas of everyday life, while also stretching out to forge relations and connections with forces at play elsewhere. Part of what is entailed here is the central importance of the 'local' – a key theme in *Disabling Globalization* to which I return below, reiterating the analytical and political importance of understanding place and the 'local' not as bounded units, but nodal points of interconnection in socially produced space (Chapter 1).

A closely related theme that connects directly with the spatio-historical dimension of passive revolution is the importance of relational forms of comparison – 'a strategy that differs fundamentally from one that deploys ideal types, or that posits different "cases" as local variants of a more general phenomenon. Instead of comparing pre-existing objects, events, places or identities, the focus is on how they are constituted in relation to one another through power-laden practices in the multiple, interconnected arenas of everyday life' (Hart 2006a: 996). In *Disabling Globalization* I used relational comparison (a) to show how links between South Africa and East Asia in the form of Taiwanese (and subsequently Chinese) investment in places like Newcastle and Ladysmith in the 1980s to 1990s dramatised the depth and extent of racialised dispossession in South Africa, and (b) to suggest delinking the powerfully resonant 'land question' from agriculture and individual restitution claims, and re-articulating it in terms of the moral and material imperatives for redistributive social change and livelihood guarantees in opposition to neoliberal capitalism.

As an inherently comparative concept, passive revolution opens the way for extending and elaborating this sort of strategy, and putting it to work in new ways. Morton, for example, suggests that what Philip McMichael (1991) called 'incorporated comparison' is directly relevant to a broader understanding of passive revolutions in different regions of the world in relation to one another.[12] Through this sort of framework, national processes of passive revolution can be understood as '*specific* instances of state transition that are internally related through the *general* world-historical conditions of uneven and combined development' (Morton 2007: 71; emphasis in original). Incorporated and relational methods of comparison share close affinities, most importantly an insistent focus on inter-connection.[13] Drawing on Lefebvre's conception of the production of space, relational comparison also directs our attention to the dialectical processes through which different regions of the world are produced in practice in relation to one another – an approach that could help extend passive revolution to encompass the Haitian revolution.

While strongly endorsing Morton's suggestion, I would add that any such project must *also* attend closely to questions of nationalism – and that Goswami's spatio-historical analysis of interconnected nationalisms outlined in Chapter 1 is powerfully salient to a comparative understanding of passive revolution in different regions of the world today. Even though she does not engage with passive revolution, her analysis builds directly on Lefebvre's (1991) understanding of the production of space, which is closely congruent with the work of Gramsci and Fanon. As we saw in Chapter 1, Goswami directs our attention to the coincidence of the period of high nationalism and high imperialism in the late nineteenth and early twentieth centuries (1870–1914), underscoring 'the synchron-icity of struggles to establish an internally homogeneous, sovereign space of nationness in a number of imperial-national . . . and colonial/semi-colonial contexts' (2002: 788). This was also the period that Gramsci identified as a Europe-wide phase of passive revolution following the defeat of the Paris Commune in 1871, closely linked to the era of imperialism, when the 'internal and international organisational relations of the State become more complex and massive' (Gramsci 1971: 243; Q13 §7). Goswami extends this analysis by insisting that, for all their 'local' specificity, the simultaneity of imperial, nationalist and anti-colonial struggles can only be understood in relation to one another in terms of their location within a single, increasingly interdependent and hier-archically organised global political economy.

Although south/ern Africa does not form part of Goswami's analysis, Chapter 1 suggests how attention to the region contributes to this spatio-historical approach to understanding nationalisms. Such an approach is essential to any Fanonian project of working through and beyond post-apartheid nationalisms in relation to political economy. In addition, as part of any project to denaturalise nationalisms, a sustained comparative understanding of South Africa's contemporary passive revolution in relation to those in other regions of the world needs to be grounded in this spatio-historical frame.

The Political Stakes of Passive Revolution

Before suggesting the political stakes of passive revolution in South Africa today, let me briefly reprise the arguments of this book, bearing in mind Gramsci's injunction to use passive revolution as 'a criterion of interpretation' that requires a dialectical under-standing of contradictions and fragilities. I use dialectics here in the sense outlined by Nash (2009) in the epigraph at the start of this chapter, an interpretation that is closely related to Fanon's and Gramsci's conceptions of dialectics. As mentioned in Chapter 1, I have also deployed what Lefebvre (1991) called a 'regressive-progressive' method, starting in the present and rethinking the past – in this case the transition from apartheid – in relation to the present, drawing on understandings of the production of space (or space-time).[14]

Chapter 2 started with the most readily available contemporary dynamics, and a search for key relations and connections in the back-and-forth processes between mounting expressions of popular discontent, official attempts to contain them and escalating conflict within the ANC Alliance. Chapter 3 pointed to local government as the key site of contradictions, tracing through in detail how official efforts to manage indigence play into and intensify popular discontent. Chapter 4 argued that, to understand fully the local dynamics that gathered force over the decade of the 2000s, we need to go back and rethink the transition from apartheid in the 1990s in terms of simultaneous practices and processes of de-nationalisation and re-nationalisation. Chapter 5 returned to the processes described in Chapter 2, drawing on the conflictual inter-relations between de-nationalisation and re-nationalisation to trace, explain and analyse the unravelling of hegemony and the proliferation of populist politics.

This approach has entailed remaining close to a Gramscian analysis of hegemony in terms of civil/political society and the integral state; but also attending to Fanonian and feminist concerns with the entanglements of race and nationalism, and their articulation with gender and sexuality. In the process I have tried to highlight the contradictions of post-apartheid passive revolution by following the interconnected dynamics of (a) the reliance of the post-apartheid state (in the sense of political society) on increasingly narrow and disciplinary articulations of race and nationalism, combined with (b) the ongoing generation of inequality and wageless life that undermine the ethico-political force of these articulations, together with (c) the inherently contradictory techno-politics of managing 'surplus' populations that play out primarily in the realm of local government but are deeply entangled with (a) and (b).

What then are the political stakes in trying, in a necessarily partial way, to understand key dynamics in post-apartheid South Africa through the lens of passive revolution? Most immediately, as mentioned at the start of this chapter, is the impossibility of reading politics directly off the structural conditions of capital accumulation. From one perspective South Africa can indeed be seen as a geographical locus in which the internal contradictions of global capital accumulation are manifest in an extreme form. Yet exposing the systemic qualities and commonalities of the depredations of global capitalism is insufficient to enable 'local particularities' to cohere and 'be articulated as a general oppositional interest', I argued in *Disabling Globalization* (2002a: 298-9) – not least because this insistence on transcending such 'particularities' abstracts from race, ethnicity, gender and other dimensions of difference that operate as constitutive forces in class processes. A key element of this argument was the historical depth and extent of racialised dispossession as the defining feature of South African political economy, and how histories, memories and meanings of colonial and apartheid dispossessions continue to operate as ongoing processes. A closely related claim was the importance of the local state as a key terrain for political action, with the 'local' understood neither as a bounded unit nor a 'space of places' as opposed to a 'space of flows' – but rather in terms of the production of space, in which 'place' and the 'local' are always understood in terms of relations and connections to that which lies 'beyond'.[15]

My turn to the concept of passive revolution in the present book has been driven by the imperative to take seriously nationalism and populism, and finding in Gramsci and Fanon the most useful resources for doing so. In thinking through the political stakes of translating their insights in contemporary South Africa, let me start with the remarkably similar things they had to say about 'spontaneity' – the simultaneous necessity and inadequacy of spontaneous movements, and the imperative for deeper, trans- formative forms of collective organisation.[16] 'Neglecting, or worse still despising, so-called "spontaneous" movements . . . may often have extremely serious consequences', Gramsci warned, going on to observe that '[i]t is almost always the case that a "spontaneous" movement of the subaltern classes is accompanied by a reactionary movement of the right-wing of the dominant class, for concomitant reasons' (1971: 199; Q3 §48). Fanon devoted a chapter to the 'Grandeur and Weaknesses of Spontaneity' during the liberation struggle noting that 'this impetuous spontaneity, which is intent on rapidly settling its score with the colonial system, is destined to fail as a doctrine' (2004: 85), and returned to the theme in the chapter on post-colonial predicaments.

Although neither Gramsci nor Fanon used the language of populism, their work speaks directly to contemporary debates that, as we have seen, have come to be dominated by Laclau (2005). Laclau's key claims in *On Populist Reason* start out with a critique of the 'manipulated mindless masses' model, but end up reiterating it (Hart 2013). As such they are sharply at odds not only with a Gramscian approach, but a Fanonian one as well. In Chapter 5, I used some of Laclau's (1977) arguments about bourgeois populism to analyse developments in South Africa over the past decade or so, but also alluded to the limits of his theory of socialist populism. According to this theory, the challenge confronting subaltern classes is to develop 'popular interpellations' antagonistic to the dominant ideology to the point that they cannot be assimilated or co-opted by the existing power bloc. Some time ago Nicos Mouzelis called attention to Laclau's failure to attend to the practices and power relations through which such interpellations might take place, pointing to a 'well-justified suspicion of movements where it is the leader . . . from whom emanates the main integrative and directive force' – a situation, he went on to note, that is very prevalent and frequently leads to adventurist tendencies (1978: 52).

By emphasising philosophy of praxis and a new humanism, Gramsci and Fanon encompass but go far beyond this critique. Fanon's comments are worth recalling:

> We must not cultivate the spirit of the exceptional or look for the hero, another form of leader . . . [P]olitical education means opening up the mind, awakening the mind, and introducing it to the world. It is as Césaire said "To invent the souls of men." To

politicize the masses is not and cannot be to make a political speech. It means driving home to the masses that everything depends on them, that if we stagnate the fault is theirs, and that if we progress, they too are responsible, that there is no demiurge, no illustrious man taking responsibility for everything, but that the demiurge is the people and the magic lies in their hands alone (Fanon 2004: 137–8).

In thinking about what this might mean in South Africa today, one key imperative is for critical interrogations of the past in relation to the present – not just by professional historians and other researchers, but also as part of collective practices and processes in the realms of everyday life, which is why the 'local' remains a key site of political practice and organisation. As Jacob Dlamini put it in his eloquent portrayal of everyday life in Katlehong township during the apartheid era, black South Africans were present at their making as citizens, and '[f]reedom was not sent . . . in a gift box from Lusaka' (2009: 13).[17] Recall here, too, Nash's (1999: 75) point about how the ANC Alliance relies heavily on invocations of symbols, sacrifices and heroes – and how this is 'a struggle only for the recovery of the past, never for its critical interrogation; it seeks inspiration, and never self-knowledge' (Chapter 5).

Even when heroic figures from the past are part of revisionist local histories, situating them within the realms of everyday life can enable new understandings of the past in relation to the present. Let me suggest here an example from my work in Ladysmith. In the late 1990s I discovered that some elderly people had been deeply influenced by the presence in Ladysmith from 1953–55 of Govan Mbeki, affectionately known as 'Oom [uncle] Gov'.[18] There was a strong oppositional political culture in the town, but 'ordinary', 'uneducated' people felt excluded until Mbeki arrived. From their accounts and from Govan Mbeki, whom I met several times before his death in 2001, he taught at the high school in Steadville, but set up a dancing school in the afternoons to divert the attention of apartheid authorities, enabling him to slip away and engage with workers in the mines and factories.[19] In the late 1990s in Ladysmith there still remained vivid local memories of 'Oom Gov's university' – memories, in other words, of what it meant to be treated as serious intellectuals; and in our conversations Mbeki gave examples of reciprocal processes of learning. Mbeki was not the lone organic intellectual; he was working closely with a group of Natal Indian Congress activists in the town.

In addition to exemplifying what Gramsci and Fanon meant by philosophy of praxis, Oom Gov's activities enable a further interrogation of the past.[20] This was the period leading up to the Freedom Charter in 1955, which entailed widespread consultation among subaltern classes of their visions for a different South Africa – and it was this process in which Mbeki was engaged in and around Ladysmith. Under the slogan 'Let us Speak Freedom', it produced thousands of slips of paper from which the Freedom Charter emerged through a process described by Rusty Bernstein (1999: 145–62). The Freedom Charter has, of course, attained legendary status, but is also the target of critique for its populist character, and more recently the butt of jokes about how it is being violated. But what Govan Mbeki was doing in Ladysmith illustrates the difference between a reified 'object', and the practices and process through which it came into being. It suggests as well the potentially radical implications of a co-ordinated process of popular consultation. The process that led up to the Congress of the People and the Freedom Charter underlines how the democratic practices in place in the 1950s gave way to vanguardism in the liberation movement from the 1960s with the turn to armed struggle, as Rusty Bernstein observed in a letter to John Saul the year before his death in 2002.[21]

It is, of course, the case that Govan Mbeki was one of the key figures in the turn to armed struggle, and was incarcerated on Robben Island for twenty-three years and four months. Colin Bundy cites an interview that Bridget Thompson conducted with Mbeki for her film *Heart and Stone*, in which she asked him about his participation in educational programmes on Robben Island: 'You know, it was such a pleasure . . . We prepared a document, it gets circulated . . . At some stage you get a feedback, somebody is posing questions . . . someone is not satisfied, and he would write back wanting a further explanation . . . It was thrilling' (Bundy 2012: 151). It was also philosophy of praxis in action.

Coda

> Unhappy is the land that needs a hero.
> [*Unglücklich das Land, das Helden nötig hat.*]
> Bertolt Brecht, Life of Galileo (1939)

As I draw this book to a close in July 2013, Nelson Mandela lies mortally ill in hospital and Julius Malema has arisen phoenix-like from the political ashes. On 11 July he launched a new political party, the Economic Freedom Fighters, calling for expropriation without compensation of white-owned land and nationalisation of the mines – and asking as well why Mandela was not being treated in a public hospital. Malema and his (all-male) lieutenants were decked out in stylish red berets reminiscent of the headgear worn by Thomas Sankara, the radical president of Burkina Faso who was assassinated in 1987. Sankara sold off the fleet of Mercedes-Benzes used to transport government officials and replaced them with the cheapest cars available; Malema in contrast 'was whisked away [from the launch] in a new model BMW 7-Series, a car famously called "a tool of the trade" by one of Malema's fiercest critics, Minister Blade Nzimande'.[22]

What becomes of Malema's professed radical turn remains of course to be seen. Throughout this book, though, I have tried to illuminate the deeper processes that have created the conditions for a populist turn of this sort. I have also refrained thus far from using what is probably the most widely cited sentence from Gramsci in South Africa today, but can do so no longer: 'The crisis consists precisely in the fact that the old is dying and the new cannot be born; in this interregnum a great variety of morbid symptoms appear' (1971: 276; Q3 §34). It is important, though, to attend to the sentence that follows: 'N.B. this paragraph should be completed by some observations which I made on the so-called "problem of the younger generation" – a problem caused by "crisis of authority" of the old generations in power and the failure of hegemony.' He was, of course, speaking here of Italy's passive revolution and the rise of fascism.

Notes

1. Gramsci argued that 'in studying a structure, it is necessary to distinguish organic movements (relatively permanent) from movements which may be termed "conjunctural" (and which appear as occasional, immediate, almost accidental)' (1971: 177; Q13 §17).

2. In his book *Nationalist Thought and the Colonial World*, Partha Chatterjee (1986: 50) emphatically declared 'passive revolution is *the* general form of the transition from colonial to post-colonial national states in the 20th century'. For reasons that I will spell out in a forthcoming paper, Chatterjee's analysis is quite limited. Goswami (2004: 21–6) delivers a severe critique of Chatterjee's theory of post-colonial nationalism, although she does not take on the question of passive revolution in relation to anti- and post-colonial nationalisms.

3. See Morton (2007, 2010, 2011) for useful elaborations of the spatio-historical and comparative dimensions of passive revolution, and their relationship to concepts of combined and uneven development.

4. See Thomas (2006) for a useful discussion of how Gramsci extended and revised the concept of passive revolution as part of a critical engagement with anodyne narratives of European history by Benedetto Croce, the enormously influential liberal philosopher-historian whom Gramsci regarded as the intellectual par excellence of Italy's passive revolution.

5. In the same notebook, Gramsci laid out what he meant by the concept of passive revolution as 'a criterion of interpretation'. Referring to Marx's Preface to *A Contribution to the Critique of Political Economy*, he argued that '[t]he concept of "passive revolution" must be rigorously derived from the two fundamental principles of political science: 1. That no social formation disappears as long as the productive forces which have developed within it still find room for further forward movement; 2. That a society does not set itself tasks for whose solution the necessary conditions have not been incubated, etc. It goes without saying that these principles must first be

developed critically in all their implications, and purged of every residue of mechanism and fatalism. They must therefore be referred back to the description of the three fundamental moments into which a "situation" or an equilibrium of forces can be distinguished, with the greatest possible stress on the second moment (equilibrium of political forces), and especially on the third moment (politico-military equilibrium)' (1971: 106–7; Q15 §17). The reference here is to 'Analysis of Situations: Relations of Force' (1971: 175–85; Q13 §17), which is clearly part of his analysis of passive revolution.

6. Adam Morton (2007: 70–2) defends Gramsci against charges of Euro-centrism, pointing out that his spatio-historical method is at odds with diffusionist understandings and that he was sharply aware of imperialism – which, indeed, formed part of his analysis of a new and intense phase of passive revolution in Europe following the defeat of the Paris Commune in 1871.

7. Kipfer and Hart (2013: 355); this point was originally suggested by Ari Sitas. Susan Buck-Morss' book *Hegel, Haiti, and Universal History* (2009) provides some provocative pointers. The classic reference is C.L.R. James' *The Black Jacobins* ([1938] 1989).

8. Lefebvre's relational conception of the production of space is of great importance here, even though his own work is limited in terms of colonisation and difference. See Kipfer and Hart (2013: 333–4) for a summary of this argument.

9. See Sekyi-Otu (1996: 171–2) for a discussion of the similarities between Fanon's open conception of dialectics and that of Gramsci, as well as how they are both different from Hegel. On the closely related spatio-historical dimensions in the work of Fanon, Gramsci and Lefebvre, see Kipfer (2007, 2011, 2013).

10. http://www.lrb.co.uk/2013/06/28/slavoj-zizek/trouble-in-paradise.

11. See for example articles and interviews with Cihan Tugal on Egypt, http://www.jadaliyya.com/pages/index/6095/egypts-emergent-passive-revolution; and Turkey, http://www.todayszaman.com/newsDetail_get NewsById.action?newsId=236197.

12. McMichael (1990: 391) explains incorporated comparison as an 'alternative to a preconceived concrete totality in which parts are subordinated to the whole . . . [From the perspective of incorporated comparison] totality is a conceptual *procedure*, rather than an empirical or conceptual premise . . . in which the whole is discovered through analysis of the mutual conditioning of the parts.' This approach is, as McMichael observes, closely related to 'Marx's historical method of developing concrete concepts in which a social

category is conceptualized as "a rich totality of many determinations and relations"' (1990: 391).

13. Philip McMichael and I are planning an article that compares incorporated and relational comparison.

14. In *Dance of the Dialectic* (2003: 157), Bertell Ollman provides a closely related exposition of this sort of dialectical method, which he summarises as falling into six successive moments: 'There is an ontological one, having to do with what the world really is (an infinite number of mutually dependent processes – with no clear or fixed boundaries – that coalesce to form a loosely structured whole or totality). There is the epistemological moment that deals with how to organize our thinking to understand such a world . . . There is the moment of inquiry (where, based on an assumption of internal relations between all parts, one uses the categories that convey these patterns along with a set of priorities derived from Marx's theories as aids to investigation). There is the moment of intellectual reconstruction or self clarification (where one puts together the results of such research for oneself). This is followed by the moment of exposition (where, using a strategy that takes account of how others think and what they know, one tries to explain this dialectical grasp of "the facts" to a particular audience. And, finally, there is the moment of praxis (where, based on whatever clarification has been reached, one consciously acts in the world, changing and testing it and deepening one's understanding of it at the same time).'

15. The recent debate between Bond (2011) and Pithouse (2012) over the 'local' makes clear that it remains a live issue.

16. See Gramsci 'Spontaneity and Conscious Leadership' (1971: 196–200; Q3 §48) and Fanon ([1963] 2004: Chapter 2).

17. Another important example of this sort of history is *Apartheid Remains*, the forthcoming book by Sharad Chari on Wentworth and Merebank townships in Durban.

18. See Hart (2002a): 83–5 and 97–8; see also Colin Bundy's biography of Mbeki (2012).

19. Here is an excerpt from an article I published in the *Sunday Independent* of 1 October 2000 entitled 'Lessons for Local Government from Oom Gov's University': 'Soon after arriving in Ladysmith [in 1953], Mbeki formed a close alliance with Achmad Sader, a medical doctor and NIC (Natal Indian Congress) activist. Sader had studied in London in the late 1940s where he met Krishna Menon and other leading figures in the Indian liberation movement. When Mbeki arrived in Ladysmith, Sader was working closely with Kallie, another NIC activist who ran a printing press on Murchison Street. It was there that the three of them planned strategies and printed

pamphlets. Much of their energy was directed towards organizing for the 1955 Congress of the People in Kliptown in 1955: "We went to the people asking them what do they want? We used to go to the coal mines to take demands from the people. Often we first had to come to agreement with the *ndunas* [headmen]". In communities around Ladysmith, one of the key concerns was land – in particular, the prospect of forced removals that were looming at the time: "These people were being removed to make way for occupation by white farmers. It was tears from families who had lived there for a long time – people who had bought the land with their own money. It was being taken away from them for no reason. At Driefontein I also met the leaders – they were being removed. We talked. The question is what can we do, what can we do? They are being shifted." In fact, Govan Mbeki did a great deal to enable resistance to removals. Participants in his regular meetings in and around Ladysmith tell of how he helped them to understand how "land, people, and politics go together" and how struggles to oppose forced removals were closely linked with struggles over wages and working conditions, as well as with opposition to injustices that people experienced in other parts of their lives.'

20. For a vivid account of philosophy of praxis, both in the past in Inanda township in Durban and in terms of its potentials in relation to nature, see Loftus (2012: Chapter 4).

21. See http://www.transformation.ukzn.ac.za/index.php/transformation/article/.../788?.

22. http://www.timeslive.co.za/thetimes/2013/07/12/juju-puts-his-hat-in-the-ring.

Select Bibliography

Adelzadeh, Asghar and Vishnu Padayachee. 1994. 'The RDP White Paper: Reconstruction of a Development Vision.' *Transformation: Critical Perspectives on Southern Africa* 25: 1–18.

Ahmad, Aijaz. 2000. *Lineages of the Present: Ideology and Politics in Contemporary South Asia*. New York: Verso.

Alexander, Neville. 1985. *Sow the Wind: Contemporary Speeches*. Johannesburg: Skotaville.

———. 2002. *An Ordinary Country: Issues in Transition from Apartheid to Democracy in South Africa*. Oxford: Berghahn Books.

———. 2010. 'South Africa: An Unfinished Revolution?' Strini Moodley Annual Memorial Lecture, University of KwaZulu-Natal, 13 May.

———. 2012. '100 Years of the African National Congress'. http://www.sahistory. org.za/archive/100-years-african-national-congress-neville-alexander.

Alexander, Peter. 2010. 'Rebellion of the Poor: South Africa's Service Delivery Protests – A Preliminary Analysis'. *Review of African Political Economy* 37 (123) (March): 25–40.

Alexander, Peter, Thapelo Lekgowa, Botsang Mmope, Luke Sinwell and Bongani Xezwi. 2013. *Marikana: A View from the Mountain and a Case to Answer*. Johannesburg: Jacana Media.

Althusser, Louis. 1971. *Lenin and History*. London: New Left.

Anderson, Benedict R. O'G. [1983] 1991. *Imagined Communities: Reflections on the Origin and Spread of Nationalism*. London: Verso.

Anderson, Perry. 1976a. 'The Antinomies of Antonio Gramsci'. *New Left Review* 1 (100): 5–78.

———. 1976b. *Considerations on Western Marxism*. New York: Verso.

Ashman, Samantha, Ben Fine and Susan Newman. 2010. 'The Crisis in South Africa: Neoliberalism, Financialization and Uneven and Combined Development'. In *Socialist Register 2011: The Crisis This Time*, edited by Leo Panitch, Greg Albo and Vivek Chibber, 174–95. London: The Merlin Press.

———. 2011. 'Amnesty International? The Nature, Scale and Impact of Capital Flight from South Africa'. *Journal of Southern African Studies* 37 (1): 7–25.

Ballard, Richard, Adam Habib and Imraan Valodia (eds). 2006. *Voices of Protest: Social Movements in Post-Apartheid South Africa*. Pietermaritzburg: University of KwaZulu-Natal Press.

Barchiesi, Franco. 2011. *Precarious Liberation: Workers, the State, and Contested Social Citizenship in Postapartheid South Africa*. Albany: State University of New York Press.

Barry, Andrew, Thomas Osborne and Nikolas Rose (eds). 1996. *Foucault and Political Reason: Liberalism, Neo-Liberalism, and Rationalities of Government*. 1st ed. Chicago: University of Chicago Press.

Bassett, Carolyn. 2008. 'South Africa: Revisiting Capital's "Formative Action"'. *Review of African Political Economy* 35 (116): 185–202.

Benit-Gbaffou, Claire. 2008. 'Local Councillors: Scapegoats for a Dysfunctional Participatory Democratic System? Lessons from Practices of Local Democracy in Johannesburg'. *Critical Dialogue: Public Participation in Review* 4 (1): 26–33.

Bernstein, Henry. 1998. 'Social Change in the South African Countryside? Land and Production, Poverty and Power'. *Journal of Peasant Studies* 25: 1–32.

Bernstein, Rusty. 1999. *Memory Against Forgetting*. London: Viking.

Bhabha, Homi K. (ed.). 1990. *Nation and Narration*. 1st ed. London: Routledge.

Bond, Patrick. 2000. *Elite Transition: From Apartheid to Neoliberalism in South Africa*. 1st ed. London: Pluto Press.

———. 2004. *Talk Left, Walk Right: South Africa's Frustrated Global Reforms*. Pietermaritzburg: University of KwaZulu-Natal Press.

———. 2005. *Elite Transition: From Apartheid to Neoliberalism in South Africa*. 2nd ed. Pietermaritzburg: University of KwaZulu-Natal Press.

———. 2011. 'What is Radical in Neoliberal-Nationalist South Africa?' *Review of Radical Political Economics* 43 (3): 354–60.

———. 2012. 'South African People Power Since the Mid-1980s: Two Steps Forward, One Back'. *Third World Quarterly* 33 (2): 243–64.

Bond, Patrick and Jackie Dugard. 2008. 'The Case of Johannesburg Water: What Really Happened at the Pre-Paid Parish Pump'. *Law, Democracy and Development* 12 (1): 1–28.

Booysen, Susan. 2007. 'With the Ballot and the Brick: The Politics of Attaining Service Delivery'. *Progress in Development Studies* 7 (1): 21–32.

Breckenridge, Keith. 2005. 'The Biometric State: The Promise and Peril of Digital Government in the New South Africa'. *Journal of Southern African Studies* 31 (2): 267–82.

Buck-Morss, Susan. 2009. *Hegel, Haiti, and Universal History*. Pittsburgh: University of Pittsburgh Press.

Buhlungu, Sakhela. 2002. 'From "Madiba Magic" to "Mbeki Logic": Mbeki and the ANC's Trade Union Allies'. In *Thabo Mbeki's World*, edited by Sean Jacobs and Richard Calland, 179–200. Pietermaritzburg: University of Natal Press.

Bundy, Colin. 2012. *Govan Mbeki*. Johannesburg: Jacana Media.

Butler, Anthony. 2009. *Contemporary South Africa*. 2nd ed. Basingstoke: Palgrave Macmillan.

Centre for Development and Enterprise (CDE). 1998. *Response to the White Paper on Local Government*. Johannesburg: Centre for Development and Enterprise.

Callinicos, Alex. 2010. 'The Limits of Passive Revolution'. *Capital and Class* 34 (3): 491–507.

Cameron, Robert. 2006. 'Local Government Boundary Reorganisation'. In *Democracy and Delivery: Urban Policy in South Africa*, edited by Udesh Pillay, Richard Tomlinson and Jacques du Toit, 76–106. Cape Town: HSRC Press.

Chabane, Neo, Andrea Goldstein and Simon Roberts. 2006. 'The Changing Face and Strategies of Big Business in South Africa: More than a Decade of Political Democracy'. *Industrial and Corporate Change* 15 (3): 549–77.

Chari, Sharad. 2010. 'State Racism and Biopolitical Struggle: The Evasive Commons in Twentieth-Century Durban, South Africa'. *Radical History Review* 108: 73–90.

Chatterjee, Partha. 1986. *Nationalist Thought and the Colonial World: The Derivative Discourse?* London: Zed Books.

———. 1993. *The Nation and its Fragments: Colonial and Postcolonial Histories*. Princeton: Princeton University Press.

———. 2004. *The Politics of the Governed: Reflections on Popular Politics in Most of the World*. New York: Columbia University Press.

———. 2008. 'Democracy and Economic Transformation in India'. *Economic & Political Weekly* 43 (16) (19 April): 53–62.

———. 2012. 'Gramsci in the Twenty-First Century'. In *The Postcolonial Gramsci*, edited by Neelam Srivastava and Baidik Bhattacharya, 119–36. New York: Routledge.

Chipkin, Ivor. 2004. 'Nationalism As Such: Violence during South Africa's Political Transition'. *Public Culture* 16 (2): 315–35.

———. 2007. *Do South Africans Exist? Nationalism, Democracy and the Identity of 'the People'*. 1st ed. Johannesburg: Wits University Press.

Comaroff, Jean and John L. Comaroff. 2011. *Theory from the South: Or, How Euro-America is Evolving Toward Africa*. Boulder: Paradigm Publishers.

Cottle, Eddie (ed.). 2011. *South Africa's World Cup: A Legacy for Whom?* Pietermaritzburg: University of KwaZulu-Natal Press.

Cottle, Simon and Libby Lester (eds). 2011. *Transnational Protests and the Media*. 1st ed. New York: Peter Lang Publishing Inc.

Coutinho, Carlos Nelson. 2012. *Gramsci's Political Thought*. Leiden: Brill.

Crankshaw, Owen. 1996. *Race, Class and the Changing Division of Labour under Apartheid*. London and New York: Routledge.

Cronin, Jeremy. 2001. Interview by Helena Sheehan. http://webpages.dcu.ie/~sheehanh/za/cronin-aah01.htm.

——. 2002a. Interview by Helena Sheehan. http://webpages.dcu.ie/~sheehanh/za/cronin02.htm.

——. 2002b. 'Post-Apartheid South Africa: Reply to John S. Saul'. *Monthly Review* 54 (7).

——. 2010. 'Whose Terrain?' *Umsebenzi Online* 9 (22) (17 November).

Crush, Jonathan. 1999a. 'Fortress South Africa and the Deconstruction of the Apartheid Migration Regime'. *Geoforum* 30: 1–11.

——. 1999b. 'The Discourse and Dimensions of Irregularity in Post-Apartheid South Africa'. *International Migration* 37 (1): 125–51.

Crush, Jonathan and Belinda Dodson. 2007. 'Another Lost Decade: The Failures of South Africa's Post-Apartheid Migration Policy'. *Journal of Economic and Social Geography* 98 (4) (September): 436–54.

Denning, Michael. 2010. 'Wageless Life'. *New Left Review* 66 (December): 79–97.

Desai, Ashwin. 2002. *We are the Poors: Community Struggles in Post-Apartheid South Africa*. New York: Monthly Review Press.

——. 2003. 'Neoliberalism and Resistance in South Africa'. *Monthly Review* 54 (8).

Dlamini, Jacob. 2009. *Native Nostalgia*. Johannesburg: Jacana Media.

——. 2011. 'Voortrekker'. In *The Smoke that Calls: Insurgent Citizenship, Collective Violence and the Struggle for a Place in the New South Africa*, edited by Karl von Holdt, Malose Langa, Sepetla Molapo, Nomfundo Mogapi, Kindiza Ngubeni, Jacob Dlamini and Adéle Kristen, 33–44. Johannesburg: Centre for the Study of Violence and Reconciliation and Society, Work and Development Institute.

Du Toit, Andries and David Neves. 2007. 'In Search of South Africa's Second Economy'. Special issue of *Africanus* 37 (2): 129–55.

Edigheji, Omano. 2005. 'A Democratic Developmental State in Africa?' Research Report 105 (May), Centre for Policy Studies, Johannesburg.

Ekers, Michael and Alex Loftus. 2013. 'Gramsci: Space, Nature, Politics'. In *Gramsci: Space, Nature, Politics*, edited by Michael Ekers, Gillian Hart, Stefan Kipfer and Alex Loftus, 15–43. Oxford: Wiley-Blackwell.

Ellis, Stephen. 2012. *External Mission: The ANC in Exile, 1960–1990*. London: C. Hurst & Co. Publishers Ltd.

Esterhuyse, Willie. 2012. *Endgame: Secret Talks and the End of Apartheid*. Cape Town: Tafelberg.

Fakier, Khayaat and Jacklyn Cock. 2009. 'A Gendered Analysis of the Crisis of Social Reproduction in Contemporary South Africa.' *International Feminist Journal of Politics* 11 (3): 353–71.

Fanon, Frantz. 1963. *The Wretched of the Earth*. Translated by Constance Farrington. New York: Grove Press.

——. 2004. *The Wretched of the Earth*. Translated by Richard Philcox. New York: Grove Press.

Fine, Ben. 2008. 'The Minerals-Energy Complex is Dead: Long Live the MEC?' http://eprints.soas.ac.uk/5617/.

———. 2010. 'Can South Africa be a Developmental State?'. In *Constructing a Democracratic Developmental State in South Africa*, edited by Omano Edigheji, 169–82. Cape Town: Human Sciences Research Council.

Fine, Ben and Vishnu Padayachee. 2000. 'A Sustainable Growth Path?' In *South African Review* 8, edited by Steven Friedman. Johannesburg: Ravan Press.

Fine, Ben and Zavareh Rustomjee. 1996. *The Political Economy of South Africa: From Minerals-Energy Complex to Industrialisation*. Boulder: Westview Press.

First, Ruth. 1978. 'After Soweto'. *Review of African Political Economy* 5 (11): 93–100.

Forde, Fiona. 2011. *An Inconvenient Youth: Julius Malema and the 'New' ANC*. Johannesburg: Picador Africa.

Foucault, Michel. 2008. *The Birth of Biopolitics: Lectures at the College de France, 1977–78*. New York: Palgrave Macmillan.

Friedman, Steven. 2009. 'An Accidental Advance? South Africa's 2009 Elections'. *Journal of Democracy* 20 (4): 108–22.

Gelb, Stephen (ed.). 1991. *South Africa's Economic Crisis*. Cape Town: David Philip.

Gellner, Ernest. [1983] 2009. *Nations and Nationalism*. 2nd ed. Ithaca: Cornell University Press.

Gentle, Leonard. 2002. 'Social Movements in South Africa: Challenges to Organised Labour and Opportunities for Renewal'. *South African Labour Bulletin* 26: 16–19.

Gevisser, Mark. 2007. *Thabo Mbeki: The Dream Deferred*. Johannesburg: Jonathan Ball.

Gibson, Nigel. 2011a. *Fanonian Practices in South Africa: From Steve Biko to Abahlali baseMjondolo*. Basingstoke: Palgrave Macmillan.

——— (ed.). 2011b. *Living Fanon: Global Perspectives*. London: Palgrave Macmillan.

Goswami, Manu. 2002. 'Rethinking the Modular Nation Form: Toward a Sociohistorical Conception of Nationalism'. *Comparative Studies in Society and History* 44 (4): 770–99.

———. 2004. *Producing India: From Colonial Economy to National Space*. 1st ed. Chicago: University of Chicago Press.

Gramsci, Antonio. 1971. *Selections from the Prison Notebooks*. Edited by Quintin Hoare and Geoffrey Nowell Smith. New York: International Publishers Co.

———. 1992. *Prison Notebooks* Vol. 1. Edited by Joseph Buttigieg and translated by A. Callari. New York: Columbia University Press.

———. 1996. *Prison Notebooks*. Vol. 2. Edited and translated by Joseph Buttigieg. New York: Columbia University Press.

———. 2007. *Prison Notebooks*. Vol. 3. Edited and translated by Joseph Buttigieg. New York: Columbia University Press.

Greenberg, Stephen. 2002. '"Making Rights Real": Where to for the South African Landless Movement after the WSSD?' Paper prepared for the Pan African Programme on Land & Resource Rights, 3rd Workshop, Nairobi, Kenya, 18–20 November.

———. 2004. 'The Landless People's Movement and the Failure of Post-Apartheid Land Reform'. A case study for the University of KwaZulu-Natal project entitled 'Globalisation, Marginalisation and New Social Movements in Post-Apartheid South Africa', Centre for Civil Society and School of Development Studies.

Gumede, William. 2005. *Thabo Mbeki and the Battle for the Soul of the ANC*. 1st ed. Cape Town: Zebra Press.

Gunner, Liz. 2008. 'Jacob Zuma, the Social Body and the Unruly Power of Song'. *African Affairs* 108 (430): 27–48.

Hall, Stuart. 1980. 'Race, Articulation, and Societies Structured in Dominance.' In *Sociological Theories: Race and Colonialism*, 305–45. Paris: UNESCO.

———. 1981. 'Moving Right'. *Socialist Review* 55: 113–37.

Hart, Gillian. 2002a. *Disabling Globalization: Places of Power in Post-Apartheid South Africa*. Berkeley: University of California Press.

———. 2002b. 'Linking Land, Labour, and Livelihood Struggles'. *South African Labour Bulletin* 23 (6): 26–9.

———. 2006a. 'Denaturalising Dispossession: Critical Ethnography in the Age of Resurgent Imperialism'. *Antipode* 38 (5): 977–1004.

———. 2006.b 'Post-Apartheid Developments in Comparative and Historical Perspective'. In *The First Decade of Development and Democracy in South Africa*, edited by Vishnu Padayachee, 13–32. Pretoria: HSRC Press.

———. 2007. 'Changing Concepts of Articulation: Political Stakes in South Africa Today'. *Review of African Political Economy* 34 (111): 85–101.

———. 2008. 'The Provocations of Neo-liberalism: Contesting the Nation and Liberation after Apartheid'. *Antipode* 40 (4): 678–705.

———. 2013. 'Gramsci, Geography, and the Languages of Populism'. In *Gramsci: Space, Nature, Politics*, edited by Michael Ekers, Gillian Hart, Stefan Kipfer and Alex Loftus, 301–20. Oxford: Wiley-Blackwell.

Hassim, Shireen. 2007. *Women's Organizations and Democracy in South Africa: Contesting Authority*. Madison: University of Wisconsin Press.

Harvey, Ebrahim. 2005. 'Managing the Poor by Remote Control: Johannesburg's Experiments with Prepaid Water Meters'. In *The Age of Commodity: Water Privatization in Southern Africa*, edited by David A. McDonald and Greg Ruiters, 120–9. London: Earthscan.

Haug, Wolfgang. 1999. 'Rethinking Gramsci's Philosophy of Praxis from One Century to the Next'. *boundary 2* 26 (2): 101–17.

———. 2000. 'Gramsci's "Philosophy of Praxis"'. *Socialism and Democracy* 14 (1): 1–19.

———. 2007. 'Philosophizing with Marx, Gramsci, and Brecht'. *boundary 2* 34 (3): 143–60.

———. 2010. 'From Marx to Gramsci, from Gramsci to Marx: Historical Materialism and the Philosophy of Praxis.' *Rethinking Marxism: A Journal of Economics, Culture & Society* 13 (1): 69–82.

Hobsbawm, Eric. 1990. *Nations and Nationalism since 1780: Programme, Myth, Reality*. Cambridge: Cambridge University Press.

Hunter, Mark. 2010. *Love in the Time of AIDS: Inequality, Gender, and Rights in South Africa*. Bloomington: Indiana University Press.

———. 2011. 'Beneath the "Zunami": Jacob Zuma and the Gendered Politics of Social Reproduction in South Africa'. *Antipode* 43 (4): 1102–26.

IDASA. 2004. 'Local Government Powers and Functions'. Paper commissioned by IDASA: Budget Information Service.

Ives, Peter. 2004. *Language and Hegemony in Gramsci*. London: Pluto Press.

Ives, Peter and Rocco Lacorte (eds). 2010. *Gramsci, Language, and Translation*. Lanham, MD: Lexington Books.

James, C.L.R. [1938] 1989. *The Black Jacobins: Toussaint L'Ouverture and the San Domingo Revolution*. New York: Vintage Books.

James, Deborah. 2002. 'Tenure Reformed: Policy and Practice in the Case of South Africa's Landless People'. Unpublished Paper.

Johnson, Krista. 2003. 'Liberal or Liberation Framework? The Contradictions of ANC Rule in South Africa'. In *Limits to Liberation in Southern Africa: The Unfinished Business of Democratic Consolidation*, edited by Henning Melber, 200–23. Cape Town: HSRC Press.

Kasrils, Ronnie. [1993, 1998, 2004] 2013. *Armed and Dangerous: From Undercover Struggle to Freedom*. Johannesburg: Jacana.

Kipfer, S. 2007. 'Space and Fanon: Colonisation, Urbanisation and Liberation from the Colonial to the Global City'. *Environment and Planning D: Society and Space* 25: 701–26.

———. 2011. 'The Times and Spaces of (De-)Colonization: Fanon's Counter-colonialism, Then and Now'. In *Living Fanon: Global Perspectives*, edited by Nigel Gibson, 93–104. London: Palgrave Macmillan.

———. 2013. 'City, Country, Hegemony: Antonio Gramsci's Spatial Historicism'. In *Gramsci: Space, Nature, Politics*, edited by Michael Ekers, Gillian Hart, Stefan Kipfer and Alex Loftus, 83–103. Oxford: Wiley-Blackwell.

Kipfer, Stefan and Gillian Hart. 2013. 'Translating Gramsci in the Current Conjuncture'. In *Gramsci: Space, Nature, Politics*, edited by Michael Ekers, Gillian Hart, Stefan Kipfer and Alex Loftus, 323–44. Oxford: Wiley-Blackwell.

Laclau, Ernesto. 1977. *Politics and Ideology in Marxist Theory: Capitalism, Fascism, Populism*. 1st ed. London: NLB.

———. 2005. *On Populist Reason*. New York: Verso.

Laclau, Ernesto and Chantal Mouffe. 1985. *Hegemony and Socialist Strategy: Towards a Radical Democratic Politics*. 1st ed. New York: Verso.

Lefebvre, Henri. [1974] 1991. *The Production of Space*. Oxford: Blackwell.

Legassick, Martin. 2007. *Towards Socialist Democracy*. Pietermaritzburg: University of KwaZulu-Natal Press.

Lemke, Thomas. 2011. *Biopolitics: An Advanced Introduction*. New York: New York University Press.

Lijphart, Arend. 1985. *Power Sharing in South Africa*. Berkeley: Institute of International Studies, University of California.

Loftus, Alex. 2005. '"Free Water" as Commodity: The Paradoxes of Durban's Water Service Transformations'. In *The Age of Commodity: Water Privatization in Southern Africa*, edited by David A. McDonald and Greg Ruiters, 189–203. London: Earthscan.

———. 2006. 'Reification and the Dictatorship of the Water Meter'. *Antipode* 38: 1023–45.

———. 2012. *Everyday Environmentalism: Creating an Urban Political Ecology*. Minneapolis: University of Minnesota Press.

MacDonald, Michael. 2012. *Why Race Matters in South Africa*. Reprint. Cambridge, MA: Harvard University Press.

Mangcu, Xolela. 2012. *Biko: A Biography*. Cape Town: Tafelberg.

Marais, Hein. 1998. *South Africa: Limits to Change: The Political Economy of Transition*. London: Zed Books.

———. 2011. *South Africa Pushed to the Limit: The Political Economy of Change*. London: Zed Books.

Marks, Shula and Stanley Trapido. 1987. *The Politics of Race, Class, and Nationalism in Twentieth-Century South Africa*. London: Longman.

Massey, Doreen. 1994. *Space, Place, and Gender*. Minneapolis: University of Minnesota Press.

Mbeki, Moeletsi. 2009. *Architects of Poverty: Why African Capitalism Needs Changing*. Johannesburg: Pan Macmillan South Africa.

McClintock, Anne. 1995. *Imperial Leather: Race, Gender and Sexuality in the Colonial Contest*. New York: Routledge.

McDonald, David A. and John Pape. 2002. *Cost Recovery and the Crisis of Service Delivery in South Africa*. London and New York: Zed Books.

McDonald, David A. and Greg Ruiters. 2005. *The Age of Commodity: Water Privatization in Southern Africa*. London: Earthscan.

McKinley, Dale T. and Prishani Naidoo. 2004. 'New Social Movements in South Africa: A Story in Creation'. *Development Update* 5 (2): 9–22.

McMichael, Philip. 1990. 'Incorporating Comparison with a World-Historical Perspective: An Alternative Comparative Method'. *American Sociological Review* 55 (3): 285–97.

Minnaar, Anthony de V., Michael Hough and Chris Paul de Kock (eds). 1996. *Who Goes There? Perspectives on Clandestine Migration and Illegal Aliens in Southern Africa*. Cape Town: HSRC Publishers.

Misago, Jean Pierre, Tamlyn Monson, Tara Polzer and Loren Landau. 2010. 'Violence Against Foreign Nationals in South Africa: Understanding Causes and Evaluating Responses'. Forced Migration Studies Programme Report.

http://www.cormsa.org.za/wp-content/uploads/2009/05/may-2008-violence-against-foreign-nationals-in-south-africa.pdf.

Mngxitama, Andile. 2002. 'The Landless Have Landed'. *Debate: Voices from the South African Left* (September): 8–10.

Mngxitama, Andile, Amanda Alexander and Nigel Gibson (eds). 2008. *Biko Lives! Contesting the Legacies of Steve Biko*. 1st ed. Basingstoke: Palgrave Macmillan.

Mohammed, Seeraj. 2010. 'The State of the South African Economy'. In *New South African Review 1: South Africa in Crisis: Development or Decline?* edited by Roger Southall, Devan Pillay, Prishani Naidoo and John Daniel, 39–64. Johannesburg: Wits University Press.

Morton, Adam. 2007. *Unravelling Gramsci: Hegemony and Passive Revolution in the Global Political Economy*. London: Pluto Press.

———. 2010. 'The Continuum of Passive Revolution'. *Capital & Class* 34 (3): 315–42.

———. 2011. *Revolution and State in Modern Mexico: The Political Economy of Uneven Development*. Lanham, MD: Rowman and Littlefield.

———. 2013. 'Traveling with Gramsci: The Spatiality of Passive Revolution'. In *Gramsci: Space, Nature, Politics*, edited by Michael Ekers, Gillian Hart, Stefan Kipfer and Alex Loftus, 47–64. Oxford: Wiley-Blackwell.

Mosoetsa, Sarah. 2011. *Eating From One Pot: The Dynamics of Survival in Poor South African Households*. Johannesburg: Wits University Press.

Mouzelis, Nicos. 1978. 'Ideology and Class Politics: A Critique of Ernesto Laclau'. *New Left Review* I/112: 48–61.

Muller, Mike. 2008. 'Free Basic Water: A Sustainable Instrument for a Sustainable Future in South Africa'. *Environment and Urbanization* 20 (1): 67–87.

Naidoo, Prishani. 2010. 'The Making of "The Poor" in Post-apartheid South Africa: A Case Study of the City of Johannesburg and Orange Farm'. D. Phil. Thesis, University of KwaZulu-Natal.

———. 2012. 'Technologies for Knowing and Managing the Poor in South Africa: The Case of Johannesburg Post-Apartheid'. Unpublished paper delivered at a seminar in the Department of Sociology, University of Johannesburg, August.

Nash, Andrew. 1999. 'The Moment of Western Marxism in South Africa'. *Comparative Studies of South Asia, Africa and the Middle East* 19 (1): 66–81.

———. 2009. *The Dialectical Tradition in South Africa*. London: Routledge.

Nattrass, Nicoli and Jeremy Seekings. 2002. 'Class, Distribution and Re-distribution in Post-Apartheid South Africa'. *Transformation* 50: 1–30.

Ndebele, Nhlanhla and Noor Nieftagodien. 2004. 'The Morogoro Conference: A Moment of Self-Reflection'. In *The Road to Democracy in South Africa: 1960–1970*, South African Democracy Education Trust, 573–600. Cape Town: Zebra Press.

Neocosmos, Michael. 2010. *From 'Foreign Natives' to 'Native Foreigners': Explaining Xenophobia in Post-Apartheid South Africa.* 2nd ed. Dakar: Codesria.

Ngwane, Trevor. 2003. 'Sparks in the Township'. *New Left Review* 22: 37–56.

Ollman, Bertell. 2003. *The Dance of the Dialectic: Steps in Marx's Method.* Urbana and Chicago: University of Illinois Press.

Osborne, Thomas. 1996. 'Security and Vitality: Drains, Liberalism and Power in the Nineteenth Century'. In *Foucault and Political Reason: Liberalism, Neo-Liberalism, and Rationalities of Government,* edited by Andrew Barry, Thomas Osborne and Nikolas Rose, 99–122. Chicago: University of Chicago Press.

Padayachee, Vishnu and Imraan Valodia. 2001. 'Changing Gear: The 2001 Budget and Economic Policy in South Africa'. *Transformation* 46: 71–83.

Peberdy, Sally. 2009. *Selecting Immigrants: National Identity and South Africa's Immigration Policies, 1910–2008.* Johannesburg: Wits University Press.

Peberdy, Sally and Jonathan Crush. 1998. 'Rooted in Racism: The Origins of the Aliens Control Act'. In *Beyond Control: Immigration and Human Rights in a Democratic South Africa,* edited by Jonathan Crush, 18–36. Cape Town: IDASA and Kingston: Queen's University.

Philip, Kate. 2010. 'Inequality and Economic Marginalisation: How the Structure of the Economy Impacts on Opportunities at the Margins'. *Law, Democracy and Development* 14: 105–32.

Pillay, Devan. 2007. 'The Stunted Growth of South Africa's Developmental State Discourse'. Special Issue of *Africanus* 37 (2): 198–215.

———. 2011. 'The Tripartite Alliance and its Discontents: Contesting the "National Democratic Revolution" in the Zuma Era'. In *New South African Review 2: New Paths, Old Compromises?,* edited by John Daniel, Prishani Naidoo, Devan Pillay and Roger Southall, 31–49. Johannesburg: Wits University Press.

Pithouse, Richard. 2012a. 'Thought Amidst Waste'. *Journal of Asian and African Studies* 47: 482–97.

———. 2012b. 'Conjunctural Remarks on the Political Significance of "The Local"'. *Thesis Eleven* 115 (1): 95–111.

Polanyi, Karl. [1994] 2001. *The Great Transformation: The Political and Economic Origins of Our Time.* 2nd ed. Boston: Beacon Press.

Posel, Deborah. 2005. 'Sex, Death and the Fate of the Nation: Reflections on the Politicization of Sexuality in Post-Apartheid South Africa'. *Africa* 75 (2): 125–53.

Roseberry, William. 1994. 'Hegemony and the Language of Contention'. In *Everyday Forms of State Formation: Revolution and the Negotiation of Rule in Modern Mexico,* edited by G. Joseph and Daniel Nugent, 355–66. Durham: Duke University Press.

Ruiters, Greg. 2007. 'Contradictions in Municipal Services in Contemporary South Africa: Disciplinary Commodification and Self-Disconnections'. *Critical Social Policy* 27: 487–508.

Satgar, Vishwas. 2008. 'Neoliberalized South Africa: Labour and the Roots of Passive Revolution'. *Labour, Capital and Society* 41 (2): 38–69.

Saul, John S. 2001. 'Cry for the Beloved Country: The Post-Apartheid Dénouement'. *Monthly Review* 52: 1–51.

Saul, John S. and Stephen Gelb. 1981. *The Crisis in South Africa*. 1st ed. New York: Monthly Review Press.

———. 1986. *The Crisis in South Africa*. 2nd ed. New York: New York University Press.

Sekyi-Otu, Ato. 1996. *Fanon's Dialectic of Experience*. Cambridge, MA: Harvard University Press.

Silver, Beverly J. and Giovanni Arrighi. 2003. 'Polanyi's "Double Movement": The Belle Époques of British and U.S. Hegemony Compared'. *Politics & Society* 31 (2): 32555.

Sitas, Ari. 1990. 'Class, Nation, Ethnicity in Natal's Black Working Class'. Collected Seminar Papers, Institute of Commonwealth Studies 38.

———. 2008. 'The Road to Polokwane: Politics and Populism in KwaZulu-Natal'. *Transformation* 68 (1): 87–98.

———. 2010. *The Mandela Decade 1990–2000: Labour, Culture and Society in Post-Apartheid South Africa*. Pretoria: Unisa Press.

Sizwe, No [Neville Alexander]. 1979. *One Azania, One Nation: The National Question in South Africa*. London: Zed Press.

Slovo, Joe. 1988. *The South African Working Class and the National Democratic Revolution*. Johannesburg: South African Communist Party.

Smith, Gavin. 2011. 'Selective Hegemony and Beyond: Populations with "No Productive Function": A Framework for Inquiry'. *Identities: Global Studies in Culture and Power* 18 (1): 2–38.

Southall, Roger. 2009. 'Understanding the "Zuma Tsunami"'. *Review of African Political Economy* 36 (121): 317–33.

———. 2010. 'The South African Development Model: Hitting Against the Limits?' *Strategic Review for Southern Africa* 32 (2).

Southall, Roger and John Daniel (eds). 2009. *Zunami! The Context of the 2009 Election*. Johannesburg: Jacana Media.

Terreblanche, Sampie. 2002. *A History of Inequality in South Africa 1652–2002*. Pietermaritzburg: University of Natal Press.

———. 2012. *Lost in Transformation: South Africa's Search for a New Future Since 1986*. Johannesburg: KMM Review.

Thomas, Peter D. 2006. 'Modernity as "Passive Revolution": Gramsci and the Fundamental Concepts of Historical Materialism'. *Journal of the Canadian Historical Association* 17 (2): 61–78.

———. 2009a. *The Gramscian Moment: Philosophy, Hegemony and Marxism*. Leiden: Brill.

———. 2009b. 'Gramsci and the Political: From the State as "Metaphysical Event" to Hegemony as "Political Fact"'. *Radical Philosophy* 153: 27–36.

———. 2012. 'The Philosophy of Praxis' and 'The Gramscian Moment: An Interview with Martin Thomas'. In *Antonio Gramsci: Working-Class Revolutionary*, edited by Martin Thomas, 14–39. London: Workers' Liberty.

Tosel, André. 2010. 'The Lexicon of Gramsci's Philosophy of Praxis. In *Gramsci, Language, and Translation*, edited by Peter Ives and Rocco Lacorte, 267–87. Lanham, MD: Lexington Books.

Tugal, Cihan. 2009. *Passive Revolution: Absorbing the Islamic Challenge to Capitalism*. Stanford: Stanford University Press.

Tutu, Desmond. [1996] 2006. *The Rainbow People of God*. 1st ed. New York: Image Books.

Von Holdt, Karl. 2011. 'Insurgent Citizenship and Collective Violence: Analysis of Case Studies'. In *The Smoke that Calls: Insurgent Citizenship, Collective Violence and the Struggle for a Place in the New South Africa*, edited by Karl von Holdt, Malose Langa, Sepetla Molapo, Nomfundo Mogapi, Kindiza Ngubeni, Jacob Dlamini and Adéle Kristen, 5–32. Johannesburg: Centre for the Study of Violence and Reconciliation and Society, Work and Development Institute.

Von Schnitzler, Antina. 2008. 'Citizen Prepaid? Water, Calculability, and Techno-Politics in South Africa'. *Journal of Southern African Studies* 34 (4): 899–917.

Watts, Michael. 2003. 'Development and Governmentality'. *Singapore Journal of Tropical Geography* 24 (1): 6–34.

Wolpe, Harold. 1975. 'The Theory of Internal Colonialism: The South African Case'. In *Beyond the Sociology of Development: Economy and Society in Latin America and Africa*, edited by Ivar Oxaal, Tony Barnett and David Booth, 229–52. London: Routledge.

———. 1988. *Race, Class & the Apartheid State*. Paris: Unesco Press.

———. 1995. 'The Uneven Transition from Apartheid in South Africa'. *Transformation* 27: 88–101.

Xulu, Nomkhosi. 2012. 'Changing Migrant Spaces and Livelihoods: Hostels as Community Residential Units, KwaMashu, KwaZulu-Natal, South Africa'. D.Phil. thesis, University of Cape Town.

Index

AIDS, *see* HIV/AIDS
Alexander, Neville, 171, 174, 178
Alexander, Peter, 48, 84
Aliens Control Act, 8, 171–2
Althusser, Louis, 216 n.7
Amajuba district municipality
    control of water, 115
    equitable shares, 116
    map, 112
    population, 111
Anderson, Benedict, 14–15
Anderson, Perry
    on Lulismo hegemony, 165
    'The Antinomies of Antonio
        Gramsci', 191–2, 215, 216 n.4,
        223
anti-colonialism, 16, 221, 226–7, 232
Anti-Privatisation Forum (APF)
    members, 31, 89 n.8
    protests, 32
    tensions with LPM, 33
apartheid
    crisis of, 6, 160
    demise of, 98
    forced removals, 20, 107, 113, 126,
        242 n.19
    forgiveness and, 7, 169
    Gramsci and Fanon's influence
        on struggles against, 18
    history and struggles of, 180
    reparations, 171
    transition from, 5–6, 20–1, 156,
        168, 232–3
articulations
    of class and populist politics,
        194–6
    concept, 157
    de-nationalisation and
        re-nationalisation relations
        and, 18
    idea of, 17, 26 n.22
    of nationalism, 9, 17, 22–3, 54,
        177

of nation and liberation, 180, 189,
    193, 200, 212
of sexuality and race, 185, 224,
    233
see also re-articulations
Ashman, Sam, 157–8, 163
'*Awaleth' Umshini Wami'* (Bring me
    my machine gun), 44, 56–7,
    59, 205–7

Barchiesi, Franco, 164
Basic Income Grant, 29, 88 n.2
    ANC rejection of, 37, 40
Bassett, Carolyn, 10–12, 162, 220
Beirut, Alexandra rampage (2008),
    65
Bench Marks Foundation, 86
Bénit-Gbaffou, Claire, 147
Bergville, 42–3, 204
Bernstein, Rusty, 237
Bhabha, Homi K., 26 n.18
Biko, Steve, 18, 27 n.25
Black Economic Empowerment
    (BEE), 52, 164, 210–11
Black Local Authorities, 98
black South Africans, 2, 4, 179, 236
    capitalist class, 7, 201
    degradation of livelihoods, 7, 159
    experiences of racism, 155
    forced removals, 20, 107, 113
    poor, 204–5
black townships, 3, 98
    amalgamations, 121–2
    resource distribution, 111
Booysen, Susan, 59
Bond, Patrick, 47, 159, 181, 241 n.15
bourgeoisie
    black, 182, 184, 198
    corporate, 10
    hegemony, 189, 191
    national/nationalism, 18, 221,
        224–5, 228
    passive revolution and, 9, 165

Morton, Adam, 217 n.24, 231, 240 n.6
Motlanthe, Kgalema, 60, 75, 150 n.6, 158
Mouzelis, Nicos, 235
'movement beyond movements', 3, 21, 49, 87, 221
Mpofu, Dali, 85-6
Mufamadi, Sydney, 105, 150 n.6
Mugabe, Robert, 81, 229-30
  LPM's support for, 33, 89 n.11
Municipal Financial Management Act, 104
municipal indigent policy, 39, 102, 107
  councillors and, 148
  debt collection and 'credit control', 104, 108, 119-20, 125-7
  qualifications, 110, 124-5
  water restrictions, 140-1, 143-4
municipalities
  ANC access to, 114
  clean audits, 105, 133
  debts, 104
  disconnection of services, 101
  equitable shares, 103-4, 115-16, 135, 150 n.1
  new demarcations, 99, 110-13, 151 n.16
  see also Ladysmith/Emnambithi; Newcastle
municipal protests
  in Harrismith, 44-8
  in Ladysmith, 95-6
  proliferation of, 48-50, 105, 135

Naidoo, Prishani, 147
Nash, Andrew
  on dialectical thought, 219, 232
  on Western Marxism, 213-14, 217 n.23, 236
nation, the
  articulations of, 180, 189, 193, 200, 212

immigration policy and, 8
making of, 166
the state and, 25 n.15
as a territorial bounded unit, 17
National Democratic Revolution (NDR)
  articulations of nationalism, 37, 177
  criticism of, 178-9, 183
  disciplinary deployment of, 198-9, 213
  re-articulations of, 177, 184, 198-9
  redefinition of, 182-5, 209
  role in two-stage revolution, 8, 176-8, 183
  struggles, 157, 174, 180, 193, 200
  working class and, 166, 201
National General Council
  conference in Polokwane (2007), 50, 54, 59-60, 65
  conference in Tshwane (2005), 50-5, 200
nationalisation, *see* de-nationalisation; re-nationalisation
nationalism
  anti-colonial and post-apartheid, 221, 226
  articulations of, 17, 22-3, 54, 177, 200
  Benedict Anderson's theory, 14-15
  democracy and, 13
  denaturalising, 24, 26 n.19, 221, 225
  of FIFA World Cup, 76-8
  left positions on, 213, 221
  liberation and, 180, 200
  Mbeki's, 185
  militant, 206-7
  neglect and disavowal of, 12-13
  passive revolution and, 225-6
  political economy and, 12
  racial, 21, 179-81
  SACP's, 211, 213, 221

privatisation, 35–6, 100–1
proletariat, 225, 229
  hegemony, 189, 192, 215 n.2
'pro-poor' measures, 22, 39, 97, 102, 156
protest rates, 48–49
public-private partnerships, 119, 164

Qabula, Alfred Temba, 168–70
Qwabe, Sibusiso, 55–6
Qwa Qwa, 46, 91 n.33

racialised geographies, 121–2
racism, 155, 156, 170, 174, 224
rainbow nation, 7, 22, 155, 177, 181
  practices and analysis of, 167–71
Ramaphosa, Cyril, 85–6, 212
Ramaphosa township, 65–7, 69
re-articulations
  of the 'land question', 20, 34
  of the NDR, 177, 184, 198–9
  of race, class and nationalism, 22, 163, 177, 199–200, 203, 208, 212
  see also articulations
Reconstruction and Development Programme (RDP), 181–3, 188 n.21
Red Ants, 29
regressive-progressive method, 19, 26 n.24, 232
re-nationalisation
  ANC hegemony and, 12
  dialectics of, 9, 17
  and immigration laws and practices, 8, 171–3
  key dimensions of, 7–8
  of post-apartheid South Africa, 8, 156, 167
  rainbow nation and, 168–71
  of sexuality and race, 185
  spatio-historical understanding of, 17, 220, 229

  see also de-nationalisation and re-nationalisation relations
Rhodes, Cecil John, 16
Risorgimento, 9, 215 n.1, 222, 225
Roseberry, William, 193, 198
Russian revolution, 222–3

Sader, Achmad, 241 n.19
Sankara, Thomas, 238
Satgar, Vishwas, 11–12
Saul, John, 10, 29, 219–20, 237
Schoeman, Willie, 115, 117, 119–20
Second Economy
  and First Economy gap, 52, 63
  launch of, 38–9, 199
  'pro-poor' measures and, 102
Sekyi-Otu, Ato, 18, 222, 225–8
Seoka, Jo, 86
service delivery protests
  over water control in Ladysmith, 95–6
  proliferation of, 3, 47–50
Shaik, Schabir, 43–4, 50
Shiceka, Sicelo, 105, 144, 150 n.6
Shivambu, Floyd, 208–9
Sitas, Ari, 28, 65, 141, 148–9
  'Class, Nation, Ethnicity in Natal's Black Working Class', 196
  on HIV/AIDS and intimacies, 186
  on indigenerality and rainbowism, 7, 168–70
  observations on cholera epidemic, 101
Sithole, Laurence, 120
Slovo, Joe, 166–7, 176
Soccer City, 76–7
socialism, 166, 174, 176, 209–11
socialist populism, 196–7, 235
Social Movements Indaba, 32–3
Sonjica, Buyelwa, 119
South African Communist Party (SACP), 8, 52, 176–7, 212

protests over, 95–6
restrictions, 138, 140–1, 143–4,
    153 n.37
see also free basic services
Watts, Michael, 98
wealth, 5, 29, 39, 82, 164
    mineral, 81, 87
West-East dichotomy, 190–1, 215 n.2
white power, 82
white privilege, 98–100, 220
Wolpe, Harold, 54, 177, 182–3, 200
working class, 34, 149, 191
    black, 182, 196
    NDR and, 166, 184, 201
    neoliberal economic policies and,
        155
    organised, 178–9
World Conference Against Racism,
    3, 31, 35
World Summit on Sustainable
    Development (WSSD), 3, 32–3

xenophobia, 4
    employment struggles and, 73
    human rights and, 173
    immigration and, 8, 172

violence, 65, 67, 71–2, 179–80, 207
    see also Nhamuave, Ernesto
        Alfabeto

Zader Municipal Services, 125–7, 136,
    140
ZANU-PF, 81, 90 n.12
Zapiro (cartoonist), 29, 65
    cartoons, 30, 36, 64, 78, 93 n.48
Zikode, S'bu, 203, 207
Zimbabwe, 35, 81, 93 n.64
Zizek, Slavoj, 229–30
Zuma, Jacob
    corruption charges, 3, 50, 61, 74
    involvement in arms deal, 42–3
    Mbeki comparison, 60–2
    meeting in East Rand, 73–4, 207
    popular support for, 3, 54, 57, 62,
        201–6, 211, 216 n.12
    public performance, 43–4
    rape trial, 56, 93 n.48, 204
    reinstatement, 50–2
    theme song, 44, 56–7, 59, 205–7
    visit to University of California,
        Berkeley, 63, 92 n.47
'Zunami', 54, 201

GEOGRAPHIES OF JUSTICE AND SOCIAL TRANSFORMATION